Creativity for Innovation I

Creativity for Innovation Management is a rigorous yet applied guide which illustrates what creativity is, why it matters, and how it can be developed at both individual and group levels. Unlike many technique-oriented studies, this book will combine theory and practice, drawing on the latest research in psychology, organizational behaviour, innovation and entrepreneurship.

This exciting new text outlines the necessary skills and competences for innovative and creative processes. It provides opportunities to explore these and also to develop via a wide variety of activities linked to relevant tools and techniques, as well as a range of case studies. By working through key competence areas at a personal and then team level, students have an opportunity to practice and enhance these skills. This will be complemented by online resources which will provide students with access to key tools and techniques plus activities to help develop their creativity.

This textbook is ideal for students of innovation, management and entrepreneurship, as well as professionals in those industries that want to excel by developing and applying their own creativity at work.

Ina Goller worked for more than twenty years as a consultant for change, teamwork and leadership development. In recent years she also works as a senior researcher at the ETH Zürich. She focuses on competence and skill development for creativity and innovation.

John Bessant holds the Chair in Innovation and Entrepreneurship at the University of Exeter. His publications include *Managing Innovation* (5th edition) and *Innovation and Entrepreneurship* (3rd edition).

This is not just another discussion of creativity and innovation; it is a call to action to think in concrete ways about how we can harness creativity to create value in everything we do. It reinforces that creativity is not the domain of just a "talented few" but is a way of thinking and behaving that is open to us all. It provides practical frameworks for applying creativity to our everyday life and challenges the myths about what it means to be creative. The text is easy to read whilst still underpinned by solid research from a range of fields. There is an impressive range of examples – both historical and contemporary – that will appeal to a wide range of readers. I commend it as "must read" for those interested in harnessing creativity to create a different future for themselves, their organizations and society at large.

Karen Becker,
Associate Professor, QUT, Australia

This book is written by two of the most accomplished experts in the field and is the one stop shop for students of creativity for innovation. It is built on rigorous and up to date research which is presented in an engaging and easy to read fashion. However, the real genius of this book lies not in its theoretical explanation of creativity, but in the comprehensive translation of that theory to a guide for its application in practice. It is an outstanding "what is" and "how to do" creativity for innovation.

Robert Galavan, *Professor and Chair of Strategic Management, Edward M. Kennedy Institute for Conflict Intervention, Maynooth University, Ireland*

If you ask people whether they are creative, they will tell you "No!". If you ask them whether they would like to be more creative, they will tell you "of course". In times where creativity and innovation is needed more than ever, here is the book for you. Ina Goller and John Bessant take the reader on an enlightening and stimulating learning journey to develop creativity for innovation individually, on a team-level and on an organizational level.

Katharina Hölzle, *Professor for Innovation Management and Entrepreneurship, University of Potsdam, Germany*

What a truly inspiring book! – *Creativity for Innovation Management* is not only a perfect reference, but provides what is needed to understand, train and develop. As the authors say: ". . . visit the 'creativity gym' and try out some exercises for yourself!".

Kathrin M. Moeslein, *Professor and Vice President for Research, Friedrich-Alexander University of Erlangen-Nuremberg, Germany*

Creativity for Innovation Management

Ina Goller and John Bessant

Routledge
Taylor & Francis Group

LONDON AND NEW YORK

First published 2017
by Routledge
2 Park Square, Milton Park, Abingdon, Oxon OX14 4RN

and by Routledge
711 Third Avenue, New York, NY 10017

Routledge is an imprint of the Taylor & Francis Group, an informa business

British Library Cataloguing-in-Publication Data
A catalogue record for this book is available from the British Library

Library of Congress Cataloging-in-Publication Data
A catalog record for this book has been requested

ISBN: 978-1-138-64130-3 (hbk)
ISBN: 978-1-138-64132-7 (pbk)
ISBN: 978-1-315-63058-8 (ebk)

Typeset in Times New Roman
by Apex CoVantage, LLC

Visit the companion website: www.routledge.com/cw/Goller

To Christoph, my partner in and for all my dreams
and
To Lara Jasmine, a constant reminder of the joy of creativity

Contents

SECTION 5

SECTION 6

Figures

Tables

Acknowledgements

A book is never written alone, especially this one because we are already two authors. We want to thank all the people around us that help us in starting and finishing this book. In particular:

- Carmen Kobe – without her we would never even have met, and she has been a big contributor to the body of research of this book. Thank you very much. With her the basic ideas for this book got developed and 'tried out' and improved with the last 'five generations' of students.
- Our friends and families for their patience and the many ways in which they supported and believed in us.
- The team at Routledge, especially Amy, Laura and Nicola.
- Lea for all her help in the background and Jonas for the figures.
- Our colleagues and students at ETH in Zürich and the University of Exeter who provided helpful feedback and were brave guinea pigs for us to try out the materials and ideas! And the many colleagues and clients of Skillsgarden AG who helped so much with understanding the challenge of putting creativity into practice.

Section 1

## Chapter 1

Creativity . . . ?

Imagine:

- An artist sitting in front of her easel, mind focused as she faces a blank canvas and thinks hard and long about where and how she will make her first mark.
- A games designer, hunched over his keyboard, frantically stabbing the keys as he creates the storyboard sketch for a new interactive game to run on smartphones.
- A team of engineers huddled round a simple mock-up of a new product, pulling it into shape, scribbling notes on the flip chart behind them as they gradually refine the idea, giving shape to what will eventually become the baby buggy of the future but which now looks like the undercarriage of a very old and rickety aeroplane.
- A nurse on the night shift, sitting alone at her desk on the hospital ward, quietly taking time to sketch out an idea she has had for a new way to handle the medication trolley to make sure she and her colleagues don't inadvertently give the wrong dose (or worse, the wrong tablets) to her patients.
- An aid worker, sitting with a group of refugees talking about the mobile phone app she is hoping to develop to help solve the problem of relocating missing members of families reconnect after they have fled a war zone.

What is the common thread running through these stories? Creativity – the ability to come up with novel solutions to problems. The context might vary widely but the core activity is still the same – creating something useful, valuable, from ideas.

The word is everywhere – creative industries, creative people, creative leaders, creative organizations and so on. But it's not just a fashion label – in a world where we face some pretty tough challenges it's a truism to say we need all the creativity we can get.

For our ancestors creativity was a matter of survival – if we couldn't think our way out of a problem (like an approaching predator) then we wouldn't be around for long! Dealing with the daily struggle to survive required us to be innovative, and the key to that was the ability to imagine and explore different possibilities.

These days we're more concerned with creating value, whether in a commercial or social sense, but the core skill remains the same. It involves finding, exploring and solving problems and puzzles – and that's where creativity comes in. Whether we are a solo start-up entrepreneur or a member of a team tasked with helping the organization to think 'outside the box', the main resource which we need is one which we already have – creativity.

Creativity and innovation

Innovation is another of those words you can't avoid bumping into these days. We talk about things being innovations – a different type of chocolate, a new form of transportation, an alternative way to shop, a radical shift in communications. Think Airbnb, Uber, Google or Apple, or take a look at the hundreds of new products which scream at you from the supermarket shelves every time you go shopping! But innovation is also the way those things came about, the process which transforms an idea, a gleam in some inventor's eye, into the new things we are being asked to buy and use. It's not a magic event; there is a long haul involving many different activities and people to create something which others will value.

Although there are many definitions of innovation at its simplest, it is the process of creating value from ideas. It's something which we have studied for a long time – not surprisingly given its importance in the economy. Without going into detail it's pretty clear that innovation – making ideas happen – is at the heart of economic growth; to take one example, the famous economist William Baumol suggested that 'virtually all of the economic growth that has occurred since the eighteenth century is ultimately attributable to innovation' [1].

It's not just about economics; innovation is also about creating social value, changing the world to make it a better place. There is a long tradition of this kind of innovation; people like Florence Nightingale, Elizabeth Fry, William Wilberforce or Albert Schweitzer are famous examples from the past, but we can also find plenty of individuals whose work today is along the same lines. The growth in social innovation has also been accelerated through enabling technologies around information and communication. These days it becomes easier to reach many different players and to combine their innovative efforts into rich and new types of solutions. For example, mobilizing patients and carers in an online community concerned with rare diseases or using mobile communications to help deal with the aftermath of humanitarian crises – reuniting families, establishing communications, providing financial aid quickly via mobile money transfers and so forth.

Whether commercially or socially motivated understanding, the innovation process is clearly important, and the good news is that we have learned a lot about how to organize and manage it [2]. Central to this is the principle that it involves human creativity; delivering innovation is primarily about building the structures and mechanisms to support this. It doesn't really matter whether we are dealing with a tiny start-up or giant Google-sized enterprise, a small family business or the UK's National Health Service (the world's biggest employer after the Chinese

People's Liberation Army), the challenge is the same: how to enable innovation as applied creativity.

Entrepreneurs, innovation and creativity

Innovation isn't an accident; anyone might get lucky once, but being able to repeat the trick and deliver a stream of new products, processes and services depends on organizing and managing it. And it's not something magical which drops out of the sky at key moments – it's the result of applied creativity. The other key part of the equation is the people who deliver it – working individually and in teams and in all sorts of different contexts. The label for this kind of activity is entrepreneurship.

As the famous management writer Peter Drucker put it, 'innovation is what entrepreneurs do' [3]. It isn't a lucky accident – evidence is that this is a skill-based activity, one which can be learned and developed. We often see entrepreneurs as a special case – famous individuals like Steve Jobs (Apple), Natalie Massenet (Net-a-Porter), Richard Branson (Virgin), Martha Lane-Fox (Lastminute.com), Jack Ma (Alibaba), Jeff Bezos (Amazon) or Elon Musk (Tesla). But – as we've shown elsewhere – everyone is an entrepreneur in the sense of being a change agent [4]. The context in which they work could be a start-up, but it could also be trying to make a change project happen in their organization. They could be working in the public or private sector or as volunteers for a charity or neighbourhood group. They might be acting as entrepreneurs – agents of change – in their wider lives – as part of an amateur theatre group, building a community shop, organizing a party. What all of these share is that they are trying to apply creativity to innovate, to create some form of commercial or social value. Figure 1.1 shows how these three are linked.

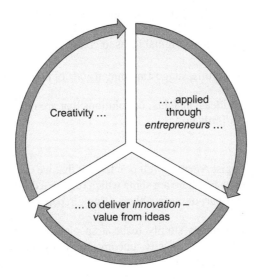

Figure 1.1 Links between creativity, entrepreneurs and innovation

In this book we want to explore creativity but not as an abstract concept. It's the fuel driving the innovation process, enabling changes which affect our lives. Creating value – whether commercial or social. And it is enabled through people – everyday entrepreneurs – working in many different contexts but sharing the ability to solve problems in novel ways. We're particularly interested in how they do so – the competences and skills which they learn and deploy to be more effective at creativity.

Creative activity

Think about the last month. Where have you been creative? Or where could you use creativity in order to reach a better outcome?

List ten situations you experienced in the last month where creativity played a role in your life.

What is creativity?

The question we want to explore in this book is not whether or not we can be creative – we already are! But research has shown that it isn't a magical flash of inspiration but rather the application of a set of skills, the development of particular competences. And there are several things we can do, as individuals, groups and organizations, to improve our capacity for it. We'll look in more detail in the following chapters, but for now let's just fly over the creativity landscape briefly to get a sense of what's involved.

So what is creativity? The Oxford Dictionary defines it as:

> the use of imagination or original ideas to create something.

Others expand a little on this, suggesting dimensions of novelty and usefulness:

> the generation of ideas, insights, or solutions that are novel and useful for a given situation or problem.

[5]

The famous psychologist Allen Newell pointed out that we can solve many problems by simple routines but there are some which require a different approach; for him creativity was this part of our problem-solving repertoire:

> creative activity appears simply to be a special class of problem-solving activity characterised by novelty, unconventionality, persistence and difficulty in problem formulation.

(p. 2, [6])

We'd add our own definition: for us creativity is a complex construct describing the ability of human beings to invent something new or behave in a novel way. It's about some key competences underpinned by a set of skills – ways of behaving – and we'll look at these through the book. It's not a luxury item – it has evolved as a human capability to help us deal with a complex and changing environment. But it's not simply about reacting in smart fashion to the unexpected; creativity is also about being proactive, finding new ways forward. Progress, whether in economic growth or the expansion of arts and culture, has creativity at the heart of the innovation engine.

It's important starting in early life – watch any group of children playing and you can't fail to be struck by the invention and joy which follows their learning through experimentation and play. But it also matters at later stages, giving us the capacity for flexibility in dealing with an increasingly complex world. In old age one of the key psychosocial factors associated with healthy ageing is again flexibility; the one organ in which cells do not wear out or stutter to a halt is the brain. Studies have demonstrated its remarkable 'plasticity' – the capability to reinvent itself through making new connections (see e.g. [7–12]).

Challenge

Creativity sometimes involves breaking rules, changing perspectives, seeing things differently. And this can set up tensions between the person coming up with this new way of seeing and the rest of the world which still has the old view.

That's not always a comfortable position because it can involve going head to head with an established view of the world. Those who hold it are likely to defend their view strongly. Creative people aren't always popular, especially when they stick to their guns and defend their crazy idea in the face of others trying to get them to conform. When Galileo the astronomer proposed a different view for the way the sun and planets operated he was imprisoned and threatened with death by the Inquisition. A version of this that was not quite so life-threatening was when Bob Dylan performed his new electric music at the Newport Festival, he was booed off the stage. Steve Jobs was portrayed in the movie of the same name as a difficult visionary and James Dyson chose an apt title for his autobiography – *Against the Odds*! [13].

> You can find a case study of James Dyson on the companion website.

This isn't to say that entrepreneurs have to go out of their way to be 'difficult' people but rather that we need to recognize and manage the conflicts which can emerge and to make sure we can bring people along with us, getting them to share in our vision rather than fighting against it.

Challenging some myths about creativity

Before we go further it's worth challenging a few of the myths around creativity.

Myth I: the instantaneous insight

First of all, it's not like in the cartoons – a 'light bulb' moment when the brilliant idea flashes on. Nor is it a spark of divine inspiration, a visit from the gods of bright ideas. Instead it's more of a journey across a landscape, one which begins in the lowland plains and fields of problem-finding. Some problems have already surfaced, thrusting themselves in front of us, blocking our path. Others are annoying and uncomfortable, nagging at our feet and snatching at our clothes, pulling us back. And others lie still buried under the ground, not yet visible but full of potential, opportunities to be harvested if we could only find some way of drawing them out.

Looking further into the distance we can see a broad river, a deep watercourse which we'll need to cross at some stage. We might swim fast across the surface or we might find ourselves drawn down into its depths, losing ourselves and sight of land in the process. Travelling in this part of the journey corresponds to incubation, of turning the idea over in both conscious and unconscious fashion, diving deeper and deeper. But eventually we reach a point at which some kind of insight bubbles to the surface – this is the flash of inspiration, the 'aha!' moment which we are familiar with.

That initial idea often needs a lot more polishing and shaping to become something that actually works and which we – and others – can use. That's the next stage in the journey, beginning the long slow climb through the foothills to the higher mountains, refining and developing our ideas along the way until finally we reach the summit!

A fanciful metaphor, perhaps, but it captures something of what we've learned about creativity. It's not a single event and it's not a simple reproducible process. Instead there are many ways in which we can travel across the landscape.

Different travellers experience it in different ways but the underlying route is the same. Writing a song, drawing a picture, developing a new product or service, finding a better way of doing something – they are all versions of the same journey. And there are lessons we can take from experienced travellers about useful things to take with us and about roadblocks and obstacles (and ways to get around them) to watch out for along the way.

The good news is also that we have a map to guide us. There is a rich body of research to draw on which can help us understand how creativity works and how we can help it happen. One of the earliest approaches was by Graham Wallas back in the 1920s. He constructed a model of creativity based on interviewing creative people to ask about the thinking process which they went through. His underlying assumption was that we can

> take a single achievement or thought – the making of a new generalization or invention, or the potential expressions of a new idea – and ask how it was brought about. We can then roughly dissect out a continuous process, with a beginning and a middle and an end of its own.

(p. 79, [14])

It's easy to see creativity as being that wonderful moment where we have a flash of inspiration. The light bulb goes on and all suddenly becomes clear. But Wallas's research (and many other studies since) showed that it is not as simple as this; there is an underlying pattern in which that light bulb moment is only a part.

It begins with us recognizing that we have a puzzle or a problem to solve. This might present itself to us as a direct challenge – how do we get out of this situation? For an artist or composer it might be the burning desire to create a new painting or symphony. To an entrepreneur it may be exploring the question of how to exploit an opportunity. But it could also be much less well formed than that – sometimes it is playing around with possibilities before the 'problem' emerges.

If it is something we have seen before we can often switch straight to applying a solution. But if it is something trickier we need to explore it further. This can be frustrating; we may wrestle with it for some time without coming up with any insight about possible solutions. Or we may try various ideas out and realize they don't or won't work. Importantly what's going on here is a process of recognizing and preparing the problem.

We might give up on the struggle and switch off our attention – but the reality is that we don't let the problem go. Our brain continues to process and explore, trying out different connections, playing with different options. When we walk away from the problem or decide to sleep on it, we are not leaving it behind but rather passing the work of trying to solve it over to our unconscious minds. This incubation stage is important; as the name suggests we are allowing something to develop and grow.

At some stage there is a moment and the insight is born. It may be that we wake up with a fresh idea in our head, or we suddenly get that flash of inspiration. The 'aha!' moment is often accompanied by feelings of certainty; even if we can't explain why, we just know this is the right solution. There's a flow of energy and a sense of direction to our thinking. The idea may still need a lot of work, elaborating and developing it, but the underlying breakthrough has been made.

The Nobel Prize winning poet T. S. Eliot reflected on this kind of experience in his work;

> it gives me the impression . . . . . of having undergone a long incubation, though we do not know until the shell breaks what kind of egg we have been sitting on. To me it seems that at these moments . . . . . what happens is something negative: that is to say, not 'inspiration' as we commonly think of it, but the breaking down of strong habitual barriers – which tend to re-form very quickly. Some obstruction is momentarily whisked away. The accompanying feeling is less like what we know as positive pleasure, than a sudden relief from an intolerable burden.
>
> (p. 47, [15])

Creativity in action: snakes on a bus

The nineteenth-century chemist Friedrich August Kekule is credited with having unravelled one of the keys to the development of organic chemistry: the structure of the benzene ring. This arrangement of atoms is central to understanding how to make a whole range of chemicals, from fertilizers through medicines to explosives, and enabled the rapid acceleration of growth in the field. Having wrestled for a long period with the problem, he eventually had a flash of inspiration on waking from a dream in which he had seen the atoms dance and then, like a snake, begin eating its own tail. This weird dream picture nudged him towards the key insight that the atoms in benzene were arranged in a ring. And that insight laid the foundations for modern organic chemistry.

This pattern can be seen in many accounts of creativity where people talk about how they came up with apparently radical new solutions. And it's a key resource for us in thinking about how we can build creativity. If it's a landscape across which we travel, then we can map the territory, understand what's going on and provide some resources to help.

Creativity activity

Pause for a moment to think about your own experience, the moments when you have had a clear sense of insight – use the Recollecting Creativity exercise on the companion website to help.

Wallas's model still offers a helpful roadmap, one that we can relate to personal experience. Although it could be criticized as relying on people's self-reporting, the core elements remain today in our theories of how creativity works: separating problem-finding/detection/redefining from incubating activity, the role of insight and the important later stages of elaboration and refinement.

Myth 2: creative people are special people

Close your eyes and imagine someone being creative. What do you see? The chances are you have begun to picture an artist, maybe a musical composer, perhaps a sculptor or a poet wrestling with his or her imagination. Maybe you have a scientist in mind, a crazy white-haired professor who has questionable dress sense but a brilliant mind and is working out solutions to the problems of the universe. Perhaps a computer geek, hunched in front of a blue screen during long, late nights, surrounded by empty pizza boxes and unwashed coffee cups.

The reality is different: what we know about creativity is that everyone is capable of it and it can be developed and deployed in a wide variety of ways. It's at the heart of being human, something we have evolved over a long period of time. Watch any group of children in a playground to be reminded of this wonderful facility fitted as standard equipment! The question is not whether or not people are creative but how to unlock what is already there and then hone and develop the skills of being creative.

But while we are all capable of creativity, we differ in how comfortable we feel about playing with new ideas or loosening up our minds to allow new thought patterns. We have a mental 'comfort zone' within which we can be creative, and we can occasionally push the boundaries and explore something significantly novel. But few of us would want to spend all of our time wrestling with the pain of trying to create something radically new. One of the characteristics associated with stereotypes of creative people is that they are often troubled and unhappy, struggling with internal conflicts. Think of Van Gogh or Tchaikovsky as examples of how painful a creative process can be.

Many studies of creative thinking have looked at two different modes of thinking – convergent and divergent. Convergent thinking is about focus, homing in on a single best answer whereas divergent thinking is about making associations, often exploring round the edges of a problem. Whereas some problems have a single right answer and only need a convergent approach, most require a mixture of the two thinking skills. We need divergent thinking to open them up, explore their dimensions and create new associations, and we need convergent thinking to focus, refine and improve the most useful solution for a particular context.

Research suggests that people differ in their approaches; some are more comfortable in divergent thinking than others. Attempts have been made to map these to personality types and characteristics like introversion and extraversion. But the emerging conclusion is that creative people have both, a predisposition for certain kind of thinking and behaviour and a developed set of competences and skills.

Another dimension of creativity is linked to experience and expertise. Creative people are often highly experienced in a field and thus able to see patterns and identify variations on a core theme that others won't see. Dorothy Leonard calls these 'deep smarts' and many studies in psychology have shown the importance of such deep knowledge as a part of creativity [16]. This raises the idea of 'domain specificity': people who may be highly creative in one field may not be so in another.

> For a 'deeper' dive on the topic of domain specificity, go to the companion website.

What all of this means is that if we want to mobilize and enhance creativity then we need to find multiple ways of doing so. It's not simply a matter of finding an 'on/off' switch but rather one of building the context in which people can deliver their particular skills. Much of what we have learned about managing creativity is about configuring tools and resources to enable different people to feel comfortable and supported in the process. For some this may be a very loose unstructured environment where crazy ideas fly around the room and bounce off each other in wild flights of fancy. For others it may be more structured and systematic, supporting people in a guided process in which they can find and solve problems in an incremental fashion.

Throughout the book we'll take an approach which looks at defining the key competences and underlying skills which we need for creativity and at how we can develop and strengthen them.

Creativity in action: skills and styles in creativity

Creativity is not about doing one single thing – researchers recognize that it is made up of many different skills. For example a study conducted by Clayton Christensen and colleagues looked the behaviour of 3,000 executives over a six-year period and found five important 'discovery' skills for innovators [17]:

- Associating
- Questioning
- Observing
- Experimenting
- Networking.

The most powerful overall driver of innovation was associating – making connections across 'seemingly unrelated questions, problems, or ideas'.

It's not just about using different skills – we also have different preferred 'styles' of behaviour – how we like to express it and what we feel comfortable with. The UK psychologist Michael Kirton carried out extensive work and developed an instrument to measure these differences [18]. He defined two points on a scale running from 'innovators' who were open to considerable flexibility in their creative thinking, to 'adaptors' who were more comfortable with incremental creativity.

Myth 3: it's all about the big bang . . .

Creativity is about breaking through to radical new ideas, new ways of framing the problem and new direction for solving it. But it's also about the hard work of polishing and refining those breakthrough ideas, debugging and problem-solving to get them to work. The pattern of innovation is one of occasional flashes of inspiration followed by long periods of incremental improvement around those breakthrough ideas. Creativity matters throughout this process.

Think about Thomas Edison – one of the great innovators of all time. He famously is supposed to have said that genius was '1% inspiration, 99% perspiration'! Whether he did or not, it certainly was a fitting motto for the way he worked. His attempts to create the electric light bulb offer a good illustration. After having shown that it was possible to make an incandescent bulb (following pioneering research by Joseph Swan), the practical challenge for Edison became one of finding the right material for the filament. The principle was to use a carbonized organic material – for example, bamboo or cedar wood – but the problem was, which one would be right for the job? Edison worked tirelessly at this, trying all sorts of things out, carbonizing anything which might offer a possible solution. He used different trees, plants, even plucking hairs out of the heads of his assistants, going through thousands of options. 'Before I got through', he recalled, 'I tested no fewer than 6,000 vegetable growths, and ransacked the world for the most suitable filament material' (p. 52, [19]).

The reality is that small steps matter; incremental innovation is a key part of making creativity happen. While there may be a flash of insight, seeing the problem in a new way and illuminating the oath towards its solution the realization of that solution involves a lot of hard work refining and elaborating it. Edison's experience is typical; for example far from instant success the Wright Brothers spent years perfecting their ideas for a flying machine. As Kevin Ashton comments,

> their glider of 1900 looked like their kite of 1899. Their glider of 1901 looked like their glider of 1900 but with a few new elements. Their glider of 1902 was their glider of 1901, bigger and with a rudder. Their 1903 Flyer – the aircraft that flew from Kitty Hawk's sands – was their 1902 glider made bigger again with propellers and an engine added. Orville and Wilbur Wright did not leap into the sky. They walked there one step at a time.
>
> (p. 57, [20])

James Dyson took five years and over 5,000 prototypes before he was able to complete the successful design for his bagless vacuum cleaner. When we talk about 'debugging' software or of ironing out teething troubles we are referring to this 'Cinderella' part of the creativity story – the need for incremental improvement along the radical trajectory.

What does research tells us about creativity?

Everyone is creative – and at times it seems as if everyone also has an opinion on how creativity happens! There are countless books and articles offering to explain what it is and how you can harness it to improve your life. YouTube channels and online websites talk of unlocking the secrets of creative potential, and there is a whole industry of workshops and seminars delivering the same message in hotel rooms and conference centres. The risk in all of this is that the message can get lost or distorted; what is offered as insight is often little more than opinion or technique without an underlying understanding.

The good news is that there is a research base on which we can draw and we can use this to build some firm foundations for enabling and enhancing creativity. Throughout the book we try and link into this, and on the companion website you can find some 'deeper dives' which shine a spotlight on the science around creativity. But let's briefly fly over the research landscape and take a look at some key insights.

Early maps

As we suggested earlier, people have been interested in creativity and how it happens for a long time, both from the standpoint of reflection (in different artists, scientists, composers, poets and inventors made attempts to describe their creative moments) and from observation and experiment – for example the work of Graham Wallas. This formed part of a wider movement around cognition – how do we think? – and the emerging field of psychology began developing experimental approaches to try and test out models around cognitive processes (see for histories of the field [21–26]). One of the pioneers in terms of bringing a systematic scientific focus to studying creativity was J. P. Guilford, president of the influential American Psychological Association, who saw creativity as 'a vital natural resource'. His studies into the structure of thinking led to the development of ideas around 'convergent' and 'divergent' thinking, and he suggested the importance of developing the ability to produce ideas ('fluency') but also to generate different directions in thinking about solutions ('flexibility') [27]. Another psychologist, Paul Torrance, built on these ideas and developed a series of psychometric tests for creative thinking ability which are still widely used today [28]. (We'll discuss this in more detail in Chapter 4.)

Cognitive psychologists have looked at many different angles on creativity – for example the role of memory, the accumulation of knowledge and the various tactics and strategies which we employ in confronting and dealing with problems [29]. For example the work of Nobel prize winner Herbert Simon included extensive research on the way experts and novices approach and solve problems and the importance of 'rules of thumb' (heuristics) in the process [30–33].

Other researchers have explored issues around why and how creativity evolved. A key theme here is the idea of a 'theory of mind' – the emergence of the ability to imagine what another human being is thinking about [34]. This allows for anticipation, for designing strategies of co-operation, for building trust and empathy and eventually for creating groups which have a better survival chance. Importantly for the study of creativity the underlying capability implied in this is one of being able to imagine – to play with ideas in the abstract and then link them to the concrete 'real' world.

Other early researchers thought that creativity results from primary drives; perhaps the most famous exponent of this model was Sigmund Freud who saw it as the result of repressed urges – wish fulfilment. 'Unsatisfied wishes are the driving power behind fantasies; every separate fantasy contains the fulfillment of a wish, and improves and unsatisfactory reality' (p. 448, [35]).

Some researchers saw links between mental illness and creativity in which creativity arises from some kind of mental disturbance, the by-product of a troubled mind. Evidence for what we might call the 'Van Gogh view' of creativity comes in part from the analysis of many creative writers, artists, composers and sculptors who produced creative work but were to a degree mentally unstable. But there is also empirical work – for example the theory developed by Hans Eysenck, suggesting that there are differences in the brain structures of people who are more or less creative [36]. His theory of personality included a dimension called 'psychoticism' and he argued that a high psychoticism score was linked to creativity; he also suggested that people with a high score might suffer some psychotic episodes during their lives.

Another research strand involves the complex physical biology of neurons and their patterns of connectivity when we are being creative. Roger Sperry's studies in the 1960s of the different hemispheres in the brain and their importance in creative thinking led to a stream of research elaborating and exploring the ways in which connectivity and association matters [37]. One of the significant findings to emerge early on was that creativity actually requires the capacities from both hemispheres, combining logic and analysis with intuition and emotion. In 1976 Silvano Arieti called this the 'magic synthesis', and writing twenty years later another researcher Albert Katz put it, 'creative activity cannot be localized as a special function unique to one of the cerebral hemispheres. Rather, productive thought involves the integration and coordination of processes subserved by both hemispheres' [38].

One of the early researchers to look at how we might mobilize creativity in systematic fashion was an advertising executive, Alex Osborn. He developed a number of techniques which he captured in his 1953 book, *Applied Imagination*; the most famous of these was the idea of brainstorming [39]. This builds on several of the emerging ideas around how creativity happens – the importance of incubation and allowing the unconscious mind the chance to express itself, the value of exploring dimensions of the problem through playing with different versions of it and the risk of an environment which is too critical too quickly. The core principle in brainstorming is separating idea generation from evaluation: suspend or postpone judgment. We'll return to this theme later in the book.

Osborn worked with a colleague, Sidney Parnes, to develop an approach which became known as Creative Problem-Solving (CPS); importantly much of their work involved developing practical tools and techniques to help support the process of creativity. The core method involved originally six stages – Objective Finding, Data Finding, Problem Finding, Idea Finding, Solution Finding and Acceptance Finding. Within each stage, there is scope for both divergent and convergent thinking. Variations on this approach spread and became widely adopted in fields as diverse as education, healthcare and business; it provided scope for what might be called 'action research' (learning in the context of doing) around creativity [40].

> The model is constantly revised and developed and has now four main stages with several sub-steps. Go to the companion website for a 'deeper dive' and for a link to the Creative Education Foundation.

Other writers offered influential models and techniques – for example Edward de Bono who coined the term 'lateral thinking' in 1967. His approach involves a systematic reasoning process that embraced multiple approaches to problem-solving, moving away from both the linear step-by-step logical reasoning and the unchecked creative imagination techniques which might lead to many wild ideas but no focus on the core problem. His ideas developed into a widely used approach for managing the thinking processes around problem-solving and stressed the importance of mental flexibility in applying different modes of thinking. (Again we'll look in more detail at his ideas later [41].)

Go to the companion website for an overview of lateral thinking.

Sharper tools, new insights

A big problem in psychology is that it is difficult to study the actual processes involved in brain activity; we can't easily get inside people's heads and rummage around! But the toolkit has been getting sharper; early studies used electroencephalograph (EEG) techniques in which electrodes are fitted to the scalp and patterns of electrical activity can be viewed as different kinds of thought take place. With the advent of computer-aided tomography (CAT) technology we have been able to probe more deeply, using techniques like positron emission technology (PET), functional magnetic resonance imaging (fMRI) and an increasingly powerful alphabet spaghetti of sharp tools!

The exciting thing is that much of this work helps confirm theories and insights proposed by earlier researchers on creativity. For example the idea that creativity somehow resided in the right hemisphere is challenged by EEG studies which show various different areas involved – and that when damage occurred in different places it inhibited creative abilities [42].

EEG research also helps confirm the stage model originally suggested by Wallas; for example a study by Colin Martindale and Nancy Hasenfus in 1978 found more alphas (a particular kind of 'spike' on an EEG readout) during the inspiration stage than in the elaboration stage, at least in notably creative individuals [43].

Interest has particularly focused on the frontal lobes (part of our cortex, the 'bit behind our foreheads') and the key role which they seem to play in integrating inputs from other parts of the brain. For example in 2005 Alice Flaherty used a mixture of imaging, drug studies and analysis of lesions (damage to brain tissue) to develop a three-factor model of the 'creative drive' which sees it as resulting from an interaction of the frontal lobes, the temporal lobes, and dopamine from the limbic system (a collection of brain structures which influences strongly our emotions) [44]. In her model the frontal lobes can be seen as responsible for idea generation, and the temporal lobes for idea editing and evaluation. Abnormalities in the frontal lobe (such as depression or anxiety) generally decrease creativity, while abnormalities in the temporal lobe often increase creativity. High activity in the temporal lobe typically inhibits activity in the frontal lobe and vice versa. High dopamine levels increase general arousal and goal-directed behaviours and reduce latent inhibition, and all three effects increase the drive to generate ideas.

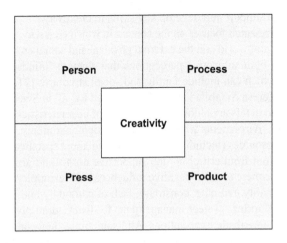

Figure 1.2 4Ps of creativity

Frameworks for thinking about creativity

A helpful way of linking the various types of research around creativity was offered by Mel Rhodes in 1961, who analyzed many different definitions and tried to characterize it in terms of four key areas of study [45]. This approach is helpful because it offers us a kind of 'periodic table', a framework for looking at creativity research in a structured fashion. His 4Ps model (see Figure 1.2) looks at person, process, press and product:

> *Person* – research focused on the traits that characterize creative persons. These typically include
>
>> high valuation of aesthetic qualities in experience, broad interests, attraction to complexity, high energy, independence of judgment, autonomy, intuition, self-confidence, ability to resolve antinomies or to accommodate apparently opposite or conflicting traits in one's self concept, and finally, a firm sense of self as 'creative'.
>>
>> [46]
>
>> It's also important to remember that there may be differences in the traits that allow creative performances in different fields. Importantly the research shows that while some people may have favourable traits, the capacity for creativity is something everyone shares and it can be developed as a set of competences and skills.
>
> *Process* – this is the strand that explores our theme from earlier that creativity is not a single flash of inspiration but some kind of journey or process. Many researchers have tried to map this and to explore relevant subprocesses which could be involved [40, 43]. As we will see throughout

the book, the use of such models can help focus particular tools and techniques to support and develop key skills in creativity.

Press – this research focuses on the context in which creativity takes place – the inner mental world and the external physical and social environment. Press involves both subjective perceptions that shape a 'mindset' and external factors which can include family and social structures [21, 47]. Researchers like Teresa Amabile in the US and Goran Ekvall in Sweden have done a great deal in this area looking at the kinds of characteristics associated with creative environments which include: freedom, autonomy, good role models and resources (including time), encouragement specifically for originality, freedom from criticism, and supportive norms and group beliefs [48]. Of course there are also negative influences – for example a lack of respect for originality, red tape, constraint, lack of autonomy and resources, inappropriate norms, project management, feedback, time pressure, competition and unrealistic expectations. And sometimes they can have two-sided effects – for example competition can both inhibit and stimulate creativity, criticism can close it down or challenge and open it up.

Work on press has led to many changes in the way we approach the design of physical and organizational environments to support creativity and we'll explore this in more detail later in the book.

Product – research here focuses on the outcomes of the creative process. Studying paintings, poems, sculpture or symphonies has the advantage of being amenable to counting and classifying – but it can also be criticized for a focus on productivity rather than creativity.

One important question raised here is whether we all have a common understanding of what is creative and if so, can we give it a value? Teresa Amabile looked at how consistently people judged creative products in different domains [49]. She gathered experts of a certain field (e.g. artists and art teachers) and had them judge newly produced works of art. She called her technique 'consensual assessment technique' and it led to the conclusion that within disciplines, creativity can be identified (and described) even if the criteria are not clearly defined. Another way to tackle that topic is by defining creative outcomes. Susan Besemer and Donald Treffinger describe three criteria: novelty, resolution, and elaboration/synthesis [50].

Novelty considers newness in materials, processes, concepts, and methods of making the product. Resolution considers aspects of how well the product works or functions. Elaboration and Synthesis describes stylistic components of the product. Making up the three factors are nine facets. These are, for Novelty, originality and surprise; for Resolution, logical, useful, valuable, and understandable; and for Elaboration and Synthesis, organic, well-crafted, and elegant.

(p. 287, [51])

Factor	Sub-Factor
Novelty	Original
	Surprise
Resolution	Valuable
	Logical
	Useful
	Understandable
Elaboration and Synthesis	Organic Qualities
	Elegance
	Well-crafted

Figure 1.3 Evaluation of creative products

The three elements are part of a three-dimensional model, the Creative Product Analysis Matrix. Susan Besemer and Karen O'Quin revised, shortened, and renamed the model the Creative Product Semantic Scale (CPSS) [52].

We'll draw on many of these research areas in the book, but for now it is worth summarizing by looking at how we can integrate what we know, and more importantly to operationalize it – that is, try to turn our understanding into practical guidelines for how we might go about being creative.

Enabling and enhancing creativity – Competences and skills

As we've seen, everyone is already capable of creativity – it's not a case of injecting them with some magic new ingredient. Instead we need to look for ways in which this natural capability can be drawn out, developed and extended. It's useful to start by thinking about what blocks this natural ability.

Creative activity: blocks to creativity

Write down all your blocks to creativity. What hinders you? Being aware of stumbling blocks does help you to see clearer and be able to see what you need to develop. Think of all four Ps of Creativity. You can use Figure 1.4 as a map to help you think about this challenge.

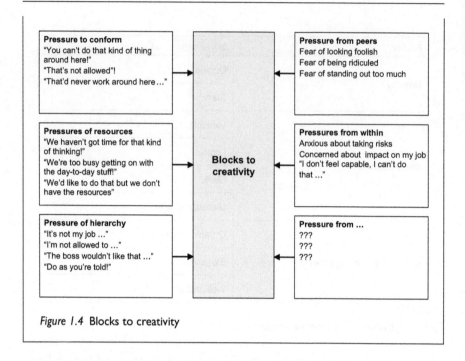

Figure 1.4 Blocks to creativity

On the companion website you can find a link to an excellent TED Talk by Ken Robinson where he powerfully explains some of the ways in which we stifle creativity.

We're interested in how to get past these blocks and barriers and how to develop skills and competences to strengthen the ways we approach creativity. So it's worth looking briefly at what we mean by these terms.

What are competences?

Competences on an individual level shed light on the skills and capabilities needed to meet expectations related to specific roles, jobs, functions or tasks. Competences describe a bundle of behaviours to cope with complex problems in situations where there are no commonly agreed guidelines existing to arrive at a solution. An example would be the competence 'attentive listening', which is needed in order to be able to handle a critical conversation. Competences are subject to learning. Every human being can acquire new competences over his or her lifespan. Competences can also be lost if they are not used on a regular basis.

One of the many wonderful characters in Lewis Carroll's *Alice in Wonderland* is Humpty Dumpty – and among his many characteristics is that he uses words 'to mean whatever I want them to mean'! Competences have become something of a Humpty Dumpty word in research on individuals and organizations. For the sake of simplicity in our competence model we only distinguish between individual competences and team competences. Individual competences are abilities and skills that everybody can make use of in a creative activity or process whether working alone or in a team. The focus is on the individual level and you don't necessarily have to be in a team in order to train and shape them. We have identified four of these competences linked to individual creativity: being open, exploring problems, building up willpower, and self-awareness. Section 2 of this book deals with team competences: creating and sharing a vision, practising psychological safety, supporting ideas, and pushing the frontiers. These competences are the backbone of a creative team.

> You can find more about this debate of what a competence really is on the companion website, where there is a 'deeper dive' exploring the issue.

Within our competence model (see Figure 1.5) there is a hierarchy; each competence involves a bundle of behaviours which allow us to be creative – skills. Webster's Dictionary defines skill as 'the ability to do something that comes from training, experience, or practice'. We've tried to identify these particular skills as 'behavioural anchors' that are measurable and trainable. So, for example, the overall competence around individual creativity is made up of four competence areas and within those a larger set of skills which can be trained and developed.

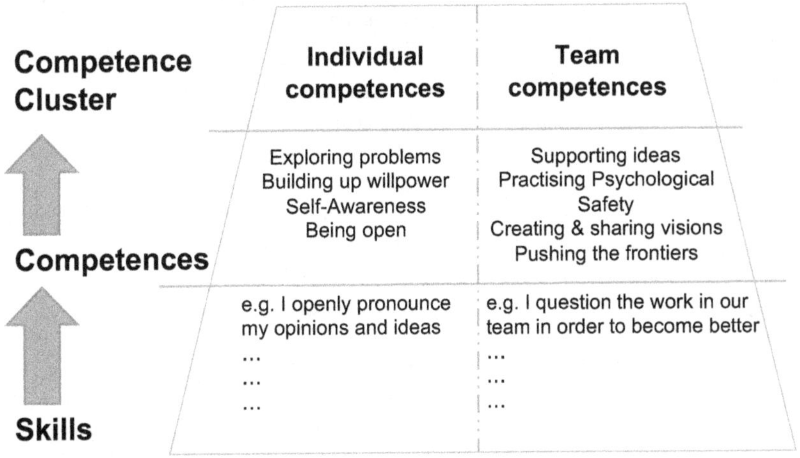

Competence Cluster	Individual competences	Team competences
Competences ⬆	Exploring problems Building up willpower Self-Awareness Being open	Supporting ideas Practising Psychological Safety Creating & sharing visions Pushing the frontiers
Skills ⬆	e.g. I openly pronounce my opinions and ideas	e.g. I question the work in our team in order to become better ... ...

Figure 1.5 Competence model

Why are competences so important for creativity and innovation?

Why are we placing emphasis on competences and skills? Because it is easy to identify factors which are associated with successful performance – but unless we can relate these to things which people actually do – translating the factors into behaviours which can be practised and developed – then these factors remain important in theory but do not make a difference in practice.

Bjarne Jensen and Hanne Harmsen wrote an article in 2001 describing this dilemma in innovation management [53]. We know quite a lot about success factors in developing innovations, drawing on decades of research and practice. Table 1.1 gives some typical factors.

But studies show that despite the fact that established and accepted lists of success factors for innovation exist, companies have a hard time implementing these [54–59]. Jensen and Harmsen get to the heart of this discussion by writing:

> despite the fact that the studies point to a fairly consistent list of success factors, it seems only a few companies have implemented these identified success factors – indicated by the fact that recent studies show companies to make the same mistakes they did 30 years ago.
>
> (p. 37, [53])

Table 1.1 List of success factors in new product development [45]

Critical success areas	Critical success factors
NPD Process	Phase or stage model of the innovation process and professionals acting within them
	Market orientation in the process
	Importance of preparatory work (e.g. initial screening)
	Continuous commercial evaluation
Organization	Cross-functional NPD teams
	Strong and responsible project leader
	NPD teams with responsibility for the whole process
	Commitment of team members and project leader towards the project
	Intensive communication
Culture	Innovation-friendly and favourable to risk-taking
	Product champions or promoters of new ideas exist
	Role and commitment of senior management
Strategy	Strategic framework with an overall long-term orientation guiding individual projects
	Defined and clear objectives

They conclude that individual competences are the missing link to successful implementation.

Developing the skills – Working Out at the creativity gym

Serious skill or competence development starts with some form of self-assessment: where are we now, what are our strengths and where are areas for improvement? Assessment helps us define a clear goal – what competence or skill do we want to improve? And it also helps us focus on how to get there – how much time/ effort do we want to put into developing it, what are our priorities and where do we start?

Underpinning any competence development is a framework like that in Figure 1.6. There is no magic wand that can suddenly move us from defining a goal to being a master – it's a process of training and a matter of development; getting feedback on the progress is a key element in this.

Developing your skills is very similar to going to the gym in order to become fitter. First of all you start with a general fitness test and use that to help setting your goal. Then you plan and undertake your training sessions, motivating yourself through different forms of inspiration. These might be visualizing yourself in the future with the perfect body, or finding a role model who you'd like to emulate. Or they might be more concrete – rewarding yourself when you reach a certain milestone.

Gradually you make progress and one wonderful day you reach your goal – great, but that sets up a new challenge. Having got to peak fitness now you need to maintain that. You need to continue training and maybe set yourself a new goal, even more stretching and challenging. Central to all of this is feedback – information on how well you are doing. At the outset this could take the form of self-assessment, but as you progress it helps to get external feedback – and maybe some coaching to help you stay focused and to push yourself to peak fitness.

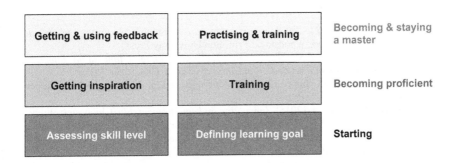

Figure 1.6 Competence development

> Go to the companion website for a model training plan for competence and skill development.

Overview of the book

The book is structured in the following way. We begin with what we know about the individual level. What are the basic elements of creativity in terms of the core neurological processes, and the key dimensions which are associated with it? In particular, why are these important for creativity and how do they play out? And what are the underlying competences and skills which can be identified and trained? Lastly we visit the gym, offering a range of 'exercises' to help develop these.

We then move to the group level – what is the evidence around creativity as a shared social process? What are the modulating effects in both a positive and a negative direction? What are the key competences and skills to enhance group level creativity and why are they important? And again, the gym and exercise options are the last part.

Then we look at context – environmental influences on creativity and how they modulate it. Again, what can we learn and implement to create contexts – what 'organizational skills' are needed?

The second half of the book is about examples, and particularly how the ideas in the first half might be organized into framework approaches. We explore several – user-led innovation, design thinking, high involvement innovation, agile and 'crisis' creativity – as examples of how the skills and competences we explore in the book can be combined to enable innovation.

Finally we take a glimpse into the future – what are new technical and social trends likely to mean for how creativity plays out in the longer term? What might the world look like when creativity is embedded in machine learning, or where we are using implants or creativity-enhancing drugs which enable more effective neurological processes? What does the digital future hold for distributed creativity?

References

[1]   Baumol, W. J. (2002). *The free-market innovation machine: Analyzing the growth miracle of capitalism.* Woodstock: Princeton University Press.
[2]   Tidd, J., Bessant, J., Pavitt, K., & Wiley, J. (1998). *Managing innovation: Integrating technological, market and organizational change.* Chichester: Wiley.
[3]   Drucker, P. (1995). *Innovation and entrepreneurship.* New York, NY: Harper Business.
[4]   Bessant, J., & Tidd, J. (2015). *Innovation and entrepreneurship.* Chichester: Wiley.
[5]   Amabile, T. M. (1996). *Creativity in context.* Boulder, CO: Westview Press.
[6]   Newell, A., Shaw, J. C., & Simon, H. A. (1959). *The processes of creative thinking.* Santa Monica, CA: Rand Corporation.

[7]   Cohen-Shalev, A. (1989). Old age style: Developmental changes in creative produc-
      tion from a life-span perspective. *Journal of Aging Studies, 3*, 21–37.
[8]   Helson, R. (1990). Creativity in women: Outer and inner views over time. In M.A.
      Runco & R.S. Albert (Eds.), *Theories of creativity* (46–58). Newbury Park: Sage.
[9]   Runco, M.A., & Charles, R.E. (1997). Developmental trends in creative potential
      and creative performance. *Creativity Research Handbook, 1*, 115–152.
[10] Dudek, S.Z., & Hall, W.B. (1991). Personality consistency: Eminent architects 25
      years later. *Creativity Research Journal, 4*, 213–231.
[11] Lindauer, M.S. (1992). Creativity in aging artists: Contributions from the humani-
      ties to the psychology of old age. *Creativity Research Journal, 5*, 211–231.
[12] Lindauer, M.S. (1993). The span of creativity among long-lived historical artists.
      Creativity Research Journal, 6, 221–239.
[13] Dyson, J. (1997). *Against the odds.* London: Orion.
[14] Wallas, G. (1926). *The art of thought.* London: Watts.
[15] Eliot, T.S. (1933). *The use of poetry and the use of criticism.* Boston: Harvard Uni-
      versity Press.
[16] Leonard-Barton, D., & Swap, W.C. (2005). *Deep smarts: How to cultivate and
      transfer enduring business wisdom.* Boston: Harvard Business Press.
[17] Christensen, C., Dyer, J., & Gregerson, H. (2011). *The innovator's DNA. Boston:
      Harvard Business School Press.*
[18] Kirton, M. (1976). Adaptors and innovators: A description and measure. *Journal of
      Applied Psychology, 61*, 622.
[19] Axelrod, A. (2008). *Edison on innovation.* Chichester: Wiley.
[20] Ashton, K. (2015). *How to fly a horse.* London: Heinemann.
[21] Albert, R.S., & Runco, M.A. (1999). A history of research on creativity. In R.J.
      Sternberg (Ed.), *Handbook of creativity* (16–31). New York, NY: Cambridge Uni-
      versity Press.
[22] Runco, M.A. (2004). Creativity. *Annual Review of Psychology, 55*, 657–687.
[23] Dewey, J. (1933/1986). *How we think: A restatement of the relation of reflective
      thinking to the educative process.* Lexington, MA: D.C. Heath.
[24] Spearman, C. (1931). The Theory of 'two factors' and that of 'sampling'. *British
      Journal of Educational Psychology, 1*, 140–161.
[25] Wallas, G. (1926). *The art of thought.* New York, NY: Harcourt-Brace.
[26] Wertheimer, M. (1945). *Productive Thinking.* New York, NY: Harper & Row.
[27] Guilford, J. (1967). *The nature of human intelligence.* New York, NY: McGraw-Hill.
[28] Torrance, P. (1962). *Guiding creative talent.* Englewood Cliffs, NJ: Prentice-Hall.
[29] The cognitive research on creativity is quite diverse. Basic cognitive processes have
      been studied:

      memory: Pollert, L.H., Feldhusen, J.F., Van Mondfrans, A.P., & Treffinger, D.J.
      (1969). Role of memory in divergent thinking. *Psychological Reports, 25*, 151–156.
      attention: Martindale, C., & Greenough, J. (1973). The differential effect of increased
      arousal on creative and intellectual performance. *Journal of Genetic Psychology,
      123*, 329–335.
      knowledge: Rubenson, D.L., & Runco, M.A. (1992). The psychoeconomic approach
      to creativity. *New Ideas in Psychology, 10*, 131–147.
      tactics, strategies, metacognition: Root-Bernstein, R.S. (1988). Setting the stage for
      discovery. *Sciences, 28*, 26–34.

[30] Simon, H.A. (1979). *Models of thought* (Vol. 1). New Haven, CT: Yale University
      Press.
[31] Simon, H. (1990). *Reason in human affairs.* Stanford, CA: Stanford University
      Press.

[32]   Langley, P. (1987). *Scientific discovery: Computational explorations of the creative processes*. Cambridge: MIT Press.

[33]   Simon, H.A. (1996). *Models of my life*. Cambridge: MIT Press.

[34]   Baron-Cohen, S. (1999). *The evolution of a theory of mind*. Oxford: Oxford University Press.

[35]   Arieti, S. (1976). *Creativity: The magic synthesis*. Oxford: Basic.

[36]   Eysenck, H. (1963). Biological basis of personality. *Nature, 199*, 1031–1034.

[37]   Sperry, R. (1969). Hemisphere deconnection and unity in conscious awareness. *American Psychologist, 23*, 723–733.

[38]   Katz, A. (1997). Creativity in the cerebral hemispheres. *Creativity Research Handbook, 1*, 203–226.

Hoppe & Kyle (1991) and TenHouten (1994) studied Sperry's patients and described how they lacked this kind of integrated thought. Hoppe & Kyle suggested that the problem was alexithymia, a lack of emotionality and affect. They found clear evidence of this in the language of the patients, and in the lack of affect-laden interpretations of experience. The patients described things rather than their reactions to things. They also 'showed a relatively impoverished fantasy life'.

Hoppe, K., & Kyle, N. (1991). Dual brain, creativity, and health. *Creativity Research Journal, 3*, 150–157.

TenHouten, W.D. (1994). Creativity, intentionality, and alexithymia: A graphological analysis of split-brained patients and normal controls. In M.D. Runco, K.D. Hoppe, & M. Shaw (Eds.), *Creativity and affect* (225–250). Norwood, NJ: Ablex.

[39]   Osborn, A. (1953). *Applied imagination: Principles and procedures of creative problem solving*. New York, NY: Scribner.

[40]   Isaksen, S.G., & Treffinger, D.J. (2004). Celebrating 50 years or reflective practice: Versions of creative problem solving. *Journal of Creative Behavior, 38*, 75–101.

[41]   de Bono, E. (1971). *The use of lateral thinking*. Harmondsworth: Penguin.

[42]   Hoppe, K., & Kyle, N. (1991). Dual brain, creativity, and health. *Creativity Research Journal, 3*, 150–157.

TenHouten, W.D. (1994). Creativity, intentionality, and alexithymia: A graphological analysis of split-brained patients and normal controls. In M.D. Runco, K.D. Hoppe, & M. Shaw (Eds.), *Creativity and affect* (225–250). Norwood, NJ: Ablex.

[43]   Martindale, C., & Hasenfus, N. (1978). EEG differences as a function of creativity, stage of the creative process, and effort to be original. *Biological Psychology, 6*, 157–167.

[44]   Flaherty, A.W. (2005). Frontotemporal and dopaminergic control of idea generation and creative drive. *Journal of Comparative Neurology, 493*, 147–153.

[45]   Rhodes, M. (1961). An analysis of creativity. *Phi Delta Kappan, 42*, 305–311.

[46]   Barron, F., & Harrington, D.M. (1981). Creativity, intelligence, and personality. *Annual Review of Psychology, 32*, 439–476.

[47]   Murray (1938) distinguished between alpha and beta pressures. The former pressures reflect the more objective aspects of press, and the latter the individual's interpretation of some contextual pressure.

Murray, H.A. (1938). *Explorations in personality*. New York, NY: Oxford University Press.

[48]   These influences create 'norms in which innovation is prized and failure not fatal' (Witt & Beorkrem, pp. 31–32).

Witt, L.A., & Beorkrem, M.N. (1989). Climate for creative productivity as a predictor of research usefulness and organizational effectiveness in an R&D organization. *Creativity Research Journal, 2*, 30–40.

Amabile, T. (1998). *How to kill creativity*. Boston, MA: Harvard Business School.

Ekvall, G. (1991). The organizational culture of idea management. In J. Henry & D. Walker (Eds.), *Managing innovation* (73–79). London: Sage.

[49]   Amabile, T.M. (1982). Social psychology of creativity: A consensual assessment technique. *Journal of Personality and Social Psychology, 43*, 997–1013.
[50]   Besemer, S., & Treffinger, D.J. (1981). Analysis of creative products: Review and synthesis. *Journal of Creative Behavior, 15*, 158–178.
[51]   Besemer, S., & O'Quin, K. (1999). Confirming the three-factor creative product analysis matrix model in an American sample. *Creativity Research Journal, 12*, 287–296.
[52]   Besemer, S., & O'Quin, K. (1986). Analyzing creative products: Refinement and test of a judging instrument. *Journal of Creative Behavior, 20*, 12.
[53]   Jensen, B., & Harmsen, H. (2001). Implementation of success factors in new product development – The missing links? *European Journal of Innovation Management, 4*, 37–52.
[54]   Ernst, H. (2002). Success factors of new product development: A review of the empirical literature. *International Journal of Management Reviews, 4*, 1–40.
[55]   Cooper, R.G. (1998). Benchmarking new product performance: Results of the best practises study. *European Management Journal, 16*, 1–17.
[56]   Cooper, R.G. (1999). The invisible success factors in product innovation. *Journal of Product Innovation Management, 16*, 115–133.
[57]   Cooper, R.G., & Kleinschmidt, E.J. (1986). An investigation into the new product process. *Journal of Product Innovation Management, 3*, 71–85.
[58]   Cooper, R.G., & Kleinschmidt, E.J. (1995). Benchmarking the firm's critical success factors in new product development. *Journal of Product Innovation Management, 12*, 374–391.
[59]   Craig, A., & Hart, S. (1992). Where to now in new product development research? *European Journal of Marketing, 26*, 1–49.

Section 2

Individual level

Close your eyes and imagine someone being creative. Or think back to a time when you did something you would consider creative. Whatever the picture, it is almost certainly not a still-life – the act of creativity is very much about action. Some of it may be visible – for example artists sketching or engineers playing with prototypes. But much of it is less visible, involving mental gymnastics and stretches, hidden from view but nonetheless of central importance.

Alongside actions like playing, exploring, reviewing, elaborating and reframing you might also list some characteristics – fluency, flexibility, curiosity, risk-taking and being tolerant of ambiguity. These are states of mind but they don't happen by accident – they too involve action. People behave in ways which stretch their thinking to be more flexible, they experiment with risky ideas, they explore to satisfy their curiosity and they learn to become more tolerant of different perspectives.

By now we hope you recognize that creativity isn't a magic gift possessed by a few lucky individuals. Nor is it merely something with which we are endowed at birth, a trait or characteristic passed on by our genes. There may be predispositions which help but research is pretty clear – creativity is something which can be practised, trained and developed by anyone. And it's very much an action, not a state of being.

Our aim in this book is to try exploring the different behaviours which are linked with creativity and particularly focus on those competencies (and their underpinning skills) which research has shown are associated with success. In the following section we'll focus on the individual level and in particular look at four areas of competence:

*   Problem exploration
*   Openness
*   Willpower
*   Self-awareness.

We'll explore each of these in the following chapters, drawing on relevant research and practical experience. In each case we'll use a common structure:

- What are the important skills – what is the competence?
- Why is it important for creativity?
- What are key skills making up this competence?
- How can these skills be trained and developed?

We'll try and illustrate with plenty of examples, and if you are interested to delve a little further we have put some 'deeper dive' material on the companion website accompanying the book. Most important, there are plenty of opportunities for you to visit the 'creativity gym' and try out some exercises for yourself!

## Chapter 2

Exploring problems

Chapter objectives

By the end of this chapter you will:

- Understand the role which problem exploration plays in creativity;
- Recognize the key skills associated with problem exploration;
- Develop awareness of tools and techniques to help build competence in problem exploration;
- Reflect on and be able to develop your own skills in problem exploration.

Introduction

'Houston, we've had a problem here.' When John Swigert reported this situation aboard the Apollo 13 spacecraft to his controllers back in Texas it triggered a fascinating demonstration of problem-solving ingenuity. At 2 a.m. on 14th April 1970 an explosion in their main oxygen tanks and the failure of a major part of the electrical system suddenly put their lives at risk. The extreme conditions in which they had to work to repair it required rapid creative thinking – novel solutions – on the part of a large group of people on the ground and aboard the ship itself. As the drama unfolded the whole world watched, holding its breath and later marvelling at this example of creativity in action.

It's worth looking a little more closely at this case. In particular, while the initial challenge was very apparent and urgently needed solving, the solutions which were developed did not immediately fall into place. This wasn't a simple case of pulling a ready-made solution off the shelf; instead it required exploring the nature and dimensions of the problem, redefining and shaping it. Only then did the solution route become apparent, emerging gradually as a direction worth travelling in.

Let's move to a different world and try, for a moment, to climb inside the mind of an artist as he or she tries to come up with something novel and of artistic value. This was what researchers Mihaly Csikszentmihalyi and Jacob Getzels did in 1971 working with a group of art students [1]. They gave them a table on which there were around 30 objects and observed them as they carried out the task of constructing a 'still life' composition from them.

The results were powerful. These artists didn't simply place the objects randomly and start to paint; instead they explored, arranged and rearranged, selected and abandoned. They took time climbing around the challenge they had been given, exploring it carefully before finally embarking on their particular journey through the landscape offered by the resources table.

When the work was evaluated (on 3 dimensions – overall creative value, originality and craftsmanship) by a group of experienced professors, there was a clear link between the quality of what they produced and the amount of time and effort they had spent in this exploration stage. Csikszentmihalyi and Getzels called this 'discovery orientation'. Perhaps of even more importance was that the researchers followed up their subjects later in their working lives as artists and found that their performance much later (and being evaluated by a much wider set of judges including people buying and exhibiting their art in homes and galleries) was also predicted by their approach shown in this early experiment. Problem exploration is correlated with high-quality creativity.

Researchers have looked at people facing creativity challenges in a variety of different settings and the same picture emerges. What we do in the early stages of working with a problem matters. We may even not be aware that it is a problem – the Apollo 13 example was a crisis which had to be solved, but the challenge to the artists was much less pressing. As the sculptor Henry Moore observed,

> I sometimes begin drawing with no preconceived problem to solve, with only a desire to use pencil on paper and only make lines, tones, and styles with no conscious aim. But as my mind takes in what is so produced, a point arrives where some idea becomes conscious and crystallises, and then control and ordering begin to take place.
>
> (p. 197, [2])

Problems aren't always what they seem . . .

Often the problem can be like a toothache, nagging away in the background but not drawing our full attention. James Dyson wasn't the first person to be frustrated at the inability of his vacuum cleaner to pick up all the dust and the need to keep changing the bag. But eventually something snapped in his engineer's mind and he took the recalcitrant machine to his workshop to try to improve things. Crawling around the apparent problem of an inefficient filtering mechanism – the particles of dust blocked the pores of the bag and so quickly reduced its effective suction – he suddenly had a flash of insight. The actual problem wasn't one of a better bag but whether or not you needed a bag at all. What if you could make a cleaner with no bag, using a different way of separating out the dust from the air being sucked through?

In other words he had *reframed* the problem – and opened up some new lines of inquiry. Just like the artists he then went through a stage of crawling around the new problem, experimenting with different approaches. It was much later, while driving by a sawmill, that he thought about the challenge they must be facing with dust. Sawing through hundreds of trees every day would generate a huge amount of sawdust – yet they didn't seem to have a problem. This led him to look at a different solution to the problem he had been carrying around – the industrial cyclone. A standard tool in manufacturing, cyclones are used to separate out particles from gas by whirling them very fast in a vortex; the gas flows through and the particles remain pressed against the side of the device. Dyson went home and began experimenting with this idea, now marching firmly in a particular direction of problem-solving.

(It's important to note that the flash of inspiration which the cyclone idea gave Dyson was not the end of the story. Rather than going home and instantly coming up with a workable solution, he spent the next five years working through 5,127 prototypes before finally making his device work. Even then he had a huge uphill battle to get his product accepted and an equally draining legal fight to stop others from copying him!)

> You can read more about this case on the companion website, and we will look in more detail at the challenge of perseverance in creativity in Chapter 4.

Reframing the problem

Reframing is a powerful tool in creativity; put simply, if we are blocked in finding a solution to an apparent problem, we try looking at it in a different way. Sometimes this is about *restating the problem* in different terms, re-expressing it in the form of another how-to statement. For example imagine you and some friends are driving out in the country when your car has a puncture in the tyre. The first thought is, 'how do we repair it?' That leads to the need to find the car jack. But when you look in the back of the car the jack is missing. So some of your friends decide that the problem is, 'how to get a replacement jack?' They start off walking towards the nearest village to see if they can borrow one. But another friend notices a tractor working in the field nearby, lifting heavy hay bales with a forklift attachment. Restating the problem as 'how can we lift up the car?' rather than finding a new jack leads your friend to ask the farmer for help and he obliges, using the forklift on his tractor to lift the car so you can quickly change the wheel. Once fixed you thank the farmer and drive on down the road to pick up your footsore friends who are still in search of the elusive jack which they thought was the problem!

A little fanciful, perhaps, but the idea is sound. Often we can find a solution, or at least the path towards one, by restating the problem in different fashion. Such thinking sometimes runs counter to conventional wisdom, but it carries the possibility of radically new solution pathways. One of the main challenges in the field of humanitarian aid is that of food – how to get it to people who need it fast and effectively? For decades the problem was seen as one of logistics – how to procure food, transport it and distribute it to where it was needed. This became the dominant logic behind a huge global effort involving agencies like the United Nations World Food Programme, and it involved a great deal of creativity around solving the problem. But another statement of the problem might be 'how to enable people to feed themselves?' and, more precisely, 'how to give them the resources to procure their own food?' This simple reformulation moves the quest for solutions along a new path; in fact in many disaster situations there is a viable food market, and the challenge is one of getting money to people to help them manage their own food and other needs. This sets up many problems along the way – how to avoid fraud and corruption, how to transmit money safely, how to ensure that the right resources reach the right people – but these can be solved.

The dreadful Indian Ocean tsunami disaster in 2004 was a tipping point in thinking about food aid; the many experiments towards a cash-based solution had matured and there was an urgent need to provide relief to victims. As the UK Overseas Development Institute (ODI) concluded,

> a strong body of evidence is starting to emerge to indicate that providing people with cash or vouchers works. It is possible to target and distribute cash safely, and people spend money sensibly on basic essentials and on rebuilding livelihoods. Cash transfers can provide a stimulus to local economies, and in some contexts can be more cost-effective than commodity-based alternatives.

(p. 2, [3])

By the time of the Haiti earthquake in 2010 this pattern had matured; dealing with this disaster was characterized by a very high level of cash-based interventions. Local food markets began functioning soon after the disaster and the government stopped food distribution interventions after only three months. In particular, this was the point at which using mobile phones as an alternative form of cash distribution came into its own [4].

The scale of turnaround in thinking about the problem became clear when in 2015 the World Food Programme reported that nearly half of its huge budget would go on providing cash-based aid rather than food aid and distribution.

You can find out more about this case, and some of the innovative solutions developed as a result of this reframing on the companion website. And you can try an activity – 'How to. . . ?' – to help you practice reframing.

Of course this kind of thinking is hard to do under conditions of crisis – the urgency of the situation often introduces a kind of 'tunnel vision' and we find it difficult to break out of our current mindset. When alligators are snapping at your legs it's hard to think about solving the problem by draining the swamp! We'll talk about this 'setting effect' later in the chapter.

Climbing the ladder of abstraction

Sometimes there is value in restating the problem at a *different level of abstraction*. Wandering round Chicago in 1912, William Klann was a man on a mission. He was part of a team set up to explore ways in which they could reduce the costs of manufacturing a car to fulfil Henry Ford's vision of 'a motor car for the great multitude'. They had already developed many of the ideas behind mass production – standardized and interchangeable parts, short task cycle work, specialist machinery – but what Klann saw while walking past the Swift Meat Packing Company's factory gave him an insight into a key piece of the puzzle. The workers were effectively *dis*-assembling meat carcasses, stripping off various different joints and cuts as the animals were led past them on a moving overhead conveyor. In a classic moment of insight he saw the possibility of reversing this process – and within a short space of time the Ford factory boasted the world's first moving assembly line. Productivity rocketed as the new idea was implemented and refined; using the new approach Ford was able to cut the assembly time for a Model T to just 93 minutes.

Not that the meat packers had invented something new – back in the early sixteenth century the Venetians had already developed an impressive line in mobile assembly. By moving ships along canals in order to fit them out for battle they were able to produce, arm and provision a new galley at a rate of one per day!

Forty years later, Ray Kroc was running the hamburger business originally established with his friends the McDonald brothers. He was looking for ways to improve productivity and began applying Ford's assembly line techniques to making hamburgers. The rest is fast food history; McDonald's now sells more than 75 hamburgers every second and feeds 68 million people every day!

In another part of the world and a further thirty years on, Dr Govindappa Venkataswamy retired. He'd worked for many years as head of ophthalmology in the main hospital in Madurai, India, and decided to use his expertise and new-found free time to try and help prevent blindness in rural communities in his home state of Tamil Nadu. This was not an insignificant problem – while the treatment itself is well developed it comes at a price: in an Indian hospital the cost works out to around $300, and in a country where most people, especially in rural environments, earn less than $2 a day, such a price tag puts treatment out of reach.

In order to achieve his dream Venkataswamy had to search outside the conventional health sector, seeking ideas from other worlds with similar challenges. Specifically he looked for low-cost ways of carrying out activities systematically, reproducibly and to a high quality standard – and eventually found inspiration in McDonald's. He saw the underlying similarities in the core processes they used and adapted their principles of assembly line manufacturing to the context of eye surgery!

Developing and refining what became known as the Aravind system has meant that the average cost of a cataract operation is now $25, and over 60% of patients are treated for free. This isn't done by compromising on quality – Aravind has better performance than many Western hospitals. It has become the world's largest and most productive eye-care service group, responsible for treating over 35 million patients with its low-cost/high-quality model.

> You can read more and watch a video about Aravind by going to the companion website.

What these stories have in common is that they are working on the same problem, just in a different context. This is a powerful resource in innovation – answers don't always have to be new to the world; they can also be adapted from different contexts. For example, when Wolfgang Dierichs, a research chemist at the German company Henkel, boarded a plane in 1967 he didn't expect to be getting off with a radical innovation in the stationery business. But when he saw a woman applying lipstick he began to see a connection between this and the possibility of selling glue not in messy pots or tins but as a stick. Pritt Stick was the result of that flash of inspiration and has since sold over 2.5 billion units in over 120 countries around the world.

To find analogous solutions in different worlds we first need to climb a 'ladder of abstraction', so that we can see the same problem being solved in different contexts. This is essentially about *translating* the problem into a higher level language.

> Try the approach for yourself – use the 'Levels of Abstraction' activity on the companion website. You'll also find some examples of tools which can help develop this skill – for example Attribute Listing.

Creativity in action: bridging different worlds

Think about the problem of turnaround time. In the low-cost airline world, much depends on being able to land a plane, disembark the passengers, clean and refuel it, load new passengers and take off again in as short a time as possible. Southwest Airlines holds the record for this, regularly managing turnarounds in less than 20 minutes. But this isn't just an issue for the airline industry – it's a version of a problem facing many others. For example in hospitals it's the challenge of using an expensive resource like an operating theatre as efficiently as possible – swiftly moving out post-operative patients, cleaning, sterilizing, preparing and getting started on the next patient as fast as possible. That has a lot in common with a very different world – fans of Formula 1 will know that a slow pit stop can ruin a driver's chances in the unforgiving world of Grand Prix motor racing.

All of these are variations on the same basic theme – and importantly the solutions developed in one world can be adapted and applied elsewhere. Turnaround time was a major challenge in the car industry, where the concern to reduce the set-up and changeover time of huge body presses led engineers at Toyota under the direction of Shigeo Shingo to develop the 'single minute exchange of die' (SMED) approach. This enabled reductions from several hours to less than five minutes. SMED principles underpin the turnaround revolution in the airline industry, and the success of Ferrari's record-breaking team, who can carry out a complete pit stop in less than six seconds!

It's not a one-way process; part of the power of recombinant innovation is the crossover learning through sharing different experience of dealing with the same basic problem. In a recent visit to the Great Ormond Street children's hospital in London the Ferrari team not only delivered some important insights for UK hospitals, but they also took back some new ideas to apply on the racetracks of the world.

You can find a number of other case examples of innovation resulting from bridging different worlds on the companion website, including NHL and Lifespring.

Abstracting problems to their essence is the basis of several powerful tools to enhance creativity. For example, 'morphological analysis' is an approach originally developed by the Bulgarian engineer Fritz Zwicky while working as an astrophysicist at Caltech in the United States. He was interested in complex multidimensional problems which have no clear solution route and developed a matrix approach to help structure and explore problems by systematically analyzing their different dimensions. Solutions can then emerge as a result of looking at new combinations (an approach similar to the one taken by the art students in the Csikszentmihalyi and Getzels study [1]). Another use of the approach is to explore underlying similarities and properties between the current problem and others sharing some of the same dimensions [5].

> You can find more about Morphological Analysis on the companion website.

Another powerful approach (called TRIZ) draws on a view of problem-solving originally developed in 1946 by a Russian engineer, Genrich Altshuller [6]. He was working in the 'inventions inspection' department of the Caspian Sea flotilla of the Soviet Navy, where his job involved reviewing thousands of patent applications. He noticed that despite the patents covering widely different fields they shared some underlying patterns; in particular, he focused on the ways in which inventive solutions seemed to emerge when there was some kind of 'unresolved contradiction'. An example might be between the weight and cost of a car engine and the power it is able to deliver. What we might call a trade-off between these elements could be resolved if we think creatively about a new solution which resolves the apparent tension.

His thinking along these lines was interrupted by his being arrested and sent to one of the notorious Gulag labour camps in 1950 where he spent three years; it wasn't until 1956 that he was able to publish 'On the Psychology of Inventive Creation' [7]. In it he suggested that the ways in which such resolution of contradictions could be handled fell into some core patterns; problems could be reduced to their essence as one or another of these.

Over the following ten years he analyzed thousands of inventions and noticed repeated patterns in the way solutions were presented even though they covered widely different fields. He suggested that all problems can be reduced to versions of a basic set of core themes (principles of invention') – he identified forty – and developed a matrix approach to help generate solutions based on reapplying solutions which shared a common problem root [8].

> You can find more about TRIZ on the companion website.

Problem-matching methods like Morphological Analysis (MA) and TRIZ lend themselves to the powerful connectivity now offered by online databases. For example the Belgian company AULive uses patent libraries to trawl through and match problems and solutions based on abstracting them to a generic level [9].

> ### Creativity in action: common problems, transferable solutions
>
> Ramon Vullings has made an extensive study of cross-industry innovation. His model is based on the idea which he summarizes as 'copy, adapt, paste' – and here are a few examples.

- Owen Maclaren, a retired aeronautical engineer and test pilot who worked on the Spitfire, developed the first foldable lightweight baby buggy to save his daughter the struggle with her cumbersome pram when getting in and out of airplanes. He drew his inspiration from the retractable landing gear on large aircraft.
- The UK company Norwich Union was the first insurance company to borrow the 'pay as you go' formula from the mobile phone industry and apply it to insurance.
- McDonald's drive-thru fast food service is based on the principles of Formula 1 pit stop layouts.
- BMW's iDrive system – which allows the driver to select and navigate various entertainment and other functions – uses the same principle as video game controllers.
- 'YoSushi' and other 'take what you want' sushi bars use the principle of the airport baggage carousel system.
- Phonebloks is a concept for a phone made of swappable components that fit together like Lego, with each component containing a different function. This means that components can be replaced or upgraded without having to throw away the phone.
- Hilti Fleet Management has a fixed monthly charge that covers all tool, service and repair costs. This new business model for the hire of tools inspired by car fleet management simplifies financial planning and results in less administrative work.

You can watch a video interview with Ramon on the companion website and find out more about his research here: http://www.crossindustryinnovation.com/.

Seeing round corners

Sometimes exploring the problem is about seeing things that others do not notice. This is the classic behaviour of the entrepreneur, spotting opportunities that others have missed – think of the low-cost airline revolution. This began by reframing the problem of air travel by asking the question, 'who doesn't fly yet but might?' Looking at the edges of the market – the underserved people – led pioneers like Southwest Airlines to develop the template of no-frills cheap flying. Muhammad Yunus (who went on to win the Nobel Peace Prize for his efforts) pioneered the idea of 'microfinance' – providing credit to the very poorest people in Bangladesh. This idea challenged the conventional wisdom that such people would not be able to repay the loans; since its foundation in 1983 Grameen has lent over $50 billion to around ten million borrowers. His model has been widely emulated around the world and similar approaches are used by Grameen to enable the poorest to access mobile phones and other services.

You can read more about Grameen and Southwest on the companion website.

As with levels of abstraction the underlying principle has been used in a variety of powerful tools for innovation search – for example, the Blue Ocean approach uses the metaphor of finding quiet 'blue ocean' spaces instead of the turbulent 'red oceans' in which many competitors thrash around fighting each other of a bite at the market prey [10]. For example, Nintendo changed the game with its Wii interface, which moved the focus of competition away from the battle over power and speed in computer games and opened up blue ocean space around engaging a wider audience in interacting in a different way with computer games. Their interface gave them several years of blue ocean before Microsoft and Sony produced their versions and now the space is again a somewhat red ocean!

There is a variety of tools which can help with the process of finding or creating blue oceans – in particular the 'value curve'. This compares valued features in the offerings of different competitors – the idea being to find features which customers would value but which are not yet offered by the competition. In similar ways the technique of competitiveness profiling can identify blue ocean space associated with process innovation.

You can find more about Value Curves and Competitiveness profiling on the companion website.

Working at the edge of what other people see is also a core feature of the theory of 'disruptive innovation' originally developed by Clayton Christensen [11]. The basic idea is that mainstream businesses focus their attention on existing markets which they can analyze, explore and work with; the trouble is that sometimes the big new idea which will overturn their industry emerges from precisely the other direction! Christensen's theory suggests that at the fringes of mainstream markets there are different groups of people with different needs; working with them and learning to solve the problems linked to meeting their needs opens up new innovation space. Sometimes the two will coexist but often the fringe solution proves attractive to the mainstream as well and so becomes the dominant design, pushing out the old incumbents in the process.

You can find more about disruptive innovation by reading the 'deeper dive' on the companion website.

Creativity in action: outcome-driven innovation

A worrying statistic about the home power tools market is that most people use such tools (electric drills, saw, etc.) for a very small percentage of time – typically less than 5%. This situation arises because the real problem they faced when making the purchase was not 'I need a power tool' but rather 'I need a hole in the wall to hang a picture/fix shelves/attach a light, etc.' In other words the solution they have chosen is only one (rather expensive) route to getting a particular job done. Thinking about that job rather than jumping to one particular solution can open up many different innovation opportunities – for example a service business based on a skilled craftsman with the appropriate tools providing exactly the size and shaped hole needed. (He would be one of the few people who did have high utilization of his expensive power tools!)

This approach – of identifying the 'jobs to be done' – is at the heart of outcome driven innovation (ODI). The idea was originally developed by Anthony W. Ulwick and forms the basis of a number of methodologies aimed at uncovering innovation opportunities and disrupting existing markets. The core of the approach is described in Ulwick's 2005 book *What Customers Want: Using Outcome-Driven Innovation to Create Breakthrough Products and Services* [12].

It is an extension of 'voice of the customer' (VOC) techniques and requires building an understanding from the customer outwards rather than making assumptions or listening to market research data. ODI can help identify important but poorly served jobs which need to be done and also overserved markets where the solutions in place exceed what is really wanted. The focus is on accurate targeting according to specific needs.

You can find more about ODI and associated tools on the companion website.

The key lesson from disruptive innovation is the importance of working with fringe users and deploying techniques to learn with them about their needs. A good example is M-PESA, a mobile payments system originally developed in Kenya which effectively offers a banking service based on mobile phones. Launched in 2007, it is now used by millions of people, and estimates suggest that up to 40% of the country's gross national product flows through the system. The name comes from the Swahili *pesa* meaning money and the original idea began as a development aid project to enable microfinance repayments. Vodafone, via its local operator Safaricom, became the project partner and rolled out the service. By 2013 over 16 million people had M-PESA accounts and the system processed more payments than Western Union did across its entire global network. Cashless payments enabled via mobile phones are now a big growth area in mainstream markets and many of the lessons from M-PESA are being transferred back.

You can find more about M-PESA on the companion website.

Creativity in action: problems hiding in plain view

A version of the 'opportunity recognition' challenge is when we already have solutions but no link to the problem. For example the discovery of penicillin didn't happen in Alexander Fleming's lab in London back in 1928. It had already been seen much earlier, perhaps as much as 1,500 years ago when observations were made about the ability of fungi to inhibit the growth of bacteria. Reportedly, Arabian stable boys stored their saddles in damp, areas which encouraged the growth of mould – they noticed that mouldy saddles prevented the development of saddle sores. In 1852, J.R. Mosse published a report on the use of yeast to treat infection, followed by Joseph Lister's unpublished observation in 1871 on the ability of *Penicillium glaucum* to inhibit bacterial growth. In 1897, French medical student Ernest Duchesne published the results of an elegant series of experiments; however, he did not publish further and his discovery lay neglected for decades thereafter. Alexander Fleming rediscovered penicillin in 1928, but it was not until 1942 that Chain, Florey, and Jennings identified patulin, the antibiotic produced by *P. glaucum*.

Problems and symptoms – getting to the root cause

Sometimes the apparent problem is actually a symptom of something deeper – the risk is that we end up solving the symptom problem rather than getting at the root cause. For example, a man might walk into a doctor's surgery complaining of feeling light-headed. The doctor might decide that he has low blood pressure and prescribe some medicine, sending the patient away. Unfortunately the patient's problem was not the light-headedness but the blood loss resulting from having cut himself while shaving!

That's an extreme picture, but it underlines the importance of making sure we are addressing the 'right' problem rather than treating a symptom. Tracing things back to their root cause might appear laborious, but it pays off. During the 1970s the problem of quality management began to surface as a challenge. Up until then people thought that quality was something which you paid extra for and that there was a trade-off between cost and quality. But even in areas like defence spending, where money wasn't the issue, there were quality problems. (An indication of the size of the problem can be gauged from the fact that in 1950 only 30% of the US Navy's electronics devices were working properly at any given time [13].)

The language of quality management at the time reflects this – people would talk about 'acceptable quality levels', implying that it was normal to expect a degree of failure in every batch of things being produced. One of the key figures who shaped thinking about quality is Philip Crosby, who began working on these issues within the giant ITT Corporation. He tried to put some numbers to the real costs of quality, and realized to his – and the company's – horror that these could account for as much as 40% of sales revenue! [14]. (For example, in 1984 when IBM first began looking at this problem they estimated that $2 billion of its $5 billion in profits was due to improved quality – not having to fix errors.)

Gradually the perspective changed – not least because of experiences with products coming from Japan. They seemed to have worked a minor manufacturing miracle, being able to offer good reliable quality without a high price tag. Manufacturers from the West flocked to Japan to try and understand the new technology behind it – only to find that it wasn't a super machine but a way of thinking and acting embedded right across the organization. 'Total quality management' (TQM) took up the challenge of quality and made it 'everyone's problem'. And at the heart of the TQM success was the seed of systematic problem exploration tools like the famous 'fishbone diagram' developed in the 1960s by Kaoru Ishikawa, one of the pioneers of the TQM approach [15].

> You can find more about the changing perspective on the quality problem in a 'deeper dive' on the companion website.

To give it its proper name, this is a cause and effect diagram, and simply offers a framework to trace problems back to their root causes. It takes its name from the resemblance to a fish skeleton, with the various bones connecting to the spine representing different contributing causes and the 'head' the problem as it first presents itself. Here's an example (Figure 2.1) of a fishbone exploring the apparent problem of poor product quality.

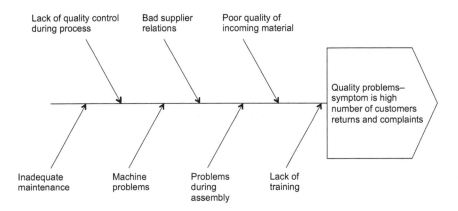

Figure 2.1 Fishbone diagram

> You can find more about fishbone tools and activities to explore them on the companion website.

Variations on this theme are in widespread use; one particularly powerful (and simple) technique originated in Toyota and consists of asking the question 'why?' often enough to drive down to underlying root causes of problems. Its application across all of their manufacturing plants around the world goes a long way to explain why Toyota has been the world's most productive car maker for nearly three decades – they continue to mobilize their workforce to drive quality problems out using simple tools like this. (We will explore 'high involvement innovation' of the kind practised at Toyota in Chapter 10.)

Creativity in action: five whys and a how

This simple but powerful tool can help strip away the apparent problem to get through to the root problem which is the one we need to solve. For example, a big problem in UK hospitals at the moment is in waiting times and delays, putting pressure on already scarce resources. Here's how one hospital applied the tool.

The apparent problem was that a patient arrived late in the operating theatre, causing a delay.

- Why? – Because they had to wait for a trolley to take them from the ward to the theatre;
- Why? – Because they had to find a replacement trolley;
- Why? – Because the original trolley had a defect – the safety rail had broken;
- Why? – Because it had not been regularly checked for wear and tear;
- Why? – Because there was no organized system of checking and maintenance.

Arriving at this root cause – the real problem is in the lack of systematic maintenance – gives plenty of clues about the 'how', the potential solutions to the problem. Setting up a simple maintenance schedule could ensure that all trolleys are regularly checked and available for use. This would mean that future delays would be avoided, flow would improve and overall system efficiency would be better. Importantly if we had just focused on the apparent problem – a single broken trolley – we would have solved that by repairing the trolley but the underlying problem would happen again.

Another widely used approach is process mapping – essentially making a physical representation of how a process actually works to deliver value to someone at the end. Very often process maps highlight particular problem 'hot spots' and help focus attention on where to focus problem-solving attention. For example anywhere there is a queue suggests that the process isn't working as smoothly as it could, so drilling down into why that queue is there – insufficient resources, too many things converging (a 'bottleneck'), imbalance with the rest of the process and so forth – can help.

Creativity in action: 'pretty in pink'

Walking through the plant belonging to Ace Trucks (a major producer of forklift trucks) in Japan, the first thing which strikes you is the colour scheme. In fact you would need to be blind not to notice it – among the usual rather dull greys and greens of machine tools and other equipment there are flashes of pink. Not just a quiet pastel tone but a full-blooded, shocking pink which would do credit to even the most image-conscious flamingo. Closer inspection shows these flashes and splashes of pink are not random but associated with particular sections and parts of machines – and the eye-catching effect comes in part from the sheer number of pink-painted bits, distributed right across the factory floor and all over the different machines.

What is going on here is not a bizarre attempt to redecorate the factory or a failed piece of interior design. The effect of catching the eye is quite deliberate – the colour is there to draw attention to the machines and other equipment which have been modified. Every pink splash is the result of a project to improve some aspect of the equipment, much of it in support of the drive towards 'total productive maintenance' (TPM), in which every item in the plant is available and ready for use 100% of the time. This is a goal like 'zero defects' in total quality – certainly ambitious, perhaps an impossibility in the statistical sense, but one which focuses the minds of everyone involved and leads to extensive and impressive problem-finding and solving. TPM programmes have accounted for year-on-year cost savings of 10%–15% in many Japanese firms and these savings are being ground out of a system which is already renowned for its lean characteristics.

Painting the improvements pink plays an important role in drawing attention to the underlying activity in this factory, in which systematic problem-finding and solving is part of 'the way we do things around here'. The visual cues remind everyone of the continuing search for new ideas and improvements, and often provide stimulus for other ideas or for places where the displayed pink idea can be transferred. Closer inspection around the plant shows other forms of display – less visually striking but powerful nonetheless – charts and graphs of all shapes and sizes which focus attention on trends and problems as well as celebrating successful improvements; photographs and graphics which pose problems or offer suggested improvements in methods or working practices; and flipcharts and whiteboards covered with symbols and shapes of fish bones and other tools being used to drive the improvement process forward.

> You can find more about process mapping and other simple tools in the Continuous Improvement Toolkit on the companion website. There are also some activities linked to using these tools and some illustrative cases.

Looking for trouble – problem anticipation

Another approach to problem exploration is to construct one! This is not a foolish attempt to worry unnecessarily but to use the fact that imagined problems might actually emerge in the future – and if we have explored them in our imaginary way we might develop some useful strategies for dealing with them when something like them does actually come along.

This is the principle behind the use of 'futures' methods in business, especially in the area of what are called 'scenario techniques'. Here a rich picture of a possible future is drawn up and then the world it represents is explored, looking for threats and opportunities for an organization to play in. Shell, the giant oil and gas company, famously employed such an approach back in the 1960s to explore what different futures might look like in the world of oil [16–17]. When the oil price tumbled the company was in a strong position to respond because it had already thought through the dimensions of the problem and what they might do in response.

> The methodology remains in place today and is at the heart of a significant programme for exploring new opportunities called 'Gamechanger'. You can read more about this on the companion website.

The essence of scenario thinking is that it makes available a 'safe' space within which people can explore potential problems in the future – it allows for openness in thinking because by definition the future hasn't yet happened and can be shaped. Hyundai, the giant Korean conglomerate, has made extensive use of an approach to problem/opportunity finding which they call 'constructed crisis', essentially using the scenario approach not only to explore but also to mobilize energy towards problem-solving to deal with imagined future challenges [18]. Many organizations use variations on this approach, sometimes constructing shared future worlds within which they can collectively explore new opportunities and develop responses to potential threats.

> You can find several resources on the companion website to explore this further – case studies of Gamechanger, video and audio clips of Helen King and Tim Jones, and some activities to try out future tools and techniques.

Messing about in problems

Part of the problem with problems is that they are messy – that is, they contain elements which are intertwined, they tangle up separate competing problems, they often appear mixed up in each other. Operations researcher Russell Ackoff coined the term 'a mess' to describe what is, in effect, a system of problems – and the key point is that the solution to a mess may not be a simple sum of the solutions to problems that can be extracted from it [19]. Viewed in this way we need to find ways of teasing out problems or 'clumps' of problems with which to work; researchers like Peter Checkland and Colin Eden have developed some helpful tools and techniques for doing so [20].

Checkland's Soft Systems Methodology (SSM), for example, starts by representing the problem mess as a 'rich picture' within which various problems can be seen. He then suggests taking a particular perspective – a *Weltanschauung*, the German word for 'world view' – and then exploring the problem from that standpoint. This leads to a definition of the problem – a 'root definition' in his terms which gives us some insights into how the problem might be approached. Repeating the exercise with a different *Weltanschauung* leads to a different root definition and a further insight. So applying the approach helps us build up a map of the messy problem and some hints about fruitful direction in which to move.

You can find more detail about SSM and the tools of rich pictures on the companion website.

Colin Eden's work on 'cognitive mapping' offers a similar approach, helping to explore complex and messy problems from different viewpoints based on how players within that problem might construct it. His toolkit allows us to represent their different 'cognitive maps' and thus open up the problem for further exploration [21].

You can find more about construct theory and cognitive mapping on the companion website.

What does research tell us about problem-finding and structuring?

Given the importance of problem-solving to our survival as a species, it's not surprising that there has been a great deal of research around the question of how we do it (and whether we might learn to do it better). But although problem definition and presentation attracted some interest, most early work focused on problem-*solving* – the strategies people used when trying to come up with answers. Until recently there was relatively little research around the phenomenon of problem-*finding*. In this section we'll try to summarize some of the key findings around problem perception, formulation and structuring [22–23].

If you'd like to know more, take a look at the 'deeper dive' on the companion website.

Perhaps the first systematic approach to the question was the 1971 study (mentioned earlier in this chapter) by Jacob Getzels and Mihaly Csikszentmihalyi looking at artists and in particular 'the way problems are envisaged, posed, formulated, created'.

Their work identified some key attributes which exceptionally creative artists seemed to share – for example a willingness to switch direction when new approaches suggested themselves. Experimentation with different perspectives and reformulating problems as they did so was another important characteristic. Importantly this group also had a degree of patience and perseverance, holding back on judging their work to be 'completed'. This didn't mean that they kept searching for perfection but rather that they were well equipped to assess where and when further improvements were possible.

Researchers began looking at these problem-finding and exploration stages and expanded their frame to look at many other settings – for example among administrators or in schools and with populations drawn from different backgrounds [24]. These studies all confirmed that 'problem-finding was the single best predictor of real world creative activities'.

It became clear that we need to differentiate between simply recognizing that there is a problem to solve (problem identification) and how to make it operational and workable (problem definition and redefinition). The influential psychologist David Kolb developed a model for problem management as part of his theory of experiential learning which had four elements; 'situation, problem, solution and implementation'. He suggested that the 'problem manager' (trying to solve a problem) is a little like a detective, 'gathering clues and information about how the "crime" was committed, organizing those clues into a scenario of "who done it" and using that scenario to gather more information to prove or disprove the original hunch' (p. 281, [25]).

Submarine thinking – the role of insight and incubation

Part of the challenge here is that unconscious processes play a part; problem-finding is often linked to moments of insight or intuition. We catch a glimpse of something about the problem which triggers an 'aha!' moment, a new way of looking at the problem (and sometimes also a fertile line of development for its solution).

This idea was first advanced in 1926 by Graham Wallas, who argued that Creative Problem-Solving involved an element of unconscious 'incubation' which was often characterized by a sense of 'intimation' as we became consciously aware of the insight which our brains had arrived at [26]. And popular writers like the polymath Arthur Koestler in the 1960s developed further ideas around the role of the unconscious in creativity; unfortunately the dominant strands of psychological research at this time disregarded this kind of thinking as non-scientific [27].

Gradually research uncovered the growing importance of neurological processes and the focus moved towards studies of cognition – what is actually going on when we think about things and how some of this does take place in unconscious mode. In particular a team led by Gordon Bower at Stanford University began developing a theory around incubation and suggested that this isn't simply a flash of inspiration – there is an underlying process going on which involves two stages:

- A 'guiding stage', where coherence or structure is unconsciously recognized and used;
- An 'integrative stage', where coherence makes it way to consciousness.

It is the transition between the two stages which we recognize as an 'aha!' feeling [28].

Some problems lend themselves to instant solution – we recognize them as something we have seen before and know how to deal with them. Others require a period of exploration and incubation before we grasp the underlying pattern and a route towards their solution. So pattern recognition is a key element in understanding what is going on in problem exploration – and a key field of research around this comes from what is termed the Gestalt school, from the German word *gestalt*, meaning 'shape' or 'form'.

The Sultan of swing – Köhler's chimpanzees

Back in early 1900s Wolfgang Köhler was working on the island of Tenerife, studying the behaviour of chimpanzees. He was particularly interested in how they solved problems and was struck by the behaviour of one of his favourites which he had named Sultan. He set a problem for Sultan involving some bananas that were outside his cage and beyond the reach of his arms. If Sultan was given a stick that was long enough he would immediately use it to reach the bananas. However if he was given two sticks, neither of which were long enough he would at first try, then give up and sulk.

But after a little while Kohler saw Sultan suddenly go up to the poles again and place one inside the other, creating a single pole long enough to reach the bananas. Kohler was fascinated by this and it provided the springboard for a new approach which challenged the then dominant psychological view of behaviourism. He suggested that problem-solving wasn't simply a matter of trial and error, a process which could be reinforced by a system of punishments or rewards. Instead it involved a degree of 'system' thinking and flashes of insight in which problem definitions and solutions emerged as a coherent whole [29].

Inspired by this view and with two other researchers, Kurt Koffka and Max Wertheimer, Köhler began to challenge the behaviourist view and replace it with an approach they termed 'Gestalt'. Gestalt psychology is primarily about how human beings perceive the world and the implications of that for problem-solving and learning.

The central principle is that the mind has the capability to form a global whole through self-organizing tendencies; this is reflected in Koffka's famous phrase 'The whole is different from the sum of its parts.' We can see this effect particularly with respect to the way we recognize things visually, seeing global figures instead of just collections of simpler and unrelated elements.

Look at the picture in Figure 2.2 (you've probably seen other examples like it). It doesn't take long before you recognize that instead of a random pattern of dots and blotches it is a Dalmatian rooting around. You didn't arrive at that conclusion by a process of elimination but rather by seeing an emerging pattern.

Figure 2.2 Example of emergence

You can find other examples of emergence on the companion website.

Gestalt psychologists call this 'emergence' and it is one of four key principles through which the brain works to create meaningful systems – holistic ways of seeing. The others are reification, multistability and invariance:

• Emergence occurs when we recognize something as a whole and get the pattern all at once rather than by identifying its parts first. (Evolutionary psychologists suggest that this was a pretty important development since it enabled our ancestors to survive. Being able to make sense of a pattern and detecting that the apparent random set of mottled light and shade in the bushes is actually a predatory animal is a pretty important skill!)
• Reification is the constructive aspect of perception, by which the perception contains more explicit spatial information than the sensory stimulus on which it is based. Look at the picture in Figure 2.3, where, for

Figure 2.3 Example of reification

example, a whole triangle can be inferred from just its corners. This can be explained by the fact that the visual system treats illusory contours as 'real' contours.

- Multistability is the tendency of ambiguous perceptual experiences to switch between two or more alternative interpretations. You've probably seen examples like those in Figure 2.4 where an image can suddenly 'flip' into something else.
- Invariance (see Figure 2.5) means that simple geometrical objects are recognized independent of rotation, translation, scale or deformations.

Our ability to see things in terms of wholes is governed by a set of rules which Wertheimer, Köhler and Koffka developed around the idea of *prägnanz* (German for 'pithiness'). In essence these rules are based on the idea that we tend to order our experience in a manner that is regular, orderly, symmetrical and simple. and that the mind understands external stimuli as whole rather than the sum of their parts. Examples of these 'laws of grouping' are shown in Figures 2.6 and 2.7.

- Proximity – objects or shapes which are close together appear to form groups. (See the picture in Figure 2.6 – you probably see a pattern because of the proximity effect!)
- Similarity – we tend to see stimuli that physically resemble each other as part of a particular pattern and things which are different as part of a different pattern. So we can pick out textures or distinguish between overlapping objects.

Figure 2.4 Example of multistability

Figure 2.5 Example of invariance

Figure 2.6 Example of proximity

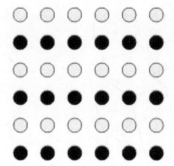

Figure 2.7 Example of similarity

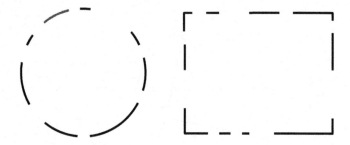

Figure 2.8 Example of closure

- Closure – the tendency we have to 'fill in the gaps' when information is incomplete. In the picture in Figure 2.8 we add in the missing detail to complete the figures.
- Continuation – we tend to perceive objects as uninterrupted and can 'read between the lines' or behind them when objects overlap. In the picture in Figure 2.9 we 'know' there are two keys even if one is obscured by the other.

Gestalt psychologists also give us another perspective on the question of insight which we discussed earlier – the 'aha!' moment often accompanied by feelings of surprise and a sense of the 'rightness' of the perception and possible solution to a problem. Looking more closely at processes before the 'revelation' of an insight, researchers suggest that people actually engage intensively with the problem, conducting thorough and systematic analyses in an attempt to find an underlying structure. Insight is not luck but the summary of various behaviours.

Figure 2.9 Example of continuation

Pattern matching and the predictive mind

An emerging model of problem-finding and solving suggests that we store a repertoire of solutions which we learn over time – and then when we are confronted with a new challenge we begin a search to see if we have something 'on file' which will offer us a solution. For example neuroscientist Jacob Hohwy's idea of 'the predictive mind' suggests that the brain constructs models of the world on the basis of past experience, and then *predicts* new experiences, which we then test out. The results either confirm our models or modify them [30].

So when we meet a problem situation our brain produces candidate solutions for this using models based on past experience. We may modify the models to suit the particular circumstances of our current problem – it's not always a simple matter of 'plug and play' – but essentially we reapply templates which we already have on file.

In other words we begin the problem search by looking for something which we recognize – problem *re*-cognition. Only if we can't find a match do we begin a secondary activity, which is searching for new solutions to the new situation.

So how do we come up with new solutions to add to our repertoire? One way is to approach the problem in a different way – to reframe it. In doing so the brain brings to bear different potential solutions from its database, offering different solution pathways. This is often important as a way of working with intractable problems – bring a new way of looking at the problem and new solutions (or rather a different set of old solutions) become available.

A simple example; suppose you are in a room which you'd like to leave. The problem is that you are on the 15th floor and the building is on fire! So the conventional set of solutions isn't going to work; instead you need to find a different answer. Reframe the problem as 'how could I fly out of here?' – and this forces the brain to explore a different set of solutions in its library and you come up with the idea of a parachute which you may be able to construct using the curtains in the room.

Learning to redefine problems – heuristics and problem perception

Another helpful contribution to our understanding of problem exploration comes from work on the ways in which problems are presented to us. Robert Kaplan and Herbert Simon did pioneering work on this back in the 1990s showing how an initial problem can baffle people, but that by changing the way the problem was represented insight became possible [31]. They set a challenge based on what became known as 'the mutilated chessboard' – see Figure 2.10.

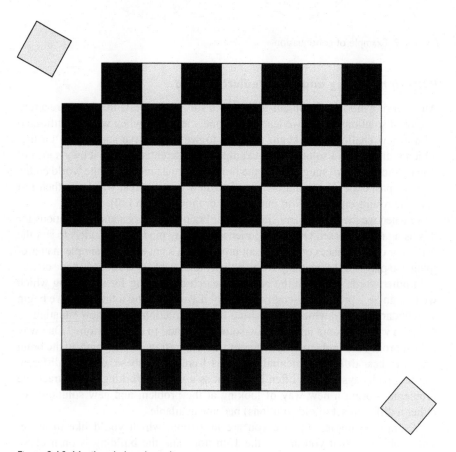

Figure 2.10 Mutilated chessboard

Suppose that a domino will cover exactly two squares on the board. Is it possible to take a set of dominos and place them so that the thirty-two squares on the board are exactly covered in dominos (that is, the dominos mustn't go off the edge of the board or overlap each other)?

Kaplan and Simon used different versions of the chessboard, from simple black and white squares to shaded with pink and black colours) to boards with the squares labelled 'pink' and 'black' through to squares labelled with different words ('bread' and 'butter'). They found that the problem became progressively harder for participants in the experiment.

In fact it is impossible to cover the board with dominoes – but what they were interested in were the processes in which people explored the problem to get to this conclusion. The simplest approach – imagining placing dominoes – is very hard because you quickly run out of memory! By using a rule of thumb which says that each domino can cover two squares (which is helped by the coloured shading or the word labelling) you can simplify the problem.

The most helpful way to solve this insight problem was through the use of *heuristics*. Heuristic techniques are rules of thumb or educated guesses, simple but efficient ways of getting a problem solved or a decision made. They mainly operate in unconscious or automatic fashion and offer practical ways of speeding up decision processes. Although they may not be perfect or always correct, most of the time they are good enough for the application they are used for.

Kaplan and Simon found that a powerful heuristic involved attending to features of the problem that remain invariant or recur repeatedly. Fast solvers not only notice more things earlier but they also notice so-called perceptual clues. They focus on *observation* rather than hypothesizing.

Learning to see – the power of observation

Importantly experts often bring an ability to 'see' things in a particular situation which others miss – they have honed their observational skills to the point where they pick up cues almost unconsciously. Malcolm Gladwell explores this idea in his book *Blink*, giving examples of art experts able to spot a fake after a few moments of observation. Importantly such experts seem to rely on intuition – on an unconscious sense that something isn't right, and intuition which we can see links to the preceding discussion of pattern recognition [32]. Expertise isn't an overnight thing – rather it seems to be the result of many hours (one commonly used figure is 10,000 hours) of practice and experience. We can see this through the lens of our pattern recognition model – after so much experience the brain has a rich stored library of templates on which to draw when trying to interpret different situations.

Importantly it isn't just simple storage and retrieval; sometimes the skill is in noticing subtle differences in a novel situation and making different connections. Dorothy Leonard in her book *Deep Smarts* gives an example of an experienced firefighting chief who was supervising a crew attending a house fire. All the signs pointed to the source of the fire being in the kitchen, but a 'sixth sense' told the chief that it was actually in the basement and he ordered his men out. Seconds later the floor collapsed into a blazing inferno below which would have claimed the lives of his crew. Such insights come from a mixture of pattern recognition and matching but also from pattern interpretation [33].

Pattern recognition of this kind is powerful since it gives us advantages in terms of speed and reduced 'cognitive load' (the effort we have to expend in working out new solutions). But there is also a risk in relying on it too much. The Nobel Prize–winner Daniel Kahneman suggests that we can loosely characterize our thinking processes as involving two systems – one fast (system 1) and one somewhat slower (system 2). System 1 is largely 'hard-wired' which gives it its speed; neuronal connections are made very rapidly and information is very quickly assimilated and processed. We have evolved system 1 to make sense quickly of complex and potentially dangerous situations – it gives rise to our best guess at what the pattern is and how we should respond. This equates to the 'gut feeling' and intuition which we often have around problem situations. System 2, by contrast, involves more cognitive assessment – we think about the information and assess it in different fashion. This process is often more accurate but also much slower; it also takes effort and we are prone to a degree of mental 'laziness' which means we often rely on system 1 to guide our decisions. In a series of elegant experiments he and his colleague Amos Tversky showed how this results in a series of cognitive biases which mean that we risk taking flawed decisions based on incorrect perception of the problem in hand [34].

For example, we are subject to what they call the 'anchoring' bias. In this we address new problems by applying decisions which we have made on similar problems in the past – effectively jumping to conclusions without exploring the 'real' problem. Its value is that it helps us respond to change more quickly but sometimes we need to pause and reframe the challenge.

You can find more examples of bias in problem-solving behaviour on the companion website.

This brings us to a paradox in problem-finding. We like to think that experience and expertise are valuable weapons in the process – if we have seen a similar problem before we are likely to have something in our repertoire to help solve it. By its nature expertise gives us a way of framing things, of seeing familiar patterns, and this can often help us get to a solution faster. But it can also act as a barrier to seeing alternative representations or structures in problems.

Getting into the box – the problem of functional fixedness

We often talk about creativity in terms of the need to 'get out of the box' in our thinking. But what is the box and how is it constructed? A number of researchers have explored this problem and one of the valuable insights which emerged came from the work of Carl Duncker on what he called 'functional fixedness' [35]. Duncker was fascinated by the way in which people approach problem-solving and devised an elegant series of experiments to explore this – for example the Stick problem (in which babies try to use a stick to reach toys, similar to the Kohler chimpanzee experiments), the Cork problem (in which participants have to fit a piece of wood into a door frame) and the ABCBAC problem (in which students find patterns in arithmetical problems). His most famous work involved the candle experiment in which participants were given a box containing various items including matches, thumbtacks and a candle. The challenge was to find ways to stick the candle to the wall to provide illumination.

Duncker found that many people in trying to solve the problem became fixated on particular properties of the objects and were not able to escape from that view to experiment with different lines of inquiry. (The 'trick' in this problem is to use the box itself and to find ways of sticking the box to the wall; it can then act as a candleholder). As he concluded, 'if a situation is introduced in a certain perceptual structure, thinking achieves a contrary structure only against the resistance of that structure.' He called this the problem of 'functional fixation'.

Recent research, following up on Duncker's approach, involves getting people to talk through their thinking as they confront the problem. It appears that there is no sudden flash of insight about using the box but rather a continuous iterative process of experiment and refinement along different avenues. But getting too locked into one way of thinking about how objects can be used often leads to frustration and a 'dead end street' in terms of progress towards a solution.

Another example of blocking our approach comes with our tendency to assume rules and boundaries to problems. For example try this challenge in Figure 2.11; using only four straight lines and not lifting your pen from the paper try to connect these dots.

Figure 2.11 Nine dot problem – task

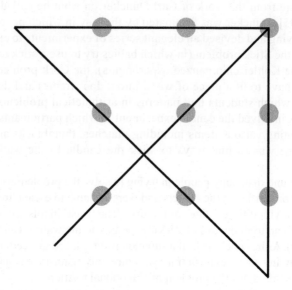

Figure 2.12 Nine dot problem – solution

People find this task difficult because they often assume a rule around keeping within the boundaries of the square which the dots represent. As soon as we relax that constraint many solutions become possible – as shown in Figure 2.12.

Getting into the box (2) – the problem of mindset

Another major challenge in exploring problems is *Einstellung* – another German word meaning 'setting'. The setting effect refers to the way in which we persist in trying a particular problem-solving strategy because it worked for us in the past. It may not be appropriate for the current problem but we find it hard to let go – 'to a man with a hammer every problem looks like a nail' might be a relevant motto to describe the situation!

In a famous series of experiments in 1945 Abraham and Edith Luchins explored what they called the *Einstellung* (= mindset) effect, using a problem based on filling and emptying water jars. Subjects were given a series of practice problems and then asked to solve some particular problems involving filling the jars; the results suggested that they were trying to solve the new problems using methods they had learned during the practice phase, even though these were inappropriate. A control group had no practice problems and developed simpler alternative approaches to the main problem more quickly and effectively. The various experiments conducted by the researchers highlighted the risk we have of falling into a pattern of what they called 'mechanized thinking' [36].

> You can try out the water jar exercises for yourself – see the companion website for the details.

Getting out of the box – The importance of incubation

So given that we have a number of forces trying to keep our thinking inside the box, how might we break out of it? One key factor seems to be time – rather than trying to rush to a solution, give the problem time to emerge. As we've seen, what appears to happen during incubation is an active suite of search behaviours in which the brain is looking for different ways of framing the problem until it finds one which 'clicks' and triggers a sense of direction – the 'aha!' moment. Research shows that insight is more likely to happen if we allow ourselves time for this to happen – incubation [37].

> You might like to try the 'recollecting creativity' activity on the companion website to help you think about how this plays out in your own experience.

Why does time make a difference? Researchers argue that it works by helping neutralize the 'setting effect'. Allowing ourselves (and particularly our unconscious) time to play around with the problem allows for different approaches to emerge. Another way of doing this is by going to sleep – Ullrich Wagner and his colleagues in Germany have shown that this can have a dramatic effect on the ability to gain insight into a problem. In their *Nature* paper, 'Sleep Inspires Insight', they showed that after giving people practice with a number sequence problem that had a hidden rule, the group that slept for eight hours had close to a 60% success rate in getting insight into the underlying rule when they got back to the task, compared to 23% for both control groups – a group that had an eight-hour waking gap during the day and another group that stayed awake for eight hours during the night [38].

Other helpful behaviours include going for a walk, immersing ourselves in a totally different activity, meditating, laughing or even (in small doses) drinking alcohol! These are all ways in which we can switch off or reduce the setting effect [36, 39–40].

Creativity in action: cheap necklaces, valuable learning

In 1971 Silveira and colleagues developed an elegant experiment in which they asked participants to solve the following problem (see Figure 2.13) [41]:

Initial State

- You are given four separate pieces of chain that are each three links in length

- It costs 2¢ to open a link and 3¢ to close a link

- All links are closed at the beginning of the problem

Goal

- Your goal is to join all 12 links of chain into a single circle at a cost no more than 15¢

- Control group: Worked on the problem for half an hour
  - 55% solved the problem

- Experimental group 1: Worked for half an hour, interrupted by a half-hour break in which other activities were performed
  - 64% solved the problem

- Experimental group 2: As 1, but with a 4-hour break
  - 85% solved the problem

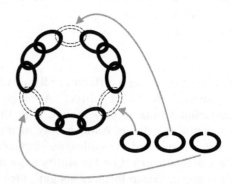

Figure 2.13 Exemplary task for problem-solving with incubation

The results show the importance of reducing setting effects by allowing for relaxation.

Putting it all together – theories of problem exploration

Look again at the nine dot problem we saw a little earlier. At one level it seems to speak about fixedness and the need for a flash of insight – a new gestalt, a new way of looking at the problem. But research suggests that people often need more than one hint to help them get there [42].

In other words we are back to our model of heuristics, of trying out previous approaches drawn from our repertoire. It seems likely that both approaches are important – and the good news is that we can draw on this research base to help us improve our problem-finding skill set.

Let's finish this research section with a couple of theories which try to integrate the way we approach problems and their solution.

The 'two tier' model

As we saw earlier, Csikszentmihalyi and Getzels identified explorative behaviour (like manipulation of the given objects for the work of art or changes in the arrangement during the process of generating the work of art) as important for a creative outcome [1]. They developed the concept of 'discovery orientation' and suggest that true creativity happens where 'the problem itself has not yet been formulated but must be identified and the appropriate method for reaching a solution and the nature of the satisfactory solution are unknown' [43]. Nickerson describes it like this: 'Problem finding involves, one might say, thinking about what to think about' (p. 395, [44]). John Baer (1993) and Mark Runco (1995) come to similar conclusions; finding problems where others have not seen any is extremely important for a creative outcome [45–46].

This is at the heart of what is often called the two-tier model of creativity – something we saw briefly in Chapter 1 (see Figure 2.14).

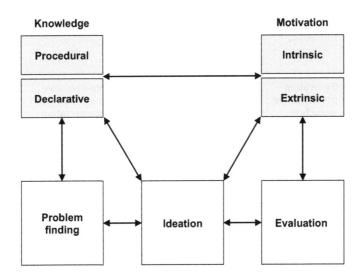

Figure 2.14 Two-tier model

In this model, originally developed by Ivonne Chand and Mark Runco, there is a core 'process' or journey involving three stages which have a high degree of interaction – problem-finding, ideation and evaluation. There are many skills linked to the front end of this which we have been looking at in this chapter, and their research (which has been replicated by others) suggests strongly that better problem definitions lead to more creative solution pathways [47–48].

Pre-inventive structures and the Geneplore model

A second influential model again focuses on the importance of the 'front end' of creativity. In 1992, Ronald Finke and colleagues proposed the 'Geneplore' (generate–explore) model, in which creativity takes place in two phases: a generative phase where an individual constructs mental representations called pre-inventive structures, and an exploratory phase where those structures are used to come up with creative ideas (see Figure 2.15). Typical generative processes involve the retrieval of existing structures from memory, the formation of simple associations among these structures, and the mental synthesis and transformation of existing structures. The new ideas resulting from these processes are explored for new or desired attributes [49]. Creative thinking can be characterized in terms of how the various processes are employed or combined.

The initial ideas are described as 'pre-inventive' because they are not complete plans, tested solutions or accurate answers. Rather they may be an untested proposal or a mere germ of an idea, but they hold some promise of yielding creative outcomes. Examples of generative processes include the retrieval of existing structures from memory, the formation of associations among those, or the synthesis and transformation of structures into new forms.

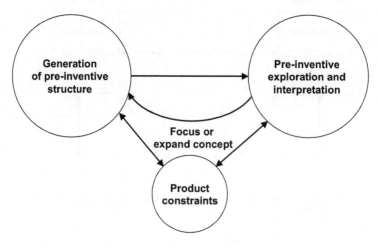

Figure 2.15 Geneplore model

Then, the pre-inventive structures are interpreted during an exploratory phase. Exploratory processes can include the search for certain attributes, implications and functions in the structures or the evaluation of these structures from different perspectives.

The Geneplore model assumes that we alternate between generative and exploratory processes, refining the structures according to the demands or constraints of the particular task. The resulting creative insights can be focused on specific issues or problems, or expanded conceptually by modifying the pre-inventive structures and repeating the cycle.

Why is exploring problems important for creativity?

From the preceding discussion we can see that 'problem exploration' (as a term to describe this 'front end' of Creative Problem-Solving) is an important element. Research shows that it's worth spending time on this preparation/finding/reframing stage because it leads to higher quality creativity [50].

How does this play out in practice? How does problem-finding link in with improved creativity? It seems obvious when we have the comfort of armchair observation to talk about the need to make sure we are working on the 'right' problem and not treating the symptom of something much bigger, or that examining the boundaries and dimensions of a problem might give us new insights about it and how to solve it. But this is often not the situation in which problems emerge – as the old observation goes, 'it's hard to think about draining the swamp when you are up to your waist in alligators!' A version of this thought was almost certainly in the minds of the Apollo 13 crew, and it is one which confronts people in organizations every day.

Well-defined problems can be solved by using standard operating procedures, whereas ill-defined problems require Creative Problem-Solving skills. The trouble is that these are not always present – for example research shows that the majority of managers lack these skills and apply processes that are suited for well-defined problems to ill-defined processes [51]. Many other studies remind us that problem-finding is a more difficult task than problem-solving [51–52].

As we saw before, several models of creativity pay attention to the importance of problem-finding and exploration. The 'two tier' model of Runco and Chand sees creativity as a three-step process moving from problem-finding, through ideation (about solutions) to evaluation. Wallas's process model talks about 'preparation' and 'incubation' as key steps. And the Geneplore approach offered by Finke and colleagues places stress on the important interplay between what they call 'pre-inventive structures' – early half-formed ideas around the problem. All of these theories suggest that a key part of our approach to developing creative skills involves generating possible ideas about the nature of the problem and its dimensions and then testing those out, exploring and elaborating just as the artists did in Mihaly Csikszentmihalyi and Jacob Getzels's study [1].

It's interesting to see that the world of practice recognizes the challenge – many organizations and researchers talk about the challenge of the 'fuzzy front end' of innovation. By this they mean the difficulties organizations face when trying to push for radical innovations which depart from the current trajectories. Under these circumstances conventional tools for project planning and execution are unlikely to work; instead organizations find themselves drawn towards the entre-preneur's toolbox, looking for techniques which can help explore the possible problem landscape. Of particular relevance here is the role of prototyping as an approach to probe and learn around the potential problem.

> At the companion website you can read a detailed case of Philips Lighting, which describes their search for radical new alternatives in their marketplace and which highlights the challenges of the fuzzy front end. The case of Colo-plast does the same from the perspective of a different sector. And Patrick McLaughlin in a video reflects on the challenges he faced when trying to build capability within his organization for working at the fuzzy front end.

This 'probe and learn', hypothesis generating and testing model – which was part of David Kolb's thinking back in the 1980s – is becoming increasingly interesting in the context of innovation and entrepreneurship [53]. The labels differ – 'agile innovation', 'lean start-up' and so forth – but the underlying prin-ciple is one which emphasizes problem exploration and finding rather than stra-tegic planning and execution. If you have an idea for a new product or service, or a social innovation, then it is unlikely to emerge perfectly formed. Indeed what you thought it might be may mutate into something very different as you dis-cover more about its characteristics and the context in which you want to launch it. So a helpful strategy is to explore and elaborate it, testing out your ideas and using feedback to shape and home in on the core things you need to deliver. It's an approach in which prototyping becomes centrally important – because pro-totypes are early sketches, possible arrangements of the problem which others can react to and help shape. They are 'boundary objects' around which a shared problem definition can emerge and from which problem-solving can then pro-ceed. We discuss lean start-up and 'agile' innovation approaches in more detail in Chapter 15.

A key theme in the lean start-up literature is the idea of a 'minimum via-ble product' – a first shot at what the originator thinks is the problem. This becomes the basis for an experiment to explore whether this hypothesis holds or not – and much of the process is one of learning what dimensions are more or less important and in what ways. It dimensionalizes the problem – and does so through the medium of a prototype. (Software development has had the idea of beta testing for a long time and it has increasingly become a label for a more open approach in which feedback and problem redefinition and shaping is a key part of the innovation process. Google, for example, talk about the importance of working in 'perpetual beta' mode, continuously learning about the problems that people actually want solved rather than making assumptions about them).

Creativity in action: the power of prototypes

Drew Houston, computer programmer, was travelling on a bus from Boston to New York when he realized he'd left his USB stick behind. Frustration at not being able to work on his current project led to him daydreaming about a file sharing/storing system online where you could work on projects at any time and from anywhere. He began to sketch out the code and came up with his good idea – but then tried to sell it to venture capitalists. They were much less enthusiastic, arguing that the market for storage was already overcrowded – where and what was his 'unique selling proposition', his USP?

He realized he would have to convince people by making the idea and its advantages real. To develop a working prototype would be hard – his software needed to integrate across many different platforms and operating systems. But what if he did some storytelling – told the story as a prototype? Help people imagine what it would be like if they had the device he was pitching? He made a video as if you were looking over his shoulder as he used the thing he was pitching – moving files around and so forth. The actions he was showing were dummies but the storyline and video experience made it real enough. From 5,000 people interested in helping with the beta test, the 'market' of interested people suddenly boomed to 75,000 overnight. More important, these were early adopters, prepared to accept bugs and help with the learning.

The product he developed became known as Dropbox and was valued in 2014 at around $10 billion.

Of particular importance in this approach is the concept of the 'pivot'. Smart entrepreneurs not only experiment with their markets to explore the problem they are trying to solve, they also are prepared to reframe it, sometimes radically. Information which comes back after an experiment may lead them in radically new directions as they discover that the real problem which people want solved is not necessarily the one the entrepreneurs began with.

For example YouTube began life as one of many new venture ideas around helping people hook up in relationships. There were plenty of ideas about how to make this happen across an online platform but when they tested them out it became clear that one feature in particular – the possibility of sending short video clips of each other – was something the market particularly liked. So they pivoted around this new information, strengthened that idea and eventually left the dating application behind to concentrate on what became a huge success. Table 2.1 gives some other examples of pivoting – reframing the problem in the light of early exploration.

Table 2.1 Examples of pivoting in start-ups

Business	History
Angry Birds	Three people decided to start a games business. Over the next six years they wrote – and abandoned – fifty-one games and nearly went bankrupt. In desperation they tried for one last push, writing ten ideas per day – and came up with Angry Birds.
Instagram	Kevin Systrom wrote a simple HTML app called Burbn and showed a prototype to friends. At a party he met some investors and decided to quit his job and try to develop the venture. He raised $500,000 and was joined by Mike Krieger; they reviewed their app and decided it was trying to do too much – everything from diary management, hotel and flight bookings through to photo organizing. They decided to focus on the photo side and prototyped a new app – which people didn't like. So they went back to Burbn but stripped it down, renamed it Instagram and eight weeks later it had attracted 100,000 users and went on to sell it for $1 billion two years later.
Airbnb	In 2007 Joe Gebbia and Brian Chesky found themselves in San Francisco unable to pay rent on their apartment. There was a big conference coming to the city and so they decided to rent out three air mattresses on their floor and to offer breakfast to visitors facing the problem of scarce hotel accommodation. They developed a simple website (a blog with maps, called 'Air Bed'n'Breakfast') to help find customers. Two men and a woman turned up, each paying $80 which solved their immediate problem but which gave them the idea to try and scale this model. They invited a former roommate, Nathan Blecharczyk (a programmer) to join them and set the venture. They hoped to succeed with their model at the 2008 Denver Democratic Convention where there was a similar problem of hotel room shortage – but although they had 800 people listing rooms they didn't make

Business	History
	any money. To help fund themselves they ran another business selling breakfast cereal to delegates! Eventually they raised $20,000 in start-up funding for the room sharing venture but had learned about the need to modify their original idea – for example in the area of payments processing. They were earning $200/week and not growing and realized part of the problem was the photos of properties they were using were not very attractive. So they went door-to-door in New York, taking their own pictures and putting them on the website; within a week they had doubled their income. They had another change in direction when that summer they rented out an entire house instead of just single rooms; the business grew further and they were able to raise $600,000 in venture funding. By 2011 they had further significant investment in their rapidly growing business, and by 2014 it was worth around $10 billion. (Brian and Joe still live in the original apartment which they rented out in 2008.)

Creativity activity: pivoting in problem exploration

Try and research successful start-ups which have gone on to become major businesses – for example YouTube, Instagram, Airbnb, WhatsApp. They didn't all start perfectly formed but changed direction many times as they experimented and learned. Look at their history and try to identify where and how they pivoted – how did they change their business model and why? How did they reframe and explore the problem?

So the idea and practice of problem exploration – finding, redefining, shaping, reframing and so forth – is of central importance in creativity. The trouble is that we don't always have the skills to enable it. That's the focus of the next section.

What is the skill set around exploring problems?

We've been using the metaphor of creativity as a journey – and this raises the question of what we might need to be a good navigator, able to traverse the landscape with confidence. In this section we'll try and answer that, offering you some co-ordinates to help program your GPS and some ideas about how to develop the different skills needed to set you up well for your particular creative journey.

As Figure 2.16 shows, problem exploration involves perceptual, cognitive and behavioural aspects.

On the cognitive side – how we think – the ability to develop and explore options is central. We also need to be able to challenge frameworks, to reframe problem definitions and sometimes explore them from a higher level of abstraction – what's the underlying common theme here? And we need to be able to and combine seemingly opposite options into new directions for problem solution. And pattern recognition matters – being able to see structures where others only see chaos is important [54].

On the perceptual side – how we take in information – key skills are around observing differences between objects or problem descriptions, distinguishing between interpretation and perception, and observing invariant features of problems.

On the behavioural side – what we do – the key skill lies in *interacting* with the environment, playing with and exploring the area. Remember the artists in Michael Csikszentmihalyi and Jacob Getzels's study? They spent a lot of time manipulating the objects they were given. Prototyping – playing with innovation – to learn about problem dimensions and allow solution options to emerge is of critical importance.

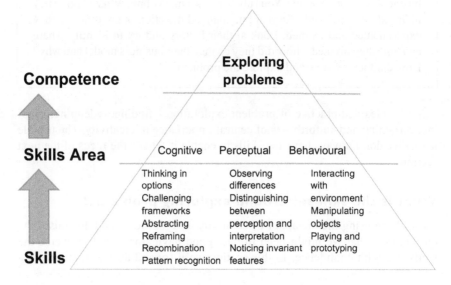

Figure 2.16 Competence exploring problems

Programming the GPS for the creativity journey – what's your position?

So how well do you stack up against this set of skills? Which ones are strengths – and which ones would you like to develop further? In this section we offer you a skills self-check on problem exploration – take a few minutes to reflect on the way you handle problems requiring creativity and rate yourself. We suggest you use a simple five-point rating scale:

1 = Not like me at all
2 = Not much like me
3 = I cannot decide if I am good or bad at it, just doing ok
4 = Describes me quite well (but not exactly)
5 = Describes me exactly

A short word about the design of this framework. People often have a hard time evaluating themselves and often think only in terms of *frequency* of behaviour – how often (or rarely) do I do this? But to get a good grasp on your current level of competence it's also important to think about how easily this behaviour comes to you – is it something you do naturally or do you have to force yourself into doing it? It's important to think about both of these elements when you are scoring yourself – and as a further aid to reflection, try and come up with some examples for the third column. That will help you avoid painting too rosy a picture, identifying the skills you aspire to rather than describing what you actually do. Try to give yourself some time and write in at least one example before you rate yourself.

Thinking about past behaviour eliminates two of the most common problems with self-check questionnaires: the central tendency and seeing oneself in a better or worse light than is true. As human beings we like the middle, the mellow landscapes, the beauty of OK. But for assessing and developing skills the middle is deceptive – it can lead us to believe that everything is OK and that we have no further need for development. As we'll see throughout the book, creativity is strongly associated with not being complacent, but with striving and stretching for better ideas and their implementation. So aiming for a higher score – and recognizing where we might not be so strong – is an important element. Our tip for filling in this self-check is to use the extremes in your ratings.

There are no prizes for getting the 'right' answer – the idea of the framework is to help you think about your creative skills in this area and to help prioritize skill areas which you'd like to develop further.

Working out at the gym – how to train your skills in problem exploration

On the following pages we'll try to provide you with some ideas and inspiration to help you train the skills associated with problem exploration. Some of them are simple recipes – food for thought. Others involve techniques and tools to stretch

Table 2.2 Self-check exploring problems

#	Core behavioural skills	Your score (1–5)	For instance ... write at least one example of your own
I	I look at the problem from different angles.		
2	I am able to reframe the problem.		
3	I challenge given frameworks.		
4	I combine differences and opposites.		
5	I explore underlying patterns and 'core problems'.		
6	I take time out to be at my best.		
7	I see differences easily.		
8	I separate between observation and interpretation.		
9	I look out for invariant features of problems.		
I0	I interact with my environment for the sake of exploration.		

your thinking muscles. Some of these are focused on developing a single skill; others have wider application, a bit like workouts where you train a while on a muscle group. Many of these development tips are linked to tools and further information on the companion website ('gym equipment').

> There is a template for a personal training plan that you can download from the companion website.

Seeing with a 'different' set of eyes

There are several useful ways of developing this, for example practising restating the problem in different ways. These include creating a series of how-to statements; using different levels of abstraction like 'climbing' above the problem, or trying to see the problem from different viewpoints. For example, try thinking about making a documentary film about your local environment as if you were a film crew from another country and culture – what would you highlight, who would you interview, how would you explain what is going on?

There is a link on the companion website to a TED Talk by Tina Seelig, a professor at Stanford University, which gives many good examples of reframing.

> See the companion website for 'how-to' statements, levels of abstraction and reversals.

You can also try using a different representational system to get a fresh perspective. Practising different ways of expressing and describing the problem, for example in the form of pictures, stories, constructions with LEGO or dramatizing it as piece of theatre, all give different perspectives on the same thing and may contribute to a flash of insight through the different representations. (For example Fabian Schlage uses a LEGO-based approach, while Henry Larsen's work uses theatre techniques to explore innovation problems through that different lens, and Nina Bozic uses dance as a medium to help people work through innovation challenges).

> See the companion website for rich pictures, serious play and innovation theatre.

Finding new ways of describing the problem

A special way of re-presenting problems that allows us to combine and link dimensions comes through the use of metaphor and analogical thinking. (Much of the early work by Alex Osborn and Sidney Parnes drew on these tools as a way of 'making the familiar strange and the strange familiar') [55]. Metaphors link one concept with another in ways we might not expect but which help us change perspective, for example 'time is money' or 'this organization works as a well-oiled machine.' With this we can see a certain quality of the problem or the status quo which is otherwise probably not so obvious. Analogies work in the same way, drawing out similarities or differences – for example in saying 'my boss and I are like fire and water.' Gareth Morgan has an excellent book which helps us understand the complex ways in which organizations work and the problem issues which emerge by considering various metaphors – for example seeing the organization as a machine, as a living organism, as a computer, as a continent of different countries and so forth. The idea is that each metaphor gives us a different lens through which to view things and highlights different aspects of the problem. He calls the skill set around using metaphors 'imagineering' [56].

> See the companion website for metaphor and analogy.

Ways of seeing

As we have seen in this chapter, Gestalt psychologists have identified various behaviours that lead to restructuring and successfully solving problems: intensive engagement with the problem including a thorough analysis and various attempts in solving the problem and a clear understanding of the goal state. Arising from this work is a deep understanding of how we perceive and interpret things and we can use some of this to help develop skills in seeing from new angles.

> See the companion website for tools to help practice different 'ways of seeing'.

Go to the source

Another powerful approach to get a different perspective involves a deceptively simple method – don't assume; go and find out! Drawing on anthropology this model recognizes that we often make assumptions about a situation and impose our own beliefs and structures on it. The method challenges this by using various tools and techniques to go and observe at the source and then interpret afterwards using real data. It's a core element in many creativity methodologies like the Creative Problem-Solving framework and Design thinking (see Chapter 13 on creativity in practice for more on this) and user-led innovation. The ways of collecting this perspective vary but they are all based on the same principle – immerse yourself in the problem, don't make assumptions about it, and don't stay behind your desk. Let the problem speak to you rather than impose a definition on it.

> See the companion website for empathic design, construct theory/repertory grid and design thinking.

What if? – exploring different scenarios

Using scenario techniques can also be a valuable starting point for changing your perspective. Exploring different alternative models in the future allows for more flexibility – and it helps us escape the setting effect of current constraints and perceptions of the problem. For example, try imagining and exploring the problem as if it were a science fiction film set in the future. Or take a radically different view and see how that affects the story you are imagining – for example, how would you handle the challenge of waste management in a world where rubbish is a high-value resource like oil?

> See the companion website for scenario techniques and Gamechanger example.

Empathize

Another way to train oneself in thinking more in options and being more flexible and adaptive in thinking is trying to 'walk in someone's shoes'. Understanding the problem and its dimensions from their point of view may open up new lines of solution thinking – and sometimes close down others. For example in the humanitarian field there are many well-meaning entrepreneurs coming up with great solutions for problems in disaster zones. The trouble is that many of these make assumptions about the lifestyle and context in which victims live – and the resulting innovations are inappropriate. Think about high tech solutions which break down because there is unreliable energy or lack of spare parts.

There are several role playing and similar approaches which can help develop skills in empathy – for example, getting people to tell the story of the problem as seen through the eyes of several different participants. Or getting inside the skin of someone else by playing their role in a simulation of the problem – how do they experience it?

> See the companion website for empathic design, design thinking, three positions and innovation theatre.

Describing problems from above

As we've seen, recombination is a powerful route to problem-solving, but it depends on skills around seeing, recognizing and combining elements. Many techniques make use of abstraction – moving to a higher level in order to see similarities which then enable new combinations to be found. Tools like TRIZ, morphological analysis and their many derivatives provide systematic frameworks for doing this. They can also help break out of the box of 'functional fixedness' by reassessing the potential of different elements in a problem. For example McCaffrey's generic parts approach lists all features of a given object and then describes these features by what they are made of rather than by their function. McCaffrey gives the example of a task: combining two metal rings by using a candle and a block of metal. For example if you describe the candle, it would goes like this: a candle is made of wax and a wick. The wick is made of string. And 'of course' now it is easy to see that strings can be used to tie things together. Problem solved [57].

> See the companion website for abstract driven search, TRIZ, morphological analysis and generic parts technique.

Exploring underlying patterns and 'core problems'

Here the skill is in 'seeing the wood for the trees' – recognizing the underlying patterns in a complex messy set of problems or drawing out a particular perspective which helps towards a useful solution. Peter Checkland's Soft Systems Methodology offers one systematic approach for this kind of skill development.

> See the companion website for rich pictures and Soft Systems Methodology.

Taking time out

Many studies highlight the problem of the 'setting effect' – our tendency to keep trying to approach problems with the same mental tools. By taking some time out, or doing something different (go for a walk, sleep on the problem, immerse yourself in something completely different) you can reduce the influence of setting effects.

Don't jump to conclusions

Separating between observation and interpretation isn't always so easy to do – as we've seen in this chapter our brains have evolved to quickly make sense of complex stimuli and so we often jump to conclusions. Teacher and artist Betty Edwards carried out some fascinating work around teaching people to draw and suggested that part of the problem is that her pupils often drew rather crude and simplistic versions of what was in front of them. Yet if she got them to use different approaches which forced them to draw what was actually there (for example by getting them to turn the picture they were copying upside down, cover it with paper and then gradually reveal it and draw the (apparently meaningless) lines and curves) they demonstrated excellent drawing ability. She concluded that the brain's ability to quickly label what it sees as a version of a concept it has already seen acts as a barrier in this context – and from this she developed a series of exercises helping to train would-be artists to 'see' [58].

You can find out more about Betty Edwards's approach – Drawing on the Right Side of the Brain – via the companion website.

In a university course one of us runs for coaching and leading innovation teams, students are asked to describe the status of the team. They should be as concrete and near to their observation as possible. Nevertheless, sentences like 'the team is motivated to do the task' are regularly used. But 'motivation' is an *interpretation*, not a behaviour that can be exhibited. Team members can be very active in a conversation, putting forward questions in order to understand the task at hand completely or they can express their willingness to start with the task. All these behaviours lead most of us to assume that a team is willing and motivated. We need to probe more deeply to discover whether this is in fact the case, and to do this we need skills in 'seeing' without instantly interpreting. Helpful questions for learning to observe are: What are people doing, what can I see, what is different in x than in y and what are features that I can see every time the problem occurs? A fascinating simple method to check if you are describing (observing) behaviour or just your interpretation is writing your observation down and then ask the following question: is this a behaviour? If not, make it one.

This development of awareness around seeing what is actually there is closely linked to the concept of 'mindfulness'. Artists speak of the negative artistic space created by the positive images painted on a surface. Psychiatrists listen for what is *not* being said in therapy as a clue to repressed material. Part of the process of human acculturation is an unconscious collusion to remain blind to the most obviously observable phenomenon, if it lies outside the realm of how we always do things. Yet the seeds of innovation and progress often lie within the domain of that which is ignored or even denied. So we need to develop awareness, see without evaluating. Although they may sound strange, sometimes we should try to listen to silence and observe the 'negative space'.

See the companion website for mindfulness and ways of seeing.

Learning to see the invariant

In their groundbreaking research Simon and colleagues highlighted the value of the rule of attending to features of a problem that remain invariant or recur repeatedly. Fast solvers not only notice more things earlier but they notice so-called perceptual clues – they focus on *observation* rather than hypothesizing [31]. Try to develop an awareness of your own heuristics – which approaches do you use, which others might you add to your repertoire?

Play, tinker and interact

The idea of play seems at odds with the serious business of coming up with something new. But there is plenty of evidence of its importance as a critical skill – something which the business world is increasingly recognizing. Books with titles like *Serious Play* and *Experimentation Matters* remind us of the importance of play as a core skill at the fuzzy front end, and this focuses our attention on ways to enable this [59–60].

Prototyping offers a way of articulating a 'boundary object' which can then be used to explore, play with the problem. Prototypes can take many forms – from physical models and mock-ups to computer simulations, stories, sketches and other devices, all of which allow for the idea to become real enough to play with and explore. Closely linked is the idea of mapping the problem – via pictures, mind-maps, cognitive maps and so forth – once again with the intention of making the hidden problem become visible so that it is available to play with.

See the companion website for prototyping, serious play, mind mapping, process mapping, rich pictures, storyboarding, simulation, business model canvas and innovation theatre.

End of chapter summary

- This chapter is about exploring the starting point of creativity: where or what is the problem?
- Different ways of exploring problems/given situations are explained: reframing, different abstraction levels, finding the right problem, finding a problem, exploring the situation in depth.
- The basis of exploring problems is problem identification and problem (re)definition.
- Research shows that there are different cognitive and perceptual processes involved: how you see the world and interpret it (e.g. Gestalt psychology); incubation and insight; overcoming mindsets and functional fixedness.

- Research also shows that interaction and tinkering with the elements of the given situation leads to more Creative Problem-Solving.
- Two basic models about problem exploration are given.
- Exploring problems is the starting point for creativity and research shows how important that first step is.
- The competence problem exploration can be subclassified into three skills sections: cognitive, perceptual and behavioural.

References

[1]   Getzels, J., & Csikszentmihalyi, M. (1976). *The creative vision: A longitudinal study of problem finding in art.* New York, NY: Wiley.

[2]   Moore, H. (1955). Notes on sculpture. In B. Ghiselin (Ed.), *The creative process* (68–73). New York, NY: Mentor Books.

[3]   Peppiat, D., Mitchell, J., & Holzmann, P. (2001). *Cash transfers in emergencies: Evaluating benefits and assessing risks.* London, UK: Overseas Development Institute (ODI).

[4]   Bessant, J., Rush, H., Gray, W., Hoffman, K., Ramalingam, B., & Marshall, N. (2014). *Innovation management, innovation ecosystems and humanitarian innovation.* London: DFID.

[5]   Zwicky, F. (1948). Morphological astronomy – The Oxford University Halley Lecture. *Observatory, 68,* 845.

[6]   TRIZ comes from the Russian acronym for 'Teoriya Resheniya Izobretatelskikh Zadatch', meaning the 'Theory of Inventive Problem Solving'.

[7]   Altshuller, G., & Shapiro, R. (1956). On a psychology of inventive creation. *Questions of Psychology* [in Russian], *6,* 37–49.

[8]   Hua, Z., Yang, J., Coulibaly, S., & Zhang, B. (2011). Integrating TRIZ with problem solving tools. *International Journal of Business Innovation and Research, 1,* 111–128.

[9]   See *http://www.aulive.com/method/*

[10] Kim, W., & Mauborgne, R. (2005). *Blue ocean strategy: How to create uncontested market space and make the competition irrelevant.* Boston, MA: Harvard Business School Press.

[11] Christensen, C. (1997). *The innovator's dilemma.* Cambridge, MA: Harvard Business School Press.

[12] Ulwick, A. (2005). *What customers want: Using outcome-driven innovation to create breakthrough products and services.* New York, NY: McGraw-Hill.

[13] Garvin, D. (1988). *Managing quality.* New York, NY: Free Press.

[14] Crosby, P. (1977). *Quality is free.* New York, NY: McGraw-Hill.

[15] Ishikawa, K. (1985). *What is total quality control?* Englewood Cliffs, NJ: Prentice-Hall.

[16] de Geus, A. (1996). *The living company.* Boston, MA: Harvard Business School Press.

[17] Wilkinson, A., & Kupers, R. (2014). *The essence of scenarios: Learning from the Shell experience.* Amsterdam: Amsterdam University Press.

[18] Kim, L. (1998). Crisis construction and organizational learning: Capability building in catching-up at Hyundai motor. *Organization Science, 9,* 506–521.

[19] Ackoff, R. (1974). *Redesigning the future.* New York, NY: Wiley.

[20] Checkland, P. (1982). *Systems thinking, systems practice.* Chichester: Wiley.

[21] Eden, C., Jones, S., & Sims, D. (1983). *Messing about in problems.* Oxford: Pergamon.

[22] Lyles, M.A., & Mitroff, I.I. (1980). Organizational problem formulation: An empirical study. *Administrative Science Quarterly, 25*, 102–119.

[23] Smilansky, J. (1984). Problem solving and the quality of invention: An empirical investigation. *Journal of Educational Psychology, 76*, 377.

[24] Runco, M.A. (1994). *Problem finding, problem solving, and creativity*. Norwood, NJ: Greenwood.

[25] McPherson, B., Crowson, R., & Pitner, N. (1986). *Managing uncertainty: Administrative theory and practice in education*. Columbus, OH: Bell & Howell.

[26] Wallas, G. (1926). *The art of thought*. New York, NY: Franklin Watts.

[27] Bower, G.H. (1981). Mood and memory. *American Psychologist, 36*, 129–148.

[28] Scheiner, C.W., Baccarella, C.V., Bessant, J., & Voigt, K.-I. (2014). Thinking patterns and gut feeling in technology identification and evaluation. *Technological Forecasting and Social Change, 101*, 112–123.

[29] Köhler, W. (1917, 3rd ed. 1973). *Intelligenzprüfung an Menschenaffen*. Berlin: Springer. / English: Köhler, W. (1927). *The mentality of apes*. New York, NY: Harcourt, Brace.

[30] Hohwy, J. (2013). *The predictive mind*. Oxford: Oxford University Press.

[31] Kaplan, C.A., & Simon, H.A. (1990). In search of insight. *Cognitive Psychology, 22*, 374–419.

[32] Gladwell, M. (2005). *Blink!* New York, NY: Sphere.

[33] Leonard, D., & Swap, W. (2005). *Deep smarts: How to cultivate and transfer enduring business wisdom*. Boston: Harvard Business School Press.

[34] Kahneman, D. (2012). *Thinking, fast and slow*. Harmondsworth: Penguin.

[35] Duncker, K. (1935). *Zur Psychologie des produktiven Denkens*. Berlin: Springer.

[36] Luchins, A.S., & Luchins, E.H. (1959). *Rigidity of behaviour: A variational approach to the effects of Einstellung*. Eugene, OR: University of Oregon Books.

[37] Gruber, H.E. (1988). The evolving systems approach to creative work. *Creativity Research Journal, 1*, 27–51.

[38] Wagner, U., Gais, S., Haider, H., Verleger, R., & Born, J. (2004). Sleep inspires insight. *Nature, 427*, 352–355.

[39] Luchins, A.S. (1942). Mechanization in problem solving: The effect of Einstellung. *Psychological Monographs, 54*, 95.

[40] Safren, M.A. (1962). Associations, sets, and the solution of word problems. *Journal of Experimental Psychology, 64*, 40–45.

[41] Silveira, J. (1971). *Incubation: The effect of interruption timing and length on problem solution and quality of problem processing*. Unpublished dissertation, University of Oregon.

[42] Weisberg, R.W., & Alba, J.W. (1981). An examination of the alleged role of 'fixation' in the solution of several 'insight' problems. *Journal of Experimental Psychology: General, 110*, 169–192.

[43] Getzels, J.W., & Csikszentmihalyi, M. (1976). *The creative vision: A longitudinal study of problem finding in art*. New York, NY: Wiley.

[44] Nickerson, R.S. (1999). Enhancing creativity. In R.J. Sternberg (Ed.), *Handbook of creativity* (392). Cambridge: Cambridge University Press.

[45] Baer, J. (1993). *Creativity and divergent thinking: A task-specific approach*. Hillsdale: Erlbaum.

[46] Runco, M.A., & Chand, I. (1995). Cognition and creativity. *Educational Psychology Review, 7*, 243–267.

[47] Chand, I., & Runco, M.A. (1992). Problem finding skills as components in the creative process. *Personality and Individual Differences, 14*, 155–162.

[48] Okuda, S.M., Runco, M.A., & Berger, D.F. (1991). Creativity and the finding and solving of real-world problems. *Journal of Psychoeducational Assessment, 9*, 45–53.

[49]   Finke, R. A., Ward, T. B., & Smith, S. M. (1992). *Creative cognition: Theory, research, and application.* Cambridge, MA: MIT Press.

[50]   Getzels, J. W. (1975). Problem-finding and the inventiveness of solutions. *Journal of Creative Behavior, 9,* 12–18.

[51]   Getzels, J. W., & Smilansky, J. (1983). Individual differences in pupil perceptions of school problems. *British Journal of Educational Psychology, 53,* 307–316.

[52]   Smilansky, J., & Halberstadt, N. (1986). Inventors versus problem solvers: An empirical investigation. *Journal of Creative Behavior, 20,* 183–201.

[53]   Kolb, D., & Fry, R. (1975). Towards a theory of applied experiential learning. In C. Cooper (Ed.), *Theories of group processes* (33–57). Chichester: Wiley.

[54]   Gick, M. L., & Holyoak, K. J. (1980). Analogical problem solving. *Cognitive Psychology, 12,* 306–355.

[55]   See website for examples of their work.

[56]   Morgan, G. (1986). *Images of organisation.* London: Sage.

[57]   McCaffrey, T. (2012). Innovation relies on the obscure: A key to overcoming the classic problem of functional fixedness. *Psychological Science, 23,* 215–218.

[58]   Edwards, B. (1993). *Drawing on the right side of the brain.* New York, NY: Harper Collins.

[59]   Schrage, M. (2000). *Serious play: How the world's best companies simulate to innovate.* Boston: Harvard Business School Press.

[60]   Thomke, S. (2002). *Experimentation matters.* Boston: Harvard Business School Press.

Chapter 3

Being open

Chapter objectives

By the end of this chapter you will:

- Understand the role which being open plays in creativity;
- Recognize the key skills associated with openness;
- Develop awareness of tools and techniques to help build openness;
- Reflect on and be able to develop your own skills in openness.

Introduction

> Minds are like parachutes – they function better when they are open.

Let's go back to our thought experiment and imagine someone creative. Leave aside their profession – artist, scientist, musician. What sort of person are they? Chances are you would say something like – curious, flexible, comfortable with new situations, perhaps something of a challenger. One word you might well use would be 'open-minded' – and that's the focus of this chapter.

An open mind is a creative mind. Sounds obvious – but what's behind this idea? And how can we develop it? What are important dimensions of openness – and why do they matter?

As we've seen creativity involves both the ability to recognize patterns in problems and the ability to retrieve and adapt solutions which we think might apply. Sometimes we can apply an old template; sometimes we may need to modify and reshape former solutions. And sometimes we need to come up with a completely different approach, generate a new solution to add to our repertoire. This generative capability implies a need to search and explore, to be open to new experiences, to absorb and assimilate new information.

We can see this clearly in the case of the artists constructing their still life arrangements in Mihaly Csikszentmihalyi and Jacob Getzels's experiments which we looked at in the previous chapter [1]. They were searching for something new, exploring the problem and trying on different directions for a solution, looking to push the frontier in some way. But doing so depends on having an open orientation, a willingness and desire to explore something new and a tolerance for the uncertainty that goes with it. It's about taking risks, jumping off a cliff without knowing for sure that the parachute you have assembled from a bed sheet will actually get you safely down to the ground!

Creativity in action: I'm not in love . . .

Released in the UK in May 1975, the song 'I'm Not in Love' became a worldwide hit for the band 10cc, reaching the top 10 in the USA, UK, Australia, Canada, New Zealand and many European charts. It won many awards (including the prestigious Ivor Novello Award for best pop song in 1976) and remains popular today, having sold in excess of 5 million physical copies and many more in downloaded formats. The song has been widely used in the soundtracks of over twenty movies, most recently *Guardians of the Galaxy*, and also features in the computer game *Grand Theft Auto*.

At the time it represented a significant breakthrough in sound, featuring a backing track made up of the band's voices painstakingly multi-tracked and layered into sheets of sound. The song was originally written by band member Eric Stewart who got the idea in response to his wife's claim that he never said he loved her. He wrote most of the melody and the lyrics on the guitar before taking it to the studio, where fellow band member Graham Gouldman suggested some different chords for the melody, and also came up with the introduction and the bridge section of the song. They spent several days writing a song (which at that point mainly involved guitars and had a bossa nova rhythm) before playing it to the rest of the band, Kevin Godley and Lol Creme.

Their response was not positive; in fact Godley's comment was 'it's not working, man. It's just crap, right? Chuck it.' So they did, throwing away the song and even erasing the early bossa nova version they had recorded. But Stewart noticed that staff members at their Strawberry Studios home were humming the melody so he persuaded the group that they should take another look at it. Godley's response was that it would only work if 'we do it like nobody has ever recorded a thing before. Let's not use instruments. Let's try to do it all with voices.'

The result was a radical departure from 'normal' recording, involving among other things the group members spending three weeks singing 'ahhh' 16 times for each note of the chromatic scale, building up a 'choir' of 48 voices for each note of the scale, 624 voices in total. In these pre-computer days they solved the problem of sustaining the notes by using tape loops strung out across the studio, wrapped around a mike stand and fed back into the tape machine! Twelve of these loops gave them the 'scale' they needed on which to build the song; they were fed separately into the mixing desk which effectively made that the 'instrument' on which the song was played! Very few 'real' instruments were used and the song's haunting effect comes from the choir they were able to create. They used a very soft drum sound to mimic a heartbeat and borrowed a child's toy music box to add another effect.

When they sang the main vocal track over the backdrop they felt something was still missing in the middle section. Stewart remembers that Lol Creme introduced a thought – he'd been saying the phrase 'Be quiet, big boys don't cry' as a test for setting up the grand piano microphones and Stewart had the crazy idea of using that but still needed a voice. 'At that point the door to the control room opened and our secretary Kathy [Redfern] looked in and whispered 'Eric, sorry to bother you. There's a telephone call for you.' Lol jumped up and said 'That's the voice, her voice is perfect!' Her whispered voice saying the phrase is one of the hallmarks of the song.

When the band played the finished version to Mercury Records their response was that it was 'a masterpiece' and the band received a five-year contract on the strength of it.

There is more about this case and a link to a video on the companion website.

That's a pattern often reported by creative artists and musicians. But it's also at the heart of the entrepreneurial journey which begins with a search for opportunities. Think about Dr Venkataswamy, searching widely beyond the health world to find the ideas that helped him establish the Aravind eye clinics. Or Muhammad Yunus, an economist working in Bangladesh who explored the hitherto uncharted space around providing finance for start-ups among the very poorest people. His idea of 'microfinancing' has gone on to change the world for millions of would-be entrepreneurs and led to his winning the Nobel Prize for Economics.

You can explore the case of Yunus and the Grameen Bank in more detail on the companion website.

Eric von Hippel at MIT has made a lifetime study of the behaviour of what are called user innovators [2]. Whether these are farmers in the Midwest modifying early Model T Fords to carry grain and cattle, aspiring sportsmen and women looking for a new thrill and bolting together rickety prototypes for their idea, or patients and carers coming up with innovative ways of living with illnesses and disabilities, user innovators share some common characteristics. First they have a high incentive to innovate – they need the solution. And second, they are prepared to explore widely and to try out different things in the hope of achieving that. In other words, they are open in their approach. (We discuss user innovation in more detail in Chapter 11.)

> You can find a 'deeper dive' around the theme of 'user innovation' and many examples of user innovators on the companion website.

It's not always the case that we need to risk life and limb – but common to all the people in these examples is an approach characterized by openness. Theories of entrepreneurship stress 'opportunity recognition' as a key stage in the process and highlight capabilities like alertness, peripheral vision, tolerance for ambiguity and network building.

Innovation is what entrepreneurs do – and the evidence is that it has always been a multiplayer game. Creating value from ideas requires abilities to acquire and deploy knowledge – and in today's knowledge-rich world even the largest organizations have to recognize that 'not all the smart guys work for us.' There's been a big shift away from seeing innovation as a process of knowledge production and accumulation towards a model which stresses knowledge flow, pulling in ideas from rich external networks and sharing our own ideas as widely as possible. This approach – which has fundamentally altered the way in which organizations large and small handle the innovation challenge – has a label originally pinned on it by US professor Henry Chesbrough in 2003, who called it 'open innovation' [3].

Creativity in action: connect and develop at Procter and Gamble

Procter and Gamble (P&G) spend about $2 billion each year and employ around 7,000 people on research to support the business. But these days they use the phrase 'Connect and Develop' instead of 'Research and Development' and have set themselves the ambitious goal of sourcing much of their idea input from outside the company. The scale of the challenge is huge; they estimate, for example, that in the 150 core technology areas which they make use of there are more than 1.5 million active researchers outside of P&G. Finding the right needle in a global haystack is a critical strategic challenge.

They achieve this through a variety of links, making particular use of internet-based sources and employing a number of people whose job it is to act as internet gatekeepers. These people use sophisticated search and visualization tools to 'mine' information about a wide range of developments in technologies, markets, competitor behaviour, social and political trends and so forth – and to bring it to the notice of others within P&G who may be able to use these signals to trigger innovation.

This search process is complemented by other ways of connecting – for example, an internet-based business (NineSigma.com) which enables client organizations 'to source innovative ideas, technologies, products and services from outside their organization quickly and inexpensively by connecting them to the very best solution providers from around the world'. They also work with another website – InnoCentive.com – which provides an online marketplace where organizations seeking solutions to problems are brought together with scientists and engineers with solutions to offer.

All of this is not to neglect the significant contribution that internal ideas can bring. The company has a wide range of active communities of practice around particular product groups, technologies, market segments and so forth and is able to draw on this knowledge increasingly through the use of intranets. A recent development has been the 'Encore' programme in which retired staff of the company – and potentially those of other companies – can be mobilized to act as knowledge and development resources in an extended innovation network.

The underlying approach is a shift in emphasis, not abandoning internal research and development but complementing it with an extensive external focus. Increasingly they see their task not just as managing 'know-how' but also 'know-who'.

You can find case studies of Procter and Gamble, Adidas, LEGO and Threadless and a 'deeper dive' on the theme of 'open innovation' on the companion website.

So what is openness?

There are two sides to openness we'll explore in greater detail in this chapter. The first is around openness as a trait, as part of our personality, something we are more or less born with. Traits are relatively stable components of our personality that shape our behaviours. The challenge here is to explore ways of developing skills associated with being open even if our predispositions are not on the side of openness.

The second is around cognitive skills – the ways we think. We've already mentioned the idea of divergent and convergent thinking and its importance in creativity. Openness is linked to our ability to think in divergent, explorative fashion, and once again the challenge is in developing and sharpening our thinking skills in this direction.

We'll look at how this skill-building might be done and what equipment we have in the gym to help you develop these 'muscles' – but first let's look in a little more detail at what research tells us about openness.

What does research tell us about openness?

Being open is sometimes about not sticking to rules and structures but about exploring in new directions, choosing different routes or just about meandering. In this book we try to describe the competence side of creativity and innovation, combining research and practical knowledge about how to train skills leading to proficiency in creative skills. But openness is a somewhat different story. There is a close link to personality traits which we do not want to neglect, so we will begin this section by looking at these before moving on to explore specific skills.

Openness as personality trait

> Openness to experience – a broad personality trait marked by an appreciation of novelty and variety and a high tolerance for ambiguity.
>
> [4]

Everyone is different but there are particular patterns in our personality – traits – which seem to be stable across many different populations and cultures. Psychologists have identified five dimensions (sometimes called 'the Big Five') that characterize the main personality traits:

* Extraversion
* Emotional instability (or neuroticism)
* Agreeableness
* Conscientiousness
* Openness to new experiences.

The Big Five were originally described in the 1970s by several researchers (among others Paul Costa & Robert McCrae), who followed two slightly different paths but ended up with the same result: personality researchers today still use this model, although they sometimes make finer distinctions [5].

'Openness to new experiences' as one of the Big Five personality traits describes the extent to which we get excited about new information and whether we seek out new experiences or try to avoid them. Research shows that it is strongly correlated with creativity in a wide range of domains; that's not to say that the other dimensions play no part but the strong links are with openness. Rather like Russian dolls, 'openness' breaks down into a number of core dimensions – things like active imagination/fantasy, aesthetic sensitivity, awareness of inner feelings, preference for variety and tolerance for ambiguity. And it can be linked with other Big Five dimensions – for example a mixture of extraversion and openness gives a dimension some researchers call 'plasticity' – a flexibility in thinking and behaviour. And linking a low score on openness with emotional stability gives a dimension around preference of security.

The important message is that openness seems to matter and is distributed in different levels across populations of people. Those who score low on openness in psychometric tests tend to be closed to new experiences, to be conventional and traditional in their outlook and behaviour, to prefer familiar routines and have a narrow range of interests. High scorers show behaviours like challenging norms, impulsivity, willingness to take risks, autonomy, imagination, curiosity, and self-confidence. One interesting behavioural aspect is around 'hostility' – people with high openness scores are not necessarily always likeable, they may be quite defensive around their particular field of activity. Think about anyone you know who is creative, always has new ideas and is seeking for new sensations – how often do they cut other people short who are arguing for the sake of the status quo, how often do they neglect social etiquette in order to rush towards their future, or how often do they fail to respond to questions or requests because they need to focus on their idea? You can probably think of someone like that; a famous recent example would probably be Steve Jobs, brilliant but sometimes quite difficult [6–7]. We could even say that in the case of people like this creativity comes with a price; as we'll see in the chapter on psychological safety, this kind of behaviour can destroy creativity in teams. So we have to find a way to integrate these different behaviours for a sustainable creative output.

Openness as divergent thinking

Apart from personality traits the other major strand of research around openness has come from the area of cognitive ability – how we think. In particular this has focused on the idea of divergent thinking, a term which was originally coined by J. P. Guilford [8]. He used it to describe the ability to generate many different possibilities for solving a problem. It is typically measured by tests of originality, fluency, flexibility and variety – for example 'how many uses can you think of for a brick'?

> You can find some examples of tests for divergent thinking and an activity based on unusual uses ('uses for . . .') on the companion website.

'Convergent thinking', as the name implies, is a style of thinking which homes in logically on a particular solution. Divergent thinking, by contrast, is all about opening up the problem, exploring different angles on it, developing associations and links (see Figure 3.1). It's important not to see these as good or bad styles of thinking but rather as two sides of a coin; we need both approaches to be effective creative problem-solvers. Divergence helps us reframe, see the problem from

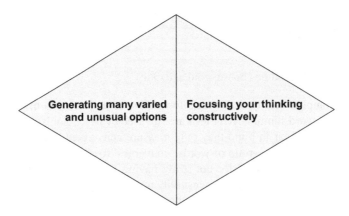

Figure 3.1 Divergent and convergent thinking

fresh angles while convergence helps us make progress towards a solution which we can implement. A helpful metaphor might be 'breathe in, breathe out' – a nice wording for how the two thinking styles work together.

Divergent thinking seems to be linked to our ability to make associations – to link together apparently unconnected thoughts and concepts. Famous examples include George de Mestral who noticed after walking through a meadow that some of the plant burrs had stuck to his clothing. Looking at them under a microscope he saw they had tiny hooks which were catching in the fibres of his clothes – and from that association Velcro was born. Alastair Pilkington made a link between the film of fat floating on the water surface of the bowl in which he was doing the washing up and the possibility of making glass by what became the revolutionary 'float glass' process. And way back in the fifteenth century Johannes Gutenberg saw a link between the wine presses he had grown up with and a new approach to pressing type onto paper, and invented the world's first printing press.

Creativity in action: think like a RAT

The Remote Associates Test (RAT) is a creativity test originally developed by Sarnoff Mednick at the University of Michigan in 1962, relying heavily on word associations [9–11]. He invented it to measure creativity, but in contrast to the Unusual Uses Test here there is only one correct answer. So, the test could be described to measure convergent creativity.

Each RAT question presents a group of three cue words and requires to provide a single extra word that links all the others together. Creative thinking is needed because the first and most obvious solution is often wrong. Instead, more remote connections need to be retrieved. The task is to come up with the correct word that links three given words.

Examples:
cottage / Swiss / cake   _____
fish / mine / rush   _____
sandwich / house / golf   _____

(the answers would be cheese, gold and club)

The complete test typically lasts forty minutes and consists of thirty to forty three-word stimulus. RAT tests are still used by psychologists to test for creativity, but bear in mind they only measure convergent thinking skills. This is because each group of words 'converges' to a single answer. RAT was very much criticized for not really having any creative correlates in practice and measuring more a sensitivity towards language than creativity.

You can try out these tests for yourself by visiting this link: http://www.creativehuddle.co.uk/the-remote-associates-test

A newer version was developed by Blaine Worthen and Philip Clark in 1971 which takes on board some of the early criticisms of the RAT tests.

One interesting strand of thinking around this area is about neural networks and connectivity. Creativity can be seen as an ability to retrieve and connect disparate concepts stored in long-term memory systems. And these concepts are connected in our brains in semantic networks. Research suggests that these networks can have different shapes – some are steeper (where associations are direct, logical and linear) whereas others are flatter (where associations are looser). Creativity seems to be linked to flatter networks where jumping across different nodes is easier than for someone with a steep network.

Recent neuroimaging research has suggested some support for the idea that different regions of the brain are involved in different aspects of creativity. Mark Beeman and John Kounios, working at Northwestern and Drexel University, suggest that steep networks are linked to activity in the left hemisphere, while flat networks seem to feature more in the right. In trying to track the elusive 'aha!' moment of insight when someone is working on a Creative Problem-Solving task they found that a region in the right temporal lobe has a spike in electrical activity just before the moment of insight is experienced. This is a region which is involved in drawing together distantly related information – lending some support to the view that creativity is strongly linked to making new associations [12].

Cognitive ability around divergent thinking is affected by physical factors and mood states. Put simply, if we are relaxed and in a positive mood we are more likely to be able to work in divergent mode. As we've seen divergence is linked to making extended associations – and arguably we can do this better when we are not working hard to focus on a task. Or if we are concentrating then sometimes taking a short break can help bring a fresh perspective and allow new links to form. Various studies have explored the ways in which things which affect our moods – for example listening to music, watching a comedy which makes us laugh, walking among beautiful scenery – can also affect our creativity. One of the early thinkers in the field, Arthur Koestler, developed a theory around 'bisociation' – the making of surprising and unexpected connections. As part of this work he analyzed the way that humour works, pointing out that it is very often based on unexpected and surprising conjunctions; importantly listening to jokes and laughing at them can also put our minds in a more receptive state for this process to happen [13].

Creativity in action: showers, strolling and not sitting still

Woody Allen, the famous film director, has been enormously productive as well as creative during his long career. Far from expecting the creative muse to suddenly visit him he recognizes the importance of regular work at the task of creativity – but also that sitting too long at the task can lead to a kind of stagnation. As a result he employs a series of strategies to break up the flow and give his brain a chance to change state – notably by moving around his apartment and even taking many showers during the day! As he comments,

> I've found over the years that any momentary change stimulates a fresh burst of mental energy. So if I'm in this room and then I go into the other room, it helps me. If I go outside to the street, it's a huge help. If I go up and take a shower it's a big help. So I sometimes take extra showers. I'll be in the living room and at an impasse and what will help me is to go upstairs and take a shower. It breaks up everything and relaxes me. I go out on my terrace a lot. One of the best things about my apartment is that it's got a long terrace and I've paced it a million times writing movies. It's such a help to change the atmosphere.

And getting a good night's sleep also matters. Studies at Jim Horne's Sleep Laboratory in Loughborough, UK, have shown that sleep affects divergent thinking performance even among highly motivated individuals [14]. Twelve subjects were deprived of sleep for thirty-two hours, while a control group of twelve others maintained a normal sleep routine. Their performance on both a word fluency task and a challenging nonverbal planning test was 'significantly impaired by sleep loss', even when the factor of personal motivation to perform well was controlled. The researchers concluded that even 'one night of sleep loss can affect divergent thinking.'

Openness and recent brain research

Some fascinating recent research suggests that openness may have strong bio-logical roots linked to dopamine systems in the brain. Dopamine is a neu-rotransmitter, a chemical which is active in enabling particular mental processes and particularly linked to reward systems. We feel good when we receive a dopamine 'hit' and this tends to reinforce a particular behaviour. Studies at the University of Pennsylvania suggest that 'people with high openness show high dopamine projections at the potential of acquiring information.' In other words, higher scores on openness are linked to a 'feel-good factor' around learning new things.

Scott Barry Kaufman draws on these studies to suggest that there is an impor-tant link with what he terms engagement in certain types of behaviour. We get involved in these things because there is a sense of pleasure attached to them coming partly from the dopamine release. His view on openness is linked to four elements [15].

Kaufman's fascinating view suggests that there may be different styles of open-ness. For example those with high intellectual engagement are driven to discover ideas as a scientist does; those with affective engagement are driven to investigate emotions as a poet does; and those with aesthetic engagement are driven to find beauty as a painter does.

It may not be quite as simple as only one chemical process inside our brains but there is a growing view that openness is linked to some kind of energizing reward which motivates people to follow these behaviour patterns.

Some researchers have looked at the idea of 'absorption' – how much we enjoy being drawn into a creative task. They make links to the idea of 'flow states' first propounded by Mihaly Csikszentmihalyi [16].

Table 3.1 Four elements of openness

Element	Description
Explicit Cognitive Ability	a baseline set of capabilities including fluid reasoning, mental rotation, verbal analogical reasoning and working memory
Intellectual Engagement	a drive to engage in ideas, rational thought and the search for truth
Affective Engagement	a preference for using emotions, gut feelings and empathy to make decisions
Aesthetic Engagement	a preference for aesthetics, fantasy and emotional absorption in artistic and cultural stimuli

Creativity in action: flow states

Flow is the high point of creative work when a person becomes fully immersed in a feeling of energized focus, full involvement and enjoyment in the process of the activity. Most people perceive this status as a strong and positive feeling linked to absorption, concentration and serenity. One is so engrossed in a question or problem that one forgets about the world. For most human beings, this is a powerful positive feeling, to be so deep in thought that concentration and relaxation are compatible together.

There are six factors encompassing an experience of flow [17]:

1   Intense and focused concentration on the present moment;
2   Merging of action and awareness;
3   A loss of reflective self-consciousness;
4   A sense of personal control or agency over the situation or activity;
5   A distortion of temporal experience; one's subjective experience of time is altered;
6   Experience of the activity as intrinsically rewarding.

A flow state can be entered while performing any activity, but it is most likely to occur when one is wholeheartedly performing a task or activity for intrinsic purposes. It's necessary to actively do something to enter a flow state.

The graph shows us that flow is linked to the needed skill level of the task at hand. Thus a feeling of confidence in one's ability to complete the task is a central precondition of flow experiences.

The argument goes that people who have a high openness to experience enjoy learning new things, which means they'll be more likely to get into the state of flow.

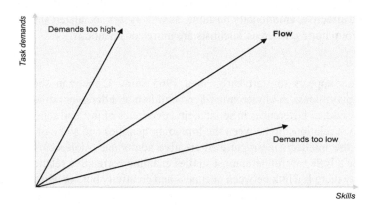

Figure 3.2 Flow chart

Another theory around the importance of openness is based on 'latent inhibition' – the tendency in our minds to filter out information as irrelevant. In one study, Harvard psychologist Shelley Carson found that college students who were high creative achievers were *seven times* more likely to have reduced instead of enhanced latent inhibition. People with high openness tend to have low latent inhibition, and thus more original ideas [18].

Researchers at the Key Laboratory of Cognition and Personality in Beijing used brain imaging to explore the links between cognitive aspects (how we think) and affective aspects (how we feel) in creativity. They found that people with high openness were more likely to be creative or creative people were more likely to have these traits. They looked at brains of people and found for some a higher grey matter volume in something called the right posterior middle temporal gyrus (pMTG). But only people who had a high score on the trait openness were more creative [19]. This raises a chicken-and-egg question of what comes first, the bigger pMTG or creativity and openness. As they summarized their studies: 'One could infer that the cultivation of the basic personality features of openness to experience in children and adolescents may increase an individual's trait creativity and, thereby, facilitate divergent thinking and creative achievement.'

Why being open is important for creativity

Many studies (using tests like those for divergent thinking and personality traits) have highlighted the links between openness and creativity in both arts and science. Feist (1999) summarizes the findings as follows:

> Creative people in art and science tend to be open to new experiences, less conventional and less conscientious, more self-confident, self-accepting, driven, ambitious, dominant, hostile, and impulsive. Creative people in art and science do not share the same unique personality profiles: Artists are more affective, emotionally unstable, as well as less socialized and accepting of group norms, whereas scientists are more conscientious.
>
> [7]

And this appears to start early; in a 1965 study Lieberman showed links between playfulness in kindergarten-aged children and divergent thinking. They 'noted individual differences in spontaneity, overtones of joy, and sense of humor that imply a relationship between the foregoing qualities and some of the factors found in the intellectual structure of creative adults and adolescents' [20]. We have to be a little careful here; most studies examine correlative relationships. So we can say there is a link between openness and creativity but not whether the one causes the other. And the assumption that creativity is equal to divergent thinking has been widely criticized as too narrow-minded [21–22].

If we look again at our picture of creativity as a journey then we can begin to see where openness would be valuable – for example:

- Openness to stimuli to trigger our creative search routines – preparation stage;
- Openness to multiple processes rational and unconscious – incubation stage;
- Openness to criticisms and new information which challenges our insight – validation and elaboration.

Openness is also important in the context of group creativity – something we will look at in more detail in the next section. Here the emphasis is on the contribution the open individual can make particularly in aspects of communication and interpersonal relationships that are probably beneficial for creative teams in terms of collaboration and co-operation.

And it matters in the wider world of 'open innovation' in which organizations are seeking new ways of making connects with different and complementary knowledge partners. Central to any open innovation strategy are ways of bridging between two different worlds, and this throws into sharp focus the need for 'boundary spanners' – people who have the ability to make connections and link things up. This is not a new insight – back in the 1970s researcher Tom Allen was studying the NASA space programme and patterns of innovation enabling it. He was fascinated by the way knowledge flowed to and within organizations and highlighted the key role played by intermediaries – people he called 'technological gatekeepers' [23]. They were open individuals who could also make connections between things they had noticed 'out there' and relevant people who could make use of that knowledge within the organization. This kind of 'knowledge brokering' is now of critical importance – and 'openness' of the kind we have been describing is a key skill set.

For more about the role of knowledge brokers and examples of them in action, see the 'deeper dive' on 'open innovation' on the companion website.

What is the skill set around openness?

In this section we'll try to help you locate where you stand in relation to navigating the creativity journey, and in particular how 'open' you are. We'll begin with a short description of the competence itself and then go on to list ten skills that are needed to master all aspects of openness. In the questionnaire you can check for yourself where you are. This self-check gives a hint what elements of openness you can further develop and what elements are already a strength. The competence description and the given skills are rooted in the research we described in the chapter.

Openness in creativity is strongly connected to personality, our relatively stable patterns and unique characteristics that give both consistency and individuality to our behaviour. Personality is much less stable than we thought in the early days of personality research, but still traits are very consistent over time and situations and hard to change. Traits that are associated with openness are intellectual curi-osity, being open to new experiences, and a preference for change and variety. If you are interested in this personal predisposition, there are some tests based on the five factor model of personality (one factor is openness) that are useful for self-evaluation.

In this section we present a very short version of a much longer questionnaire (almost 100 questions!) which will give you a glimpse in five minutes.

Ten-item personality inventory (TIPI) [24]

Here are a number of personality traits that may or may not apply to you (see Table 3.2). Please write a number next to each statement to indicate the extent to which you agree or disagree with that statement. You should rate the extent to which the pair of traits applies to you, even if one characteristic applies more strongly than the other.

1 = disagree strongly
2 = disagree moderately
3 = disagree a little
4 = neither agree nor disagree
5 = agree a little
6 = agree moderately
7 = agree strongly

For your scale scoring, please fill in Table 3.3. The question number marked with R is a so called reverse-scored item. Therefore please reverse your score here: A 7 will be a 1, and so on.

Table 3.2 Personality questionnaire (big five)

#	I see myself as:	Your score (1–7)
1	Extraverted, enthusiastic	
2	Critical, quarrelsome	
3	Dependable, self-disciplined	
4	Anxious, easily upset	
5	Open to new experiences, complex	
6	Reserved, quiet	
7	Sympathetic, warm	
8	Disorganized, careless	
9	Calm, emotionally stable	
10	Conventional, uncreative	

Table 3.3 Evaluation personality questionnaire (big five)

Extraversion	Agreeableness	Conscientiousness	Emotional Stability	Openness to Experiences
I	2R	3	4R	5
6R	7	8R	9	I0R
Sum =	Sum =	Sum =	Sum =	Sum =

R = Reversed item. Please reverse score before entering (e.g. score of 7 in Table 3.2 will become score of I in Table 3.3).

Programming the GPS for the creativity journey – what's your position?

In this definition we focus on the competence of openness. There are two main skill-areas of openness as a competence: divergent thinking and interpersonal openness skills. Divergent thinking skills are about producing new ideas. The more varied and the more original the ideas, the better. Interpersonal openness is concerned about how one reacts towards other people, differences in views, thoughts, and ways of thinking.

There is a strong link between openness in individuals and supporting ideas of others in teams. If you want to develop your openness we recommend that you also look closely at Chapter 8 which deals with supporting ideas.

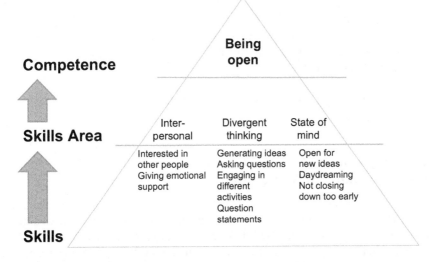

Figure 3.3 Competence being open

Table 3.4 Self-check being open

#	Core behavioural skills	Your score (1–5)	For instance write at least one example of your own
1	I am open for new ideas		
2	I question statements that are well tried or taken for granted		
3	I have lots of original ideas		
4	I generate diverse ideas		
5	I ask questions frequently		
6	I like to have 'daydreams'		
7	I engage in a variety of activities		
8	I am interested in other people		
9	I give emotional support when needed		
10	I would rather look at another idea before coming to an early conclusion		

Next we offer you a skill self-check on being open (Table 3.4). We suggest you rate yourself with a five-point rating scale:

1 = Not like me at all
2 = Not much like me
3 = I cannot decide if I am good or bad at it, just doing OK
4 = Describes me to a good extent (but not exactly)
5 = Describes me exactly

For tips on filling in a self-check questionnaire please go to Chapter 2 on problem exploration.

Working out at the gym – how to train the skills of being open

The first question one has to ask is what aspects of openness are truly there to train. The skill description section about openness is the only one we put a trait questionnaire in next to our skill descriptions, being well aware that openness as competence is closely linked to a personality trait. But as you can see with our skill descriptions, there is a big part that you can change by training.

Once again, there is a template for a personal training plan that you can download from the companion website.

Following are some 'workouts' for developing openness.

Overcome your routines

Use every opportunity to try something different from your normal routine – it will help. This can be a different way to work, a different routine than normal on your Fridays (getting ready for the weekend), or just a different place to sit on the sofa or at your dining table. You very probably won't feel different after the first time you do this, but after a while you are not so stuck to your usual routines. It's a start.

Use multiple representational systems

Openness isn't only about using a different route to work every day – it's also about training unused 'mental muscles'. For example try playing with different representational systems. If you are a word person, try to sing a song about the problem instead – or draw the problem. You will probably not earn an award for it, but by using different representational systems you will get new insights. One of the most widely used techniques for resolving conflicts is to use a visualization of the conflict because you see different connections; sometimes you see a different world from the world you are hearing while listening to the conflict parties. The same is true for creative problems and your openness.

Train your divergent thinking skills

There are many tests you can not only use to measure your divergent thinking but also to train it. The most famous tests are Torrance Tests of Creative Thinking (TTCT) [25–27]. There are three parts to it: verbal tasks using verbal stimuli (e.g. imaginative stories task), verbal tasks using non-verbal stimuli (e.g. unusual uses task), and non-verbal tasks (e.g. incomplete figures tasks). The Wallas and Kogan Test is basically another version of the unusual uses task by Torrance or the Alternate Uses Task by Guilford [28–29].

You can find links to these tests on the companion website.
   Specific tools to help develop divergent thinking (all available on the companion website) include:

- Lateral thinking tools
- SCAMPER
- Six thinking hats

Fertilize your mindsoil

Researchers Edward Necka and Teresa Hlawacz have studied the importance of openness to new experiences and its relation to creativity and found (in a study comparing artists with bankers) that what made the artists most creative was a 'tendency to initiate numerous activities that lead to, or provoke, rich external stimulation' [30]. This richness of input creates a corresponding richness of output. They use the metaphor of 'mindsoil' – the layer where ideas are able to take root. Steve Jobs once similarly spoke of the benefits of a tendency towards diverse inputs: the bigger your 'bag of experiences', the more varied the connections you can make between things.

Give yourself a whack on the head!

Not literally – but you can use various stimuli to help change your thinking state – for example change your environment, go for a walk, look for stimuli in pictures or through music, and so forth. One very powerful method is to try and force connections between random elements and your particular challenge – this lateral thinking technique helps create novel associations in the brain.

You can find this tool and another, the HIT Matrix, on the companion website.

Amplify your openness

Alfred Bandura, a social learning psychologist, describes different ways of social learning: one is to imitate a *role model*. Think back to your teenage days how you imitated your favourite music star or the girls or boys you thought were cool. You probably not only tried to dress like them but also to walk, gesture or talk like them. This is learning by imitation. So look around you and find somebody with high openness, find out what they are doing to be open, and start to learn and imitate.

Develop your questioning skills

Divergent thinking is promoted by creating lists of questions on topics (regardless which). You can use it in two different ways. Take a topic for which you need a creative solution, and before starting with brainstorming or any other solution-finding technique start by asking yourself questions (and writing them down). Try and generate a long list rather than stopping after a handful.

Another way to use questions is as a different form of brainstorming – what we might term 'q-storming'. Jon Roland has a useful website which describes this technique – for a link go to the companion website.

Many problems which present themselves are actually symptoms or consequences of something deeper. Various methods have been developed to help peel away these layers and get to the root cause, the core problem.

On the companion website there are several tools to help explore by questioning and mapping – see, for example:

- Five whys
- Fishbone (Ishikawa) diagram
- Process mapping.

Free your writing

Creative writing techniques are not just for would-be writers; they can also help creativity-seekers. Free writing is a good example. Start with writing a paragraph or a page each day about what you've seen or felt; it's not like writing a 'normal' journal where you reflect and think about the experiences of the day but more like writing a doodle. Focus on a particular topic and write non-stop about it for a short period of time, in a stream of consciousness fashion.

Relax your mind

There is a Chinese proverb: if you are in a hurry, take your time. This also applies to creativity. Relaxation is incubation time, allowing some of the setting effect to dissipate. After a hard day working on a problem we need to rest and let our mind wander off. Mindful meditation is a technique that enhances our ability to be open and creative.

You can find some tools for mindfulness on the companion website.

Get some sleep

As described earlier, even one night's sleep deprivation impacts severely on our capacity for divergent thinking. So getting enough sleep seems to be one of the ways to at least get back to a baseline of creative capability.

Deliberate daydreaming

Most of us have had the experience of sitting in a chair, looking out the window and, while doing nothing in particular, thinking about the world. And this state can sometimes help us to come up with a new insight, a creative idea, or a question that leads one further on in the creative journey. Deliberate daydreaming, as the name suggests, is trying to harness this experience in more systematic fashion. Doing so begins with finding a suitably relaxing but stimulating environment – for example sitting on a park bench idly watching people pass by, or at a desk in a library, surrounded by books on diverse topics. The second step is to formulate a concrete question: your challenge. And you will use this as a focus for the day-dreaming which hopefully follows.

End of chapter summary

- This chapter is about being open as one of the major elements of creativity.
- Openness can be defined as a personality trait or as a cognitive process.
- Recent research shows correlates in our brain linked to being open and creative.
- Being open is important for creativity in many ways, for example:

    - Open to stimuli to trigger our creative search routines – preparation stage;
    - Open to multiple processes rational and unconscious – incubation stage;
    - Open to criticisms and new information which challenges our insight – validation and elaboration.

- The competence can be subcategorized into three different set of skills: inter-personal, divergent thinking and state of mind.

References

[1] Csikszentmihalyi, M., & Getzels, J. W. (1971). Discovery-oriented behavior and the originality of creative products: A study with artists. *Journal of Personality and Social Psychology, 19*, 47–52.

[2] Von Hippel, E. (2005). *The democratization of innovation.* Cambridge, MA: MIT Press.

[3] Chesbrough, H. (2003). *Open innovation: The new imperative for creating and profiting from technology.* Boston, MA: Harvard Business School Press.

[4] McCrae, R. (2011). *Encyclopaedia of creativity* (Vol. 1) (Eds.), M. A. Runco & S. R. Pritzker. London: Elsevier.

[5] Costa, P. T., & McCrae, R. R. (1976). Age differences in personality structure: A cluster analytic approach. *Journal of Gerontology, 31*, 564–570.

[6] Feist, G. J. (1998). A meta-analysis of personality in scientific and artistic creativity. *Personality and Social Psychology Review, 2*, 290–309.

[7] Feist, G. J. (1999). Influence of personality on artistic and scientific creativity. In R. J. Sternberg (Ed.), *Handbook of creativity* (273–296). New York, NY: Cambridge University Press.

[8] Guilford, J. P. (1950). Creativity. *American Psychologist, 5*, 444–454.

[9]   Mednick, S.A. (1964). An associative interpretation of the creative process. In C.W. Taylor (Ed.), *Widening horizons in creativity* (54–68). New York, NY: Wiley.

[10] Mednick, S.A. (1968). The Remote Associates Test. *Journal of Creative Behavior*, *2*, 213–214.

[11] Mednick, S.A., & Andrews, F.M. (1967). Creative thinking and level of intelligence. *Journal of Creative Behavior*, *1*, 428–431.

[12] Kounios, J., & Beeman, M. (2015). *The eureka factor*. London: Penguin Random House.

[13] Koestler, A. (1964). *The act of creation*. London: Hutchinson.

[14] Horne, J.A. (1988). Sleep loss and 'divergent' thinking ability. *Sleep*, *11*, 528–536.

[15] Kaufman, S. (2013). *Ungifted: Intelligence redefined*. New York, NY: Basic Books.

[16] Csikszentmihalyi, M. (1996). *Creativity: Flow and the psychology of discovery and invention*. New York, NY: Harper Perennial.

[17] Nakamura, J., & Csikszentmihalyi, M. (2014). The motivational sources of creativity as viewed from the paradigm of positive psychology. In M. Csikszentmihalyi (Ed.), *The systems model of creativity* (195–206). Dordrecht: Springer Netherlands.

[18] Shelley Carson, see her website *http://www.shelleycarson.com/*

[19] Li, W., Li, X., Huang, L., Kong, X., Yang, W., Wei, D., . . . Liu, J. (2015). Brain structure links trait creativity to openness to experience. *Social Cognitive and Affective Neuroscience*, *10*(2), 191–198.

[20] Lieberman, J.N. (1965). Playfulness and divergent thinking: Investigation of their relationship at the kindergarten level. *Journal of Genetic Psychology*, *107*, 219–224.

[21] Gardner, H. (1993). *Multiple intelligences: The theory in practice*. New York, NY: Basic Books.

[22] Weisberg, R.W. (1993). *Creativity: Beyond the myth of genius*. New York, NY: WH Freeman.

[23] Allen, T., & Henn, G. (2007). *The organization and architecture of innovation*. London: Routledge.

[24] Gosling, S.D., Rentfrow, P.J., & Swann, W.B. (2003). A very brief measure of the Big-Five personality domains. *Journal of Research in Personality* 37, 504–528.

[25] Torrance, E.P. (1972). *Torrance Tests of Creative Thinking. Directions manual and scoring guide. Figural test booklet A*. Bensenville, IL: Scholastic Testing Service.

[26] Torrance, E.P. (1972). Predictive validity of the Torrance Tests of Creative Thinking. *Journal of Creative Behavior*, *6*(4), 236–252.

[27] Torrance, E.P. (1974). *Torrance Test of Creative Thinking: Norms and technical manual*. Bensenville, IL: Scholastic Testing Services.

[28] Christensen, P.R., Guilford, J.P., Merrifield, P.R., & Wilson, R.C. (1960). *Alternative uses*. Beverly Hills, CA: Sheridan Psychological Services.

[29] Wallach, M.A., & Kogan, N. (1965). *Modes of thinking in young children: A study of the creativity intelligence distinction*. New York, NY: Holt, Rinehart & Winston.

[30] Nęcka, E., & Hlawacz, T. (2013). Who has an artistic temperament? Relationships between creativity and temperament among artists and bank officers. *Creativity Research Journal*, *25*, 182–188.

Chapter 4

Building up willpower

Chapter objectives

By the end of this chapter you will:

*   Understand the role which willpower plays in creativity;
*   Recognize the key skills associated with willpower;
*   Develop awareness of tools and techniques to help build willpower;
*   Reflect on and be able to develop your own skills in willpower.

Introduction

> It's not that I'm so smart, it's just that I stay with problems longer.
>
> —Albert Einstein

By now we hope you are familiar with the idea of creativity as a journey rather than a single lightning flash event. There's often a long period of frustration, of wrestling with a problem at the outset before a clear definition emerges. Sometimes we move quietly on to solving the problem which has come into view, sometimes this moment of insight is accompanied by an emotional charge, a sense of 'aha!', a flash of inspiration. But in either case this point is not the end of the journey; it is followed by a long period of elaboration and refinement, getting that solution to work. Throughout the journey we need mental energy and commitment to sustain us, a degree of perseverance and persistence. That's the focus of this chapter; while there are several different words to describe it, we will make use of the term 'willpower' since that describes well the focused and purposeful commitment which creativity needs.

Think (again) about someone being creative – and it's easy to fall into the trap of seeing them as gifted, inspired and instantaneous producers of something novel and useful. In fact, when you ask them how they go about writing a novel, building a sculpture, painting a picture or imagining the orderly distribution of notes on the page of a symphony, they will tell you it is mostly hard work. It's the same with science and technology – remember Thomas Edison's famous comment that 'genius is 1% inspiration and 99% perspiration'! A hundred years later, Drew Houston, founder of Dropbox, makes a similar observation about innovation:

> It is a very gruelling experience. . . . one day you are on the top of the world. . . . the next day there is a huge bug and the site is down and you are tearing your hair out.

This isn't just a matter of putting pen to paper or paintbrush to canvas; it's also about a wrestle with the problem at hand, trying to force it into shape. And much of that is learning to work with failure – recognizing the blind alley that you have been walking down, the mistakes and flaws in your original thinking which force you to retrace your steps and try a different tack. Thomas Stearns Eliot, the famous poet, captured this well in trying to explain the challenge of writing poetry [1]:

> So here I am, in the middle way, having had twenty years—
> Twenty years largely wasted, the years of l'entre deux guerres—
> Trying to use words, and every attempt
> Is a wholly new start, and a different kind of failure
> Because one has only learnt to get the better of words
> For the thing one no longer has to say, or the way in which
> One is no longer disposed to say it.
>
> ('East Coker', 1943)

In the very different world of domestic appliances James Dyson has literally become a household name – vacuum cleaners, hand dryers and cooling fans bearing his name appear in homes and offices, shops and restaurants, airports and theatres all around the world. His autobiography is called *Against the Odds*, and it sums up well the approach he has taken to creativity – constantly wrestling with problems and winning through hard work. Central to this is acceptance of failure as a series of steps on the journey to success. His breakthrough product, the bagless vacuum cleaner, took him over five years to bring to life, discarding over 5,000 prototypes along the way. Even then the challenge didn't end; he had to spend more time and energy fighting a major court case to stop competitors copying his idea.

> You can find more about Dyson and his struggles in the case study on the companion website.

'If at first you don't succeed, try, try, try again' is not just a trite saying – it's a pretty accurate description of what is needed to sustain effective creativity. It's a life lesson that an impressive array of successful players would share – think about Walt Disney who beavered away at the laborious process of animating cartoons before his first major success with *Snow White and the Seven Dwarfs*. The Wright Brothers didn't just put an aeroplane in the air – the 1903 flight at Kittyhawk Sands was the product of five years of experimentation and failure with different designs for gliders and flying machines. Kevin Ashton (the man who first introduced the idea of the 'Internet of Things' to the world) reflects on these examples and suggests that 'creation is not a moment of inspiration but a lifetime of endurance' [2].

A key part of the story seems to be around attitudes towards failure. Psychologist Adam Grant has made a detailed study of what he calls 'creative originals' – people in different fields who are known for the novelty and usefulness of their work [3]. He observes that:

> the greatest originals are the ones who fail the most, because they're the ones who try the most . . . You need a lot of bad ideas in order to get a few good ones.

You can find a link on the companion website to a TED Talk by Adam Grant about this topic.

PERSISTENCE.

So creativity is about persistence, perseverance and the willingness to keep going in the face of failure, sustained by the belief in the end goal of a solution which works. We call this cluster 'willpower' – and it involves a mixture of strong internal motivation and the skill to mobilize our energies and keep going.

What does research tell us about willpower?

Willpower is important in many areas of activity and it has been the subject of some detailed research. One interesting finding is that it isn't simply something we can turn on and off; it takes effort and we get tired when we use it. Roy Baumeister and colleagues use the analogy of a muscle which can become fatigued through use; they talk about 'ego depletion', describing it as people's diminished capacity to regulate their thoughts, feelings, and actions' (p. 264 [4, 5–8]). And, like a muscle, we can learn to develop 'stamina'; through training we can strengthen the muscle so that the time until depletion gets longer.

Psychologist Angela Duckworth has made a detailed study of what she calls 'grit' – the tendency to sustain interest in and effort towards very long-term goals. There are strong correlations between achievement and high levels of grit and there are important links to factors like self-control (being able to forgo short term rewards for the longer term higher prize).

GRIT

You can find a link to a fascinating TED Talk by Angela Duckworth on the companion website.

In a groundbreaking study Terrie Moffit and a team of researchers studied a group of 1,000 people from their birth to the age of thirty-two. They could show that self-control in childhood is the most important predictor for physical health, substance dependence, personal finances, and criminal offending outcomes. This means that willpower is more important than intelligence and social class [9]. These results fall in line with research by Walter Mischel who studied kids with the now so-called Marshmallow Test (where children have to choose between eating one marshmallow straight away or waiting a while and then having more than one). He found similar outcomes [10].

You can find a link to a 'reproduction' of the original marshmallow test on the companion website.

FLOW STATES

Creativity theory also recognizes the value of persistence. A core principle in Alex Osborn's original concept of brainstorming was 'no criticism' – a rule specifically intended to remove barriers to persistence during group idea generation [11]. And Mihaly Csikszentmihalyi's research suggests that creativity is powerfully facilitated by the experience of flow because in the state of flow, people 'persist . . . single-mindedly, disregarding hunger, fatigue, and discomfort' (p. 89, [12]).

Creativity in action: the role of motivation

Willpower depends in part on the underlying motivation to keep going, and this too has been studied extensively. One of the important distinctions lies between 'intrinsic motivation' – the incentives to effort provided by the nature of the thing we are engaged upon – and 'extrinsic motivation', where the incentive is provided by expectations of some kind of reward or concerns about negative consequences. This is the famous 'stick or carrot' side of motivation theory. Research suggests that creative persons tend to follow intrinsic interests, and that tasks that are intrinsically motivated tend to be free from the evaluations and constraints that can inhibit creativity [13]. People may have certain traits or abilities which are favourable for creativity but whether these will actually result in something depends strongly on their intrinsic motivation and their willpower.

Extrinsic motivation seems to be more of a two-edged sword; it can reinforce the power of intrinsic motivation (for example by providing a supportive environment in which there are rewards for creative behaviour) but it can also have strong negative impacts (for example when there is a fear of blame or punishment for risky behaviour).

PERSEVERENCE

Several theories which try to draw relevant research on creativity together stress the importance of willpower. For example, Teresa Amabile's componential model of creativity includes skills such as the ability to 'concentrate effort for long periods of time' and to 'persever[e] in the face of frustration' (p. 361, [14]).

Another theory – the stochastic approach – suggests that creativity is, to some extent, a product of random variations in our thinking which allow new ideas to emerge. This is important for evolutionary survival – as we find new ways and remember them so our ability as a species to survive in a complex environment increases. One important factor in this model is the idea of 'productivity' – the more ideas we produce the better our chances of finding the good ones and holding on to them. So persistence becomes important to keep the flow of ideas coming even when the task seems difficult or the outcome uncertain. Researchers like Dean Simonton, again studying creative people, found links between sheer productivity (the number of ideas and the persistence in searching for them over time) and creative originality [15–16]. This could be described as the 'kissing frogs' model – the underlying message in the famous fairy tale of the Brothers Grimm is that you need to kiss a lot of frogs before you find your fairy-tale prince!

There is also an observed tendency for us to follow the 'path of least resistance' when it comes to creative thinking. Try the activity in the following box – then read on.

Creativity activity

An alien flying saucer arrives and the door opens – what comes out? Try and draw a picture of this creature from outer space.

Research shows that when given a task of this kind more people come up with something which builds on concepts we already know – variations on earthly birds or animals. They would have features we would recognize – arms or legs, bilateral symmetry, eyes and so forth. Psychologist Tom Ward carried out a range of studies on this effect and argued that when developing new ideas, most people retrieve a specific instance of a known concept from memory (e.g. a bird), and then use its features in the subsequent creative product. He suggested that when trying to be creative most people follow the 'path of least resistance': they will generate a few highly accessible ideas with the least effort possible and then stop [17]. But if people were pushed or stimulated to explore further they might find other more creative possibilities; for example, when people were asked to think a bit more about their creatures (by instructing them to consider the environment of the imagined planet) participants made more creative drawings. Once again persistence pays off!

Intriguingly some research suggests that, counter to the accepted view of divergence being the key pathway to creative insight, there may be times when focus and convergence is the key [18]. Researchers at the Universities of Amsterdam and Groningen in the Netherlands found that 'systematic and focused thinking can and does result in high levels of creativity under some circumstances' [19]. They propose a 'dual pathway' model of creativity in which creativity is linked both to cognitive flexibility – being able to explore and associate in different directions – and cognitive persistence [20]. Like many others they stress the importance of cognitive flexibility – being able to think in divergent mode. But they also examine the role of persistence – in their terms being able to explore an idea pathway in depth. Not only did they find that persistence was an important component of creativity, it is also linked to stimulating cognitive flexibility. In other words there is a link between the two, the one skill set reinforcing the other.

Importantly it is not a case of a trade-off – either you have the advantage of divergent thinking to come up with a new insight or you have the persistence to follow it through to realize the potential in the new line of thinking. Instead they suggest that there is a positive interrelationship – it is possible to get the best of both worlds. As the team suggest, 'a person might employ the flexibility pathway to discover new and promising approaches to a task, and then switch to a more systematic approach to further explore these approaches.'

Creativity in action: the dual pathway model [21]

The dual pathway model is shown in Figure 4.1. At the core of the figure are the two pathways through which creativity might be achieved: the flexibility pathway and the persistence pathway. Cognitive flexibility is defined as the ease with which people can switch to a different approach or consider a different perspective, and cognitive persistence as the degree of sustained and focused task-directed cognitive effort.

The pathways are influenced by situational (denoted with Xi) as well as dispositional (denoted with Pi) variables. However, some situational and dispositional variables affect the flexibility pathway more strongly than the persistence pathway, and vice versa. The arrows are therefore drawn in solid (stronger relation) or dotted (weaker relation, or even a negative relation) lines.

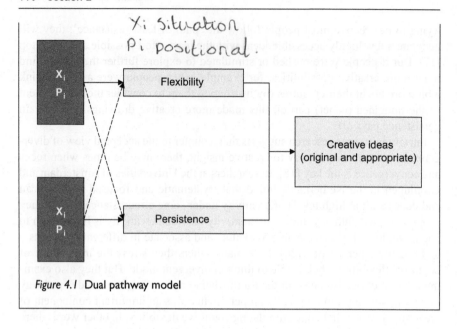

Figure 4.1 Dual pathway model

Why is building up willpower important for creativity?

We've been using the metaphor of a journey to describe the experience of creativity – and going on a journey can be tiring. We run the risk of getting lost and feeling 'stuck', and even if we do know where we are going and can see the destination in the distance we sometimes feel too tired to put one more step in front of another. And that feeling is not only disheartening, it might be enough to make us revise our aspirations downwards. Maybe going those extra steps just isn't worth it? As Brian Lucas and Loran Nordgren point out, 'when creative challenges start to feel difficult, most people lower their expectations about the performance benefits of perseverance, and consequently, underestimate their own ability to generate ideas' [22].

That's why we need willpower. It provides the energy, the fuel, the ability to enable persistence through the necessary iterations to build a good idea and to go through the frustration that accompanies this.

One other important aspect of willpower is learning to deal with failure. By its nature innovation is all about experimentation and that means we will often fail – 'you can't make an omelette without breaking eggs' is a pretty applicable motto. The skill lies in managing that experience of failure – learning to see each failure as a learning opportunity and maintaining enough inner resilience to keep going.

Creativity in action: failure and innovation

There are more people who stop early than those who fail.

—Henry Ford

Next time you scrawl a message on a Post-it Note you might pause for a moment to reflect on the value of failure in innovation. Because Post-its – like many of the breakthrough innovations produced in over a century by the 3M company – actually evolved from a failed innovation. Spence Silver, a polymer chemist, was working on adhesives when he came up with glue which was not particularly sticky. Viewed through the single lens of developing glue this represents bad news – but change the lens, reframe the problem, and the question becomes what other uses might there be for non-sticky glue? And the answer they came up worth led to a thriving new business. 3M is a company which has learned from its very beginnings that innovation is all about taking risks and learning from failure – their origins as the Minnesota Mining and Manufacturing Company (hence 3M) were less than glorious, since the mine they bought for the purpose of extracting carborundum abrasives turned out to contain the wrong kind of rock! It took some rapid reframing to recover but they did – and have grown consistently on the back of a relentless commitment to innovation.

Most companies work on the assumption that of 100 new product ideas only a handful will make it through to success in the market, and they are comfortable with that because the process of failing provides them with rich new insights which help them refocus and sharpen their next efforts. The problem is not with failure – innovations will often fail since they are experiments, steps into the unknown.

Failure is important in at least three ways in innovation:

- It provides insights about what not to do. In a world where you are trying to pioneer something new there are no clear paths and instead you have to cut and hack your own way through the jungle of uncertainty. Inevitably there is a risk that the direction you chose was wrong, but that kind of 'failure' helps identify where not to work – and this focusing process is an important feature in innovation.
- Failure helps build capability – learning how to manage innovation effectively comes from a process of trial and error. Only through this kind of reflection and revision can we develop the capability to manage the process better the next time around. Anyone might get lucky once but successful innovation is all about building a resilient capability to repeat the trick. Taking time out to

review projects is a key factor in this – if we are honest we learn a lot more from failure than from success. Well-managed post-project reviews where the aim is to learn and capture lessons for the future rather than apportion blame are one of the most important tools for improving innovation management.

- Failure helps to learn from each other. Sharing failure stories – a kind of 'vicarious learning' – provides a road map for others, and in the field of competence building that's important. Not for nothing do most business schools teach using the case method – stories of this kind carry valuable information that can be applied elsewhere.

Experienced innovators know this and use failure as a rich source of learning. Most of what we've learned from innovation research has come from studying and analyzing what went wrong and how we might do it better next time – Robert Cooper's work on stage gates; NASA's development of project management tools; Toyota's understanding of the trial-and-error learning loops of their *kaizen* system, which has made it the world's most productive carmaker. Google's philosophy is all about *perpetual beta* – not aiming for perfection but allowing for learning from its innovation. And IDEO, the successful design consultancy, has a slogan which underlines the key role learning through prototyping plays in their projects – 'fail often, to succeed sooner'!

Significantly much of today's renewed interest in 'artificial intelligence' is around the concept of 'machine learning', in which computers emulate the approaches human beings take in learning and problem-solving. A key element in this is the idea of iterative experimentation, learning through multiple probe and learn cycles and using failure to help home in on successful strategies.

Creativity in action: iterative innovation

Unilever's sprawling complex at Port Sunlight near Liverpool is the source of much of the detergent used to wash the nation's clothes. Keeping the machinery operating effectively is a key challenge – and back in the 1970s the company found it had a particular problem with the nozzle of one machine responsible for spraying boiling detergent out at high pressure so that it settles as a powder. The nozzles kept blocking up, meaning that the powder was made up of grains of different sizes, sometimes clumping together. The challenge was clearly one of improving the nozzle design.

The company turned first to 'experts' – mathematicians and chemical engineers skilled in fluid mechanics and flow theory – but despite their best efforts the project failed. An alternative route was taken by a small group of biologists who began a series of experiments, taking ten nozzles and then trying out all sorts of variations, making them bigger, smaller, longer, shorter and so on. Where they found a design which made a small improvement to performance they built on that, refining and extending the experiments.

This approach built on one of the core tools of their trade – evolutionary theory. Organisms evolve by mutation and variation and the fittest survive to carry these traits on to the next generation. Applying this different lens to the nozzle problem worked – after forty-five 'generations' and 449 'failures' they came up with a design which looked very different to the conventional but which improved performance radically.

(This story comes from Matthew Syed's 2015 book *Black Box Thinking*, published by John Murray, London.)

Failing Intelligently

At its heart, managing 'intelligent failure' is about self-perception – managing the experience of failure not as a judgment or criticism of ourselves as people but as a necessary precondition on our way to accomplish what we want to do. We'll look at this in more detail in Chapter 5.

What is the skill set around willpower?

As with previous chapters in this section we will first summarize the key skills underpinning the competence around willpower and then give you the chance to assess yourself against a framework of reflective questions.

Willpower is linked to being persistent. People with a lot of willpower seem to have a kind of extra energy that lets them go on, even if others are more than ready to give up. Willpower skills not only enhance our perseverance, but help us not to start things that we do not want to do. Willpower skills help us to control our impulses. Think about the famous marshmallow task and how the kids tried to evade the impulse to just gulp this marshmallow down and not wait in order to get a second one. The better you are at withstanding these impulses the more willpower you have. Another aspect of skills connected to willpower is being able to get a balance between speed and accuracy. Here the ability to concentrate and not let yourself be distracted is needed.

Figure 4.2 shows the key skills underpinning the willpower competence.

Programming the GPS for the creativity journey – what's your position?

Here we offer you a skill self-check on willpower. If you are interested in finding out where you stand and what are you good at or where you want to improve, just fill in the questionnaire. We suggest you rate yourself with a five-point rating scale:

1 = Not like me at all
2 = Not much like me
3 = I cannot decide if I am good or bad at it, just doing OK
4 = Describes me to a good extent (but not exactly)
5 = Describes me exactly

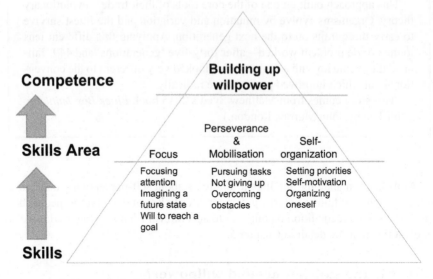

Figure 4.2 Competence building up willpower

We've tried to keep the skill-check short so that you do not have to spend all your willpower on filling it in! But be assured for improving your skills you will need at least some willpower. So reading up on our training session will help you not only for your willpower development but also for the improvement of the other skills.

For tips on filling in a self-check questionnaire please refer back to the skills section in Chapter 2 (Programming the GPS for the creativity journey – what's your position?). For the self-check on willpower, fill in Table 4.1.

Working out at the gym – how to train the skills around willpower

The good news is that, while willpower is exhaustible, it is also renewable and extendable. Here are some tips that can help you to increase your willpower.

Put your brain on autopilot

Think about situations where your willpower often fails and come up with a rule that guides you to the behaviour you want to show. This sounds like hard work, but when you discover how much mental stress these rules can save you, you'll be glad you did. These rules can be about doing something (every day I do one divergent thinking exercise for 15 minutes to train my openness) or about avoiding something (I do not turn on my TV before 7 p.m.). Another way of using this is by developing routines. A routine to increase your willpower can be for example clearly regulated study periods (up to 90 minutes). You can start with

Table 4.1 Self-check willpower

#	Core behavioural skills	Your score (1–5)	For instance..... write at least one example of your own
1	I pursue tasks with energy		
2	I seldom give up before the task is finished		
3	I do not give up when confronted with resistance or setbacks		
4	I find ways to overcome obstacles when I get stuck		
5	I am able to focus my attention		
6	I focus on priorities and manage the important tasks		
7	I am good at motivating myself		
8	I organize myself to keep a high energy level and focus on the task		
9	I can imagine a future state in such a desirable way that I make it impossible for myself not to do nothing		
10	I can get myself into a state of mind where I have the absolute will to reach the goal		

30 minutes and increase them over time. You will see being fully concentrated that 90 minutes can be easy. This tip helps to reduce the amount of stress you feel when that choice comes up. And it helps you to spend your willpower on the things you really want to accomplish and free your mind for the really important stuff like creativity.

Arrange your environment to make the right choices easy

If you have to clean off your desk before you can start writing your novel, how likely are you to work on the novel? Would you channel surf less if your television was hidden away in your cellar? Could you hide the junk food in the back of a cabinet and put the healthy food right up front? The more your environment supports the habits you're trying to cultivate, the easier it is to stick to those habits.

Do the important things first

There's a reason so many successful writers recommend getting up early in the morning and writing first thing. If your reserve of willpower is exhausted, you're likely to skip your scheduled writing session altogether. Another approach is the so called Pomodoro Technique. Put your timer on 25 minutes and just start on the project – write, draw, whatever the task involves. Don't worry about the quality, just concentrate on getting into the rhythm. The famous crime writer Raymond Chandler had another approach, giving himself two choices. Sitting in front of your workspace – your desk, your computer, your easel, whatever, you can choose to do nothing (literally nothing – stare at a wall) or you can work as you planned. Try it out. It works because working is in the end much more interesting than doing nothing. Both approaches help with the hurdle of starting a demanding process like writing a book, coming up with a new ad campaign or having an idea for the next family dinner speech.

Make starting easier

Taking the first step on a project often involves overcoming many mental hurdles, and each of those hurdles requires a bit of willpower to get past. What's the simplest first step you could take? A phone call? A Google search? A quick-and-dirty list that breaks the project down into simple steps? Gathering all the materials you'll need in one place? Anything that makes you feel like you've gotten a grip on the project today can make it easier to do the next step tomorrow.

Keep going!

Ignore your first instinct to stop. When working on a tough creative challenge, you will likely face a moment when you feel stuck and can't come up with any more ideas. Temporarily ignore this instinct, especially if you're still in the early stages of the work. Try to generate just a few more ideas, or consider just a few more alternatives. Quantify your extra effort in time, just another 10 minutes, or in percentage, plus 10%, in order to push yourself a little further.

Frustration is normal

Think about that if you get stuck. Just accept the frustrating feelings as part of the process, learn to recognize them as positive signs of progress (even if they don't feel that way!). Suppress your instinct to interpret these feelings as a signal that you just aren't creative or that you've run out of good ideas up when confronted by resistance or setbacks. Remember that creative problems are *supposed* to feel difficult. Most involve setbacks, failures, and that 'stuck' feeling. Reaching your creative potential often takes time, and persistence is critical for seeing a challenge through to the end.

Expand your comfort zone

Take on a task you dislike (and do so regularly), correcting your posture whenever you think of it. This has nothing to do with feeling bad or being in a bad mood; actually thinking about challenges and hurdles increases your willpower and your will to stay focused until the end. If you look at our training plan you will find the idea of 'wooping' as one way to increase application of what you want to do. Gabriele Oettingen has done research in various fields such as academic achievements, interpersonal relationships, or health issues and found that positive thinking without also thinking about risk and possible hurdles does not help in the implementation of an idea or a wish. She established a four-step process to overcome upcoming challenges [23]. For more see Table 4.2.

Table 4.2 WOOP [24]

Steps	Explanation
What is your wish?	What is your most important creative challenge or your current idea you want to implement? Pick one that feels challenging but that you can reasonably fulfil within the next four weeks.
What is the best outcome?	If your creative challenge or your idea is fulfilled, where would that leave you? What would be the best, most positive outcome? How would fulfilling this make you feel?
	Identify your best outcome and take a moment to imagine it as fully as you can.
What is your main inner obstacle?	What is it *within* you that holds you back from implementing your idea? It might be an emotion, an irrational belief or a bad habit.
	After you wrote down the first answers – think more deeply: what is it really?
	Identify your main inner obstacle and take a moment to imagine it fully.
Make a plan: 'If ... (obstacle), then I will ... (action or thought).'	What can you do to overcome your obstacle? Identify one action you can take or one thought you can think to overcome your obstacle.

Manage your motivation and your moods

On any creative project, your mood will rise and fall. The thrill of a brilliant idea soon gives way to the slump of actually getting it done. One moment we're inspired, the next we're questioning our competence. Sometimes we think that there is just no way forward. But it's worth trying to stay positive, as several studies show that positive mood is associated with greater creativity. One study took the following approach to inducing different moods. Another way to stay on track is reward. It is not just about the big event at the end of a successful project but about finding a mix of frequent small prizes with occasional big ones.

Accept failure as a learning opportunity

Many methodologies now build in the idea of 'fast intelligent failure' – creating something new is likely to involve experimentation and sometimes you won't get the results you expected. The important point is to recognize that it is not you who is the failure but rather that the experiment has generated useful information to help you move forward. For this reason taking time out to review what went wrong and what lessons might be learned is a key step.

On the companion website you can find some tools for managing post-project reviews to capture learning. The lean start-up is also described as a powerful systematic method for designing and learning from experiments on the way to creating new products, services or ventures.

Take care of your body

One of the biggest factors in how much willpower you have is your health. Physical vitality translates into mental energy that's available for making choices. Lack of sleep, poor nutrition, and other things that drain your body don't just affect how you feel; they also affect how much self-control you have available. Getting a good night's sleep, taking a fifteen-minute walk, a few minutes of deep breathing, eating a healthy meal: these are just a few of the small steps you can take to increase your physical vitality, and at the same time, your willpower.

Nourish your mind

Mental stress – sensory overstimulation, an environment that's full of distractions, having too much on your mind – also reduce your available willpower. There are many small steps you can take to reduce mental stress too: meditation, journaling, talking with a good friend, losing yourself in a good book for a few minutes, listening to relaxing music.

Develop your creative confidence

An important field in psychology deals with what is called 'self-efficacy' – the belief in your own abilities. In our terms this links with a degree of confidence in our creative abilities and can help sustain our willpower.

End of chapter summary

- Willpower has many names: perseverance, persistence and grit. It is an aged concept that is now again wholly embraced because of the overpowering research results. Willpower seems to be a precondition for basically a happy and fulfilling life.
- But willpower is also important for creativity. The obvious connection is the one between willpower and overcoming frustration and failures that are prone to happen in the creative process. Without perseverance there will be no one last step to make it really happen. But this has also to do with controlling our impulses, another element of willpower. Not only being able to overcome frustrations but to get ourselves going, starting the job and 'squeeze our brain' for that wow idea we are looking for.
- Not quite so obvious is the positive influence persistence or willpower has on cognitive flexibility. In the dual pathway a 'virtuous circle' is described between divergent thinking and willpower.
- On the skill level willpower consists out of three clusters: not giving in or up; being able to focus and imagining a future state; and being able to organize oneself – setting priorities, managing our moods and motivation, and looking for ways to go ahead and start with the creative journey.

References

[1] Eliot, T.S. (1943). *Four quartets.* New York, NY: Harcourt Brace.
[2] Ashton, K. (2015). *How to fly a horse.* London: Heinemann.
[3] Grant, A. (2016). *Originals: How non-conformists move the world.* New York, NY: W.H. Allen.
[4] Baumeister, R.F., & Tierney, J. (2011). *Willpower: Rediscovering the greatest human strength.* New York, NY: Penguin.
[5] Muraven, M., Baumeister, R.F., & Tice, D.M. (1999). Longitudinal improvement of self-regulation through practice: Building self-control strength through repeated exercise. *Journal of Social Psychology, 139,* 446–457.
[6] Oaten, M., & Cheng, K. (2004). *Longitudinal gains in self-control.* Poster session presented at the annual meeting of the Society for Personality and Social Psychology, Austin, TX.
[7] Oaten, M., & Cheng, K. (2004). Academic study improves regulatory strength. *Australian Journal of Psychology, 56,* 84–84.
[8] Gailliot, M.T., Plant, E.A., Butz, D.A., & Baumeister, R.F. (2004). Increasing self regulatory strength can reduce the depleting effect of suppressing stereotypes. Manuscript submitted for publication.

9]   Moffitt, T. E., Arseneault, L., Belsky, D., Dickson, N., Hancox, R. J., Harrington, H., . . . Sears, M. R. (2011). A gradient of childhood self-control predicts health, wealth, and public safety. *Proceedings of the National Academy of Sciences, 108*, 2693–2698.

[10]   Mischel, W. (2015). *The Marshmallow Test: Understanding self-control and how to master it.* New York, NY: Random House.

[11]   Osborn, A. F. (1953). *Applied imagination: Principles and procedures of creative problem solving.* New York, NY: Scribner's.

[12]   Nakamura, J., & Csikszentmihalyi, M. (2002). The concept of flow. In C. R. Snyder & S. J. Lopez (Eds.), *Handbook of positive psychology* (89–105). New York, NY: Oxford University Press.

[13]   Amabile, T. M. (1996). *Creativity in context: Update to the social psychology of creativity.* Boulder, CO: Westview Press.

[14]   Amabile, T. M. (1983). *The social psychology of creativity.* New York, NY: Springer.

[15]   Simonton, D. K. (1997). Creative productivity: A predictive and explanatory model of career trajectories and landmarks. *Psychological Review, 104*, 66.

[16]   Simonton, D. K. (2003). Scientific creativity as constrained stochastic behavior: The integration of product, person, and process perspectives. *Psychological Bulletin, 129*, 475.

[17]   Ward, T. B., Smith, S. M., & Finke, R. A. (1999). *Creative cognition.* Cambridge, MA: MIT Press.

[18]   Martindale, C. (1995). Creativity and connectionism. In Smith, S. M., Ward, T. B., & Finke, R. A. (Eds.), *The creative cognition approach* (249–268). Cambridge, MA: MIT Press.

[19]   Rietzschel, E. F., De Dreu, C. K., & Nijstad, B. A. (2007). Personal need for structure and creative performance: The moderating influence of fear of invalidity. *Personality and Social Psychology Bulletin, 33*, 855–866.

[20]   De Dreu, C. K. W., Baas, M., & Nijstad, B. A. (2008). Hedonic tone and activation in the mood–creativity link: Towards a dual pathway to creativity model. *Journal of Personality and Social Psychology, 94*, 739–756.

[21]   Nijstad, B. A., De Dreu, C. K., Rietzschel, E. F., & Baas, M. (2010). The dual pathway to creativity model: Creative ideation as a function of flexibility and persistence. *European Review of Social Psychology, 21*, 34–77.

[22]   Brian, L. J., & Nordgren, L. F. (2015). People underestimate the value of persistence for creative performance. *Journal of Personality and Social Psychology, 109*, 232–243.

[23]   Oettingen, G. (2015). *Rethinking positive thinking: Inside the new science of motivation.* New York, NY: Current.

Chapter 5

Self-awareness

Chapter objectives

By the end of this chapter you will:

*   Understand the role which self-awareness plays in creativity;
*   Recognize the key skills associated with self-awareness;
*   Being able to use techniques to facilitate self-awareness;
*   Using reflection to learn and train self-awareness.

Introduction

'Know thyself'

These words were engraved above the entrance of the ancient Greek temple of Delphi – the place people went for insight and knowledge.

By now we hope you are comfortable with the view of creativity as a journey, not a single flashbulb moment. And you have some idea of the landscape – exploring the wide sprawling plains in search of problems before gradually or suddenly finding ourselves with a clear path forward. Swimming the river of incubation, sometimes diving deep and long below the surface, sometimes skimming the surface and quickly reaching the other side. And the long trek up through the mountains of solution elaboration and refinement, the hard slog of iterative innovation.

As we have suggested there isn't a single pathway but a set of possible routes across this landscape. But there are skills we can acquire and develop as we become frequent travellers, experienced in making the journey and knowing what might help us along the way. We've tried to capture some of this knowledge and condense it into a kind of hitch-hiker's guide to creativity, drawing on research and experience. And there's real value in preparing for the journey by going to the gym, getting our mental muscles into shape to ensure we have the stamina and fitness to make it.

In this chapter we're going to look at how we can use self-awareness to help us repeat the trick. To stay with the travelling metaphor, experienced travellers know how to pack, how to prepare themselves, carry a repertoire of tricks and techniques they have learned through earlier journeys – and they also are open to learning new experiences which they feed back into their travelling repertoire. We suggest that creativity is like that – we can learn to repeat the trick and to be more successful at it, but for this we require the skill set around self-awareness.

Look at Table 5.1 which offers some reflective statements from people across a wide spectrum. What they share is the ability to look at themselves as creative people and reflect on how they are able to make creativity happen – in other words, they demonstrate self-awareness. This isn't simply a matter of armchair reflection – it's a competence made up of several components like taking time to analyze, seeking and using feedback, experimenting and varying their behaviour and distilling from those experiments a working pattern to apply in the future. And it matters in effective innovation – anyone might get lucky once, but to repeat the trick you need self-awareness. 'Serial innovators' understand that in order to be able to come up with a stream of new products or processes they need to reflect on what they do and begin to capture, codify and reuse that knowledge gained from experience. (In innovation management these learned patterns of behaviour are called 'routines' – not in the sense of being boring rituals but rather like the idea of a dance routine – a rehearsed pattern of steps which helps create something [1–2].)

Self-awareness involves reflection and introspection to gain insights. Charles Carver and Michael Scheier define it as the ability to judge the self, and it's essential to help us identify our progress towards goals and to target areas for self-improvement [3–4].

In essence self-awareness is thinking about thinking – and this kind of reflection has been the focus of many studies. Unlike most other species, human beings can have a concept of self and use this as the basis for self-improvement [5–7]. Such self-awareness involves the ability to reflect upon oneself, and researchers break this down into three components:

- The cognitive self – how do we think?
- The affective self – how do we feel?
- The executive self – how do we behave?

Often self-awareness is mistaken for self-evaluation or self-monitoring – but these really refer to the current state [8–10]. Self-awareness goes beyond this, offering a higher level reflection – it's a bit like pausing on a journey and looking down from a hilltop, looking at the map and at the road stretching behind and ahead of us, working out where we are.

Table 5.1 If you want to repeat the trick ...

Reflections on creativity	Underlying key message
'Some men give up their designs when they have almost reached the goal; While others, on the contrary, obtain a victory by exerting, at the last moment, more vigorous efforts than ever before.' —Herodotus	Learn to manage persistence, keep on going
'Creativity comes from looking for the unexpected and stepping outside your own experience.' —Masaru Ibuka	Learn to develop skills around openness and go beyond your comfort zone
'A problem well stated is a problem half solved.' —Charles F. Kettering	Learn to explore and develop problem exploration skills
'Creativity is just connecting things. When you ask creative people how they did something, they feel a little guilty because they didn't really do it, they just saw something. It seemed obvious to them after a while. That's because they were able to connect experiences they've had and synthesize new things.' —Steve Jobs	Learn to apply recombinant search approaches, openness skills
'An essential aspect of creativity is not being afraid to fail.' —Edwin Land	Learn to 'manage' failure, develop skills around willpower
'Creativity is a habit, and the best creativity is the result of good work habits.' —Twyla Tharp	Learn to develop the habit through reflection and experimentation
'One who fears failure limits his activities. Failure is only the opportunity to more intelligently begin again.' —Henry Ford	Learn to deal with failure, develop skills to manage this
'An idea, like a ghost, must be spoken to a little before it will explain itself.' —Charles Dickens	Learn to explore problems, don't rush ideas
'An idea is a point of departure and no more. As soon as you elaborate it, it becomes transformed by thought.' —Pablo Picasso	Learn to allow for elaboration, the effort of refinement and also learn the skill of knowing when to stop
'Life is not easy for any of us. But what of that? We must have perseverance and above all confidence in ourselves. We must believe that we are gifted for something and that this thing must be attained.' —Marie Curie	Learn to be persistent and motivate ourselves to keep going

(Continued)

Table 5.1 (Continued)

Reflections on creativity	Underlying key message
'A hunch is creativity trying to tell you something.' —Frank Capra	Learn to trust your instincts and work with them – not as divine inspiration but as part of a managed process. Learn when to ignore them as well!

What does research tell us about self-awareness?

To take a computing analogy, self-awareness allows us to reprogram ourselves to be more effective [11–12]. And it matters in creativity.

For example, there are links to studies of personality traits and dimensions – 'rumination' is part of the neuroticism dimension and reflection is linked to the openness dimension. Being able to reflect in a systematic fashion and use the insights generated to develop changes in our behaviour is at the heart of many models of learning.

Research note: double loop learning

The term 'double loop learning' describes a learning process in which the goals or decision-making rules are modified in the light of experience [13]. In the first loop, the goals or decision-making rules are implemented, whereas the second loop enables their modification.

Double loop learning stands in contrast to 'single loop' learning, in which we try to solve the same problem by repeatedly using the same method without questioning the goal (see Figure 5.1). Chris Argyris, one of the founders of organizational development, states that most people define learning too narrowly as mere 'problem-solving', that is, they focus on identifying and correcting errors in the external environment. There are cognitive rules or reasoning to design and implement one's actions. These rules are a kind of 'master program'

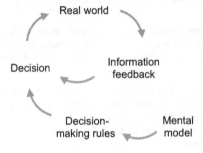

Figure 5.1 Single loop learning

---

stored in the brain, governing all behaviour. The problem lies in attributing the blame for any problems to external factors instead of internal ones. The purpose is to avoid embarrassment or threat, feeling vulnerable or incompetent. Consequently, single loop learning does not enable people to learn from failure.

To enable continuous learning, it is necessary to look inward and to reflect critically on one's own behaviour, and then change it if required. In particular, one must learn that the way of defining and solving problems can be a source of problems itself. In double loop learning, feedback from the situation is used to examine critically and change one's own theories in use (see Figure 5.2).

Chris Argyris used the following analogy to capture the distinction between the two kinds of learning: a thermostat that automatically turns on the heat whenever the temperature in a room drops below a certain value, for example 20 degrees, is a good example of single loop learning. In contrast, if the thermostat could ask why it is set at 20 degrees, and then explore whether some other temperature might more economically achieve the goal of heating the room, would be engaging in double loop learning [13].

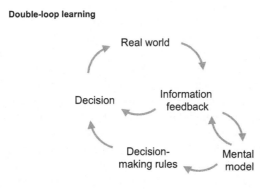

Figure 5.2 Double loop learning

Reflecting on how we approach creative tasks can help us accumulate skills for the next one – by developing new cognitive strategies, by learning to deal with negative emotions (fear of failure, anxiety about risk, etc.), and by building a repertoire of behaviours which we deploy when faced with a challenge requiring creativity [12]. It's an important element in ensuring that training – for example in the use of creative techniques – actually makes a difference. Without self-awareness we never take stock and improve our creative competences and skills.

But it can also have a downside – self-reflection can lead us into a state of thinking that we lack the competence to be creative and paralyze our ability to act. Studies suggest that:

- Self-evaluation may reduce creativity because it disrupts the divergent thinking processes needed for generating creative ideas [14].
- Thinking about how well one is doing can interfere with doing well [15].
- Expansive cognition is impeded when the person focuses narrowly on how the self stands in relation to personal and social standards.
- Worrying about whether the self will live up to important standards reduces intrinsic motivation, a critical element in creativity [16–17]. For example, self-evaluation brought about by self-awareness reduced intrinsic motivation by promoting an externally controlled motivational orientation [18].
- Even the prospect of evaluation can have an impact. For example, Teresa Amabile's studies of motivation and creativity suggested that this prospect led participants to produce collages that were judged to be less creative (control group without evaluation) [19].

Richard Deci and Edward Ryan attribute these negative elements to the effects of feedback. They reason that feedback or the fear of negative feedback undermines intrinsic motivation. But as we discussed earlier, self-awareness is not necessarily connected to fear of getting feedback; it is rather a general competence to evaluate oneself. Researchers Paul Silvia and Ann Phillips found a link between people's perception of their ability to improve and their creativity (as measured by tests of fluency, flexibility, etc.) [4]. They concluded that feeling able to improve helps 'buffer against the detrimental effects of self-evaluation on creativity. . . . . when people felt able to improve, self-evaluation did not affect creativity.' In other words we can develop skills around self-awareness which help counter the effects of evaluation – both by others and by ourselves.

In summary, too much or the wrong kind of self-evaluation can have negative effects on creativity. But, as we suggested earlier, self-evaluation is not the same than the competence self-awareness. It is not only about asking the question 'do we match up to standards?' but also asking questions like 'how do I improve, what is my skill set and how able am I to go forward?' [3, 20].

Why is self-awareness important for creativity?

Let's go back for a moment to the idea of self-awareness as involving three components:

- The cognitive self – how do we think?
- The affective self – how do we feel?
- The executive self – how do we behave?

As we've seen in the previous chapters, there are skills which can be developed around openness, problem exploration and willpower, and these work on all three of these aspects of self. For example, we can stretch and train our cognitive skills in the direction of more divergent thinking, using tools and techniques to practise. We can use strategies to help us reframe and explore problems from different angles. And we can deploy different representational frameworks to help us gain new insights and form new associations.

In similar fashion we can learn to manage our feelings around creativity. The anxiety about taking risks or fear of being judged, the mood states which help us with the challenge of persistence, the concerns we feel about 'moving out of our comfort zone' are all areas of the 'affective self' which we can learn to manage through practising and reinforcing new approaches linked to tools and techniques.

And we can change the way we approach the creative challenge, learning to try new behaviours and vary our habits. But all of these skill sets depend on our being able to take that step back, reflect and reassess how we manage the creativity journey. So self-awareness becomes a higher order set of skills around learning to be more effective – and that takes a mixture of motivation to change and the tools and skills around reflection and rethinking our approach.

Research note: self-efficacy and learning how to be creative

An important field in psychology deals with what is called 'self-efficacy' – the belief in your own abilities. It describes a person's belief in his/her own ability to perform a certain task or exhibit a specific behaviour. This belief about one's own competences and skills affects the way people think, feel and behave in different situations. It is a requirement throughout any creative process; without it people will usually not even attempt to be creative. After all, without the belief that you can be creative, you would probably not even start to think about something new. The concept of self-efficacy also works at the group level (termed collective self-efficacy) and may, by extension, also be applied to organizations [21].

On the companion website there is a link to a TED Talk by David Kelley of IDEO where he discusses this and suggests some strategies for building your 'creative confidence'.

Managing 'intelligent failure' is an important skill for self-awareness. By its nature innovation is all about experimentation and that means we will often fail – 'you can't make an omelette without breaking eggs' is a pretty applicable motto. The skill lies in managing that experience of failure – learning to see each failure as a learning opportunity and maintaining enough inner resilience to keep going.

Creativity in action: failure and innovation

Accidents will happen – and as far as innovation is concerned, that's a good thing. Whilst much of our attention is on the focused efforts to bring new ideas to market or to effect process changes in systematic, planned and strategically targeted fashion, there are some times when Fate takes a hand. What might appear to be a failed experiment or a strange but ultimately useless outcome can sometimes turn out to be the basis of a game-changing innovation. Think about these examples . . . .

- Roy Plunkett was working on chlorofluorocarbons in DuPont's labs in 1938 trying to improve refrigeration materials. Returning to examine the results of his latest experiment he was bitterly disappointed to find one canister no longer contained the gas he expected but some white flaky material. But he took time to play with it and realized its incredible properties as a lubricant with a very high melting point – perfect for a host of military applications and, eventually, for making omelettes in frying pans coated with Teflon.

Or metallurgist Harry Brearly, working hard in his lab in 1912 trying to improve the design of guns. He needed an alloy which wouldn't erode over time as bullets spinning fast along grooved barrels rubbed against their walls – but his efforts proved fruitless. After months next to a growing pile of steel scrap representing failed efforts he noticed one particular piece had managed to retain its original shine rather than oxidizing. He explored this 12% chromium alloy a little further and found it also resisted marks and scratches as well; not very useful in gun-making but 'stainless steel' had an impressive future elsewhere.

Or Harry Coover In 1942 who was working in Eastman Kodak labs trying to perfect material for a precision gun sight. Unfortunately the cyanoacrylate he experimented with was a bitter disappointment – sticking annoyingly to everything it touched. But six years later in trying to use it for cockpit canopies he suddenly realized the incredibly strong bonding powers could have a different application – and Superglue was born. The final version of his product hit the market sixteen years after his original experiments.

'*Failure is not an option*' is a phrase usually meant to inspire people to focus on not making mistakes. But in the world of innovation it's the reverse – failure is an essential part of the process. Without experimentation and the chance that things will go wrong there is no opportunity to move in new directions.

Failure matters because it helps us explore – and it also offers opportunities to learn for next time. For example Thomas Edison had problems with interesting people in his phonograph – it took him over twenty years to get widespread acceptance. This failure was due in large measure to promoting it as a device for listening to voices rather than music. But he learned from that (and many other failures) so that when he came to launch electric lighting he had a much better understanding of the challenges. As he is famous for saying 'I have not failed. I've just found 10,000 ways that it won't work.'

Innovation research has been carried out for over a century, trying to understand what are the most valuable levers in enabling the process of realising value from ideas. Whilst there have been many elegant approaches to this study one of the most powerful sources has been reflection on the failures of the past and the mobilisation of that knowledge to design ore effective methods and systems. Well-managed post project reviews where the aim is to learn and capture lessons for the future rather than apportion blame are one of the most important tools for improving innovation management.

Examples of such failure-driven lessons include Robert Cooper's work on stage gates, NASA's development of project management tools and Toyota's understanding of the minute trial and error learning loops which their *kaizen* system depends upon and which have made it the world's most productive car-maker. The essence of the lean start-up approach for entrepreneurs or of 'agile innovation' methods in software development is, once again the idea of trying things out and quickly capturing the lessons of failure so that the next cycle of development can be improved.

You can find more information on structured evaluation frameworks used in companies like ABC Electronics on the companion website.

What is the skill set around self-awareness?

In this section we give you some help to find out where you stand with respect to the challenge of developing self-awareness. We begin with a short description of the competence itself and then follow with a list of ten key skills linked to self-awareness. In the questionnaire you can carry out a self-check and identify elements of self-awareness where you already have strengths and those where you might wish to develop further (see Figure 5.3). The competence description and the given skills are rooted in the research we described in the chapter.

Programming the GPS for the creativity journey – what's your position?

Self-awareness is about taking stock of our strengths and weaknesses, about knowing what we can build in and what we need to develop further. Carver and Scheier described it as the ability to judge the self [3]. It's about taking on feedback and using it to understand oneself. But the competence goes beyond pure evaluation, it's about installing a learning cycle of reflection, reconceptualization and experimentation with new approaches.

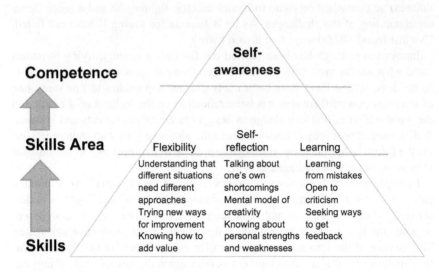

Figure 5.3 Self-awareness

Next we offer you a skill self-check on self-awareness – we suggest you rate yourself with a five-point rating scale:

1 = Not like me at all
2 = Not much like me
3 = I cannot decide if I am good or bad at it, just doing OK
4 = Describes me to a good extent (but not exactly)
5 = Describes me exactly

In this self-check you are doing something like looking in the mirror of the mirror. Self-awareness basically means in the first place that you are able to be honest with yourself about your strengths but also about your weaknesses. Filling in a questionnaire about your skills is exactly something that needs self-awareness, otherwise it is a wish list and not an evaluation of your current state. And again thinking about recent behavioural examples help to have a look in the mirror.

For tips on filling in a self-check questionnaire please go to Chapter 2.

Working out at the gym – how to train your skills in self-awareness

Self-analysis

Self-awareness is more than self-assessment or self-analysis but it always starts with it. So if you have not done the self-check, now is the time for it. The outcome of self-analysis is knowing about your limitations and weaknesses.

Table 5.2 Self-check self-awareness

#	Core behavioural skills	Your score (1–5)	For instance write at least one example of your own
1	I know my personal strengths and weaknesses		
2	I can talk about my shortcomings and explore them with others		
3	I actively seek ways of getting feedback to improve my behaviour		
4	I am open to (constructive) criticism		
5	I learn from my mistakes by reflecting my behaviours and their outcome		
6	I understand that different situations require different approaches and have developed flexibility to match my approach to them		
7	I keep trying new ways to improve my creative behaviour		
8	I know when and where my contributions are needed and will add value to the creative process		
9	I am able to learn and to improve		
10	I have a mental model of how I can be creative and I constantly review and revise this		

The next step is to develop strategies to compensate for the weaknesses and using the strengths.

Self-reflection – watch yourself and learn

Self-reflection moves a little further on from self-analysis; for example doing the self-check and then using the outcome is pure self-analysis. Self-reflection involves thinking about the process, asking questions of yourself like which

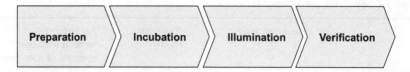

Figure 5.4 Wallas's creative process

questions do you find hard to answer? (These are probably the ones which take you longer to make up your mind on a score). Which skills in the self-check do you think are not central to the overall competence? Which skills do you hesitate in answering about because you'd like to think you are better than the score you were about to put? This kind of reflection helps move your review to a higher level and may identify some new direction to explore and develop.

Another way to increase your self-reflection is keeping a reflective journal. List in there what worked and why it did – or what didn't work out and what you learned from that. In the classic *Harvard Business Review* article, 'Managing Oneself', Peter Drucker wrote, 'Whenever you make a decision or take a key action write down what you expect will happen. Nine or 12 months later, compare the results with what you expected' [23]. Drucker called this self-reflection process *feedback analysis* and credited it to a fourteenth-century German theologian. He said it was the 'only way to discover your strengths'. The key to the effectiveness of feedback analysis is to (1) codify rationale and motivations and (2) reflect and assess outcomes. This forces one to focus not just on the *what*, but also on the *why* (see [24]).

Use a mental model of creativity

Having a mental model of how you can be creative helps you become aware of how you do what you do – it gives you some anchors to hold down and explore what is otherwise a fuzzy process. We've tried to give some models in the book, and you could also use some of those offered by frameworks like design thinking (see Chapter 13). You could start with a simple model like that offered by Wallas – it links the creative process to four key stages of preparation, incubation, insight and validation/elaboration (see Figure 5.4) [25].

Try the activity 'Recollecting Creativity' on the companion website.

Get feedback about yourself

Self-analysis and self-reflection are very good instruments but we have to be aware that we are only looking at ourselves from the inside out. To get a 360° view we need to talk to other people and use external sources, looking from the outside

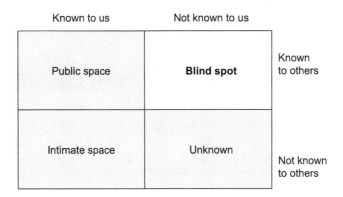

Figure 5.5 Johari window

in. You can do this by asking in a general sense for feedback or getting people to comment and rate you on the self-check questionnaire.

Dealing with feedback isn't always easy – it's another important skill. The problem for most people is that they do not like (everything) what they hear and start to devalue the feedback given to them. So it's helpful to remember that your goal is simply to get to know yourself better. It's not a competition to be best in everything. When getting feedback, take it all in, write it down if possible, ask for specific examples (if needed) and try to understand what the other person is telling you. (See the next section on 'Active listening' for more on that). Then you can begin to organize the feedback, cluster it and sort it in ways which help you focus on what it means and how you might use it. One helpful tool is something called the 'Johari Window': essentially try to use the feedback to help you see the things you find difficult – your 'blind spots' (see Figure 5.5). Our reaction here is often not to believe the feedback – but rather than just rejecting it, try to amplify it, ask for examples, search for more data.

Active listening

This is a useful technique to get the most out of feedback; when receiving it try not to judge it (wrong or right) immediately but concentrate on listening to the other. What is it that he/she is really trying to tell you? Why is he/she coming up with this kind of feedback? Where did you hear it before? This helps you to separate out the threat to identity from the development of skills.

Use a learning cycle

The psychologist David Kolb developed a helpful model of how people learn, pointing out that it isn't simply a matter of injecting them with new knowledge. Instead it is a cyclic process with different stages, running from active experimentation (trying something out) through experience (what happened there?),

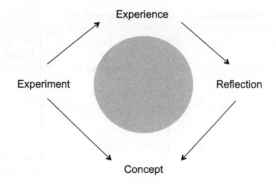

Figure 5.6 Kolb's learning model

reflection (stepping back and reviewing it) through to conceptualization (distilling learning from it which we can then use in the future). It's a simple but helpful framework and reminds us of the need to pause for self-reflection but also of the value of tools and time to carry this out (see Figure 5.6).

Use structured reflection frameworks

We've offered a simple self-check in this chapter but there are many others which can help you dig down into particular areas to explore and develop your self-awareness.

> You can find examples (including the Innovation Fitness Test and the Entrepreneur's Audit) on the companion website together with tools like post-project reviews to help capture learning in a structured reflective fashion.

End of chapter summary

- This competence is more like a meta-competence; looking down from a hill and seeing what is going on, where are you standing, and what to do to go on.
- In innovation research there was for a long time a debate whether self-awareness is helpful or not. Looking closer at research it becomes clear that self-monitoring and self-evaluation can become harmful for creative action because people tend to focus more on impression and evaluation than at the task at hand.
- Self-awareness is the ability to reflect upon oneself, the approaches taken so far, and the ability to look at one's image in the mirror are enhancing creativity.

- One can conclude that self-awareness comes in three 'forms': cognitive, affective and executive.
- Self-awareness as skill set therefore has three components: having self-reflection skills, being able to learn (from mistakes) and of course being flexible enough to take different approaches.

References

[1] Nelson, R., & Winter, S. (1982). *An evolutionary theory of economic change.* Cambridge, MA: Harvard University Press.

[2] Tidd, J., & Bessant, J. (2013). *Managing innovation: Integrating technological, market and organizational change.* Chichester: Wiley.

[3] Carver, C. S., & Scheier, M. F. (2004). Self-regulation of action and affect. In K. D. Vohs & R. F. Baumeister (Eds.), *Handbook of self-regulation: Research, theory, and applications* (13–39). New York, NY: Guilford Press.

[4] Silvia, P. J., & Phillips, A. G. (2004). Self-awareness, self-evaluation, and creativity. *Personality and Social Psychology Bulletin, 30*, 1009–1017.

[5] Povinelli, D. J., & Prince, C. G. (1998). When self met other. In M. D. Ferrari & R. J. Sternberg (Eds.), *Self-awareness: Its nature and development* (37–107). New York, NY: Guilford Press.

[6] Silvia, P. J., & Duval, T. S. (2001). Predicting the interpersonal targets of self-serving attributions. *Journal of Experimental Social Psychology, 37*, 333–340.

[7] Wicklund, R. A. (1975). Objective self-awareness. *Advances in Experimental Social Psychology, 8*, 233–275.

[8] Szymanski, K., & Harkins, S. G. (1992). Self-evaluation and creativity. *Personality and Social Psychology Bulletin, 18*, 259–265.

[9] Ryan, R. M., & Deci, E. L. (2000). Intrinsic and extrinsic motivations: Classic definitions and new directions. *Contemporary Educational Psychology, 25*, 54–67.

[10] Snyder, M. (1974). Self-monitoring of expressive behavior. *Journal of Personality and Social Psychology, 30*, 526–537.

[11] Clapham, M. M. (1997). Ideational skills training: A key element in creativity training programs. *Creativity Research Journal, 10*, 12.

[12] Grote, S., Kauffeld, S., & Frieling, E. (Eds.). (2006). *Kompetenzmanagement. Grundlagen und Praxisbeispiele.* Stuttgart: Schäffer-Poeschel.

[13] Argyris, C. (1991). Teaching smart people how to learn. *Harvard Business Review, 4*, 4–15.

[14] Runco, M. A. (1991). The evaluative, valuative, and divergent thinking of children. *Journal of Creative Behavior, 25*, 311–319.

[15] Baumeister, R. F., & Heatherton, T. F. (1996). Self-regulation failure: An overview. *Psychological Inquiry, 7*, 1–15.

[16] Amabile, T. M. (1996). *Creativity in context.* Boulder, CO: Westview Press.

[17] Hennessey, B. A. (2003). The social psychology of creativity. *Scandinavian Journal of Educational Research, 47*, 253–271.

[18] Plant, R. W., & Ryan, R. M. (1985). Intrinsic motivation and the effects of self-consciousness, self-awareness, and ego-involvement: An investigation of internally controlling styles. *Journal of Personality, 53*, 435–449.

[19] Amabile, T. M. (1979). Effects of external evaluation on artistic creativity. *Journal of Personality and Social Psychology, 37*, 221–233.

[20] Silvia, P. J., & Duval, T. S. (2004). Self-awareness, self-motives, and self-motivation. In *Motivational analyses of social behavior: Building on Jack Brehm's contributions to psychology* (57–75). Mahwah, NJ: Lawrence Erlbaum.

[21]   Bandura, A. (1997). *Self-efficacy: The exercise of control*. New York, NY: Freeman.
[22]   Cooper, R. (2001). *Winning at new products* (3rd ed.). London: Kogan Page.
[23]   Drucker, P. F. (2008). *Managing oneself*. Boston: Harvard Business Review Press.
[24]   Tjan, A. K. (2012). How leaders become self-aware. *Harvard Business Review*. See *https://hbr.org/2012/07/how-leaders-become-self-aware/*
[25]   Wallas, G. (1926). *The art of thought*. New York, NY: Harcourt-Brace.

Section 3

Group level

Let's pause for a moment and take stock. We've seen that creativity matters and that we all have it and that it is not a magical moment but a journey. And we've mapped the landscape a little, understanding some of the different kinds of terrain that we have to cross in that journey. We've looked at the key skills underpinning being more effective as creative travellers – problem exploration, openness, willpower and becoming self-aware. And we've seen how important this is in innovation – creating value from our ideas. Whether in a start-up or a giant organization, whether in social or commercial, public or private sectors, we need this set of skills.

Now we move to a further consideration – what happens when we combine our creativity? And in particular, what happens when we interact, not simply adding our individual approaches together but combining them? We are all different in personality, experience and approach, and these differences mean that we see problems and solutions from different perspectives. Combining our approaches, sparking ideas off each other, building on shared insights are powerful ways of amplifying creativity. The old proverb that 'two heads are better than one' is often true; think about creative partnerships in the musical world like Lennon and McCartney, Rogers and Hammerstein, Rice and Lloyd Webber, the Gershwin brothers. Look at the world of theatre and film and see how much of the success is not the product of a lone genius but a team of co-creators front and backstage who help make it happen. Look at business ventures and very often you'll find more than one person involved – Eric Schmidt and Sergei Brin (Google), Bill Gates and Paul Allen (Microsoft), Andy Grove and Gordon Moore (Intel), Steve Jobs and Steve Wozniak (Apple).

Go to the companion website for some activities around shared problem-solving.

Teams matter

It's not just pairs but teams that are important – groups of individuals who come together to create something on a shared basis. Teams matter for many reasons – not just because they assemble a diverse mixture of skills and background but also because being in a team creates ways of working which are not possible alone. Diversity amplifies our openness, different cognitive styles increase the chance of novel associations, groups can provide support for the perseverance skills when the going gets tough, and feedback within the group can help us develop self-awareness. Not for nothing do organizations focus on the team as the core unit to deliver innovation.

Whether it is project teams working on new product or service development or shop-floor teams helping to improve quality and productivity through their shared ideas and efforts; whether it is a special task force set up to drag the organization 'out of the box' or a dedicated community of practice that works together to bring their different insights to a common problem – the picture is still the same. Shared effort, shared creativity and a higher outcome.

And it's often at the heart of entrepreneurial start-ups. By now we have enough stories to recognize a pattern – the small group of friends huddled round pizza and coffee late into the night, the excited experimentation and review in the incubator, the full-on shouting matches which lead to the flash of new insight. High energy groups bringing (and often clashing) their ideas and enthusiasm to create the next cool thing.

Creativity in action: the power of groups

Take any group of people and ask them to think of different uses for an everyday item – a cup, a brick, a ball and so forth. Working alone they will usually develop an extensive list – but then ask them to share the ideas they have generated. The resulting list will not only be much longer but will also contain much greater diversity of possible classes of solution to the problem. For example, uses for a cup might include using it as a container (vase, pencil holder, drinking vessel, etc.), a mould (for sandcastles, cakes, etc.), a musical instrument, a measure, a template around which one can draw, a device for eavesdropping (when pressed against a wall) and even, when thrown, a weapon!

The psychologist J. P. Guilford classed these two traits as 'fluency' – the ability to produce ideas – and 'flexibility' – the ability to come up with different types of ideas [1]. The preceding experiment quickly shows that working as a group people are usually much more fluent and flexible than any single individual. When working together people spark each other off, jump on and develop each other's ideas, encourage and support each other through positive emotional mechanisms like laughter and agreement – and in a variety of ways stimulate a high level of shared creativity.

If we think back to our early days trying to survive on a hostile planet we can see why teamwork evolved. When you face daily challenges like how to defend yourself or how to hunt down and bring home the evening's meal, then pooling resources seems like a good idea. Bringing different skills, different experiences, different ideas and approaches helped us deal with these problems and survive – and gradually built into our way of life recognition of the value of creative teamwork.

It's important to recognize the importance of what are called 'emergent properties' – the whole becomes greater than the sum of the parts. In research this is often referred to as the 'interactionist perspective', and it explores the ways in which individual skills and competencies often 'come alive' in the context of a group, and how certain properties – like 'psychological safety', which we need to feel when we are trying out new and risky ideas – only emerge as something which the group creates for itself.

This 'interactionist perspective' stresses that creativity is a complex interaction between the individual and his or her work situation at different levels of organization. At the individual level, individual creativity is the result of antecedent conditions (e.g. biographical variables), cognitive style and ability (e.g. divergent thinking), personality (e.g. self-esteem), relevant knowledge, motivation, social influences (e.g. rewards) and contextual influences (e.g. physical environment). At the team level, creativity is a consequence of individual creative behaviour, the interaction between the group members (e.g. group composition), group characteristics (e.g. norms, size), team processes and contextual influences (e.g. organizational culture, reward systems). At the organizational level, innovation is a function of both individual and group creativity.

Teams are made not born

Behind all of this is the question of how a group of diverse individuals can come together effectively and become a creative team. The answer is that this is not some magic chemical reaction but a consequence of effort, of learning and building capability. Teams are made, not born. There's a rich research literature about group dynamics, roles, structures and so forth, and it all points to the same conclusion. The whole can be greater than the sum of the parts – but only if we work at it.

This isn't a one-off training session but the result of a continuing process of interaction and learning among the team members. Creative performance is increasingly considered a group process that takes place within teams, and an increasing number of studies focus on facilitating team-oriented processes such as group interaction or motivation.

Part of this is recognizing that there are tensions to be resolved in group creativity – it is not simply an additive process where the more minds on the job means the greater the creativity. It's more like learning to walk a tightrope, handling the difficult balancing act between various tensions which doesn't always come off.

Groups can be less than the sum of their parts; they can fragment, explode or hinder individual creativity. Creativity involves conflicts, clashes about objectives, differences in motivation and values, arguments about where and how to go forward. As we'll see the skill in building creative teams is finding a way of handling shared risk-taking, building trust, developing ways of handling 'constructive controversy', building a climate of psychological safety and mobilizing individual efforts towards a shared goal.

It's easy to put a note on your CV – 'good team worker' – and it probably helps since so much work today is accomplished through teams. But what does it mean and what are the skills involved in being an effective creative team?

Four core competence areas

As we have suggested this question has occupied researchers for a quite some time now, and the good news is that there is quite a lot of common ground around the answer. In particular, a helpful framework was developed by psychologist Michael West, Neil Anderson and colleagues and we'll make use of that in structuring this section. We defined four competence areas:

- Creating and sharing visions;
- Building psychological safety;
- Supporting ideas;
- Pushing the frontiers (with constructive conflict).

As in Section 2 we explore each of these competences in the following chapters, drawing on relevant research and practical experience. In each chapter we'll use the same structure as in Section 2. We will also provide you with exercises to develop and improve your competences and skills, but in this section we are also offering team exercises and techniques and tools to develop your 'fitness' as a team player.

Reference

[1]   Guilford, J., *The nature of human intelligence*. 1967, New York: McGraw-Hill.

## Chapter 6

Creating and sharing visions

Chapter objectives

By the end of this chapter you will:

- Understand the role which creating and sharing visions plays in creativity;
- Recognize the key skills associated with vision building;
- Develop awareness of tools and techniques to help develop vision and set challenging goals;
- Reflect on and be able to develop your own skills and those of the team around creating and sharing visions.

Introduction – the vision thing

> If you want to build a ship, don't herd people together to collect wood and don't assign them tasks and work, but rather teach them to long for the endless immensity of the sea.
>
> —Antoine de Saint-Exupery

Innovation is partly about making dreams real. Sounds fanciful perhaps, but that's what many entrepreneurs start with. A dream, an idea about something they want to achieve which might sound at first hearing to be impossible. But somehow they manage to keep that picture in mind, share it with others who help elaborate it, refine it in the face of changes on the road to making it become real. It acts as a guiding star, something fixed in the distance towards which they can focus their efforts and energies. Think about some examples:

- Dr Venkataswamy, retiring eye surgeon, who believed he could bring safe, low-cost eye care to the poor of India. His Aravind Eye System has returned sight to millions and continues to expand around the world.
- Henry Ford, whose vision was to create 'a car for Everyman' at a price everyone could afford.
- Toyota's global environmental challenge for 2050: zero emissions.

• Ray Anderson, founder and CEO of Interface, a global floor coverings company which has made radical progress towards sustainability, cutting greenhouse gas emissions by 82%, fossil fuel consumption by 60%, waste by 66%, water use by 75% – all while increasing profits by 60%. Using a powerful metaphor for the challenge, he explains that

> as we climb Mount Sustainability with the four sustainability principles on top, we are doing better than ever on bottom-line business. This is not at the cost of social or ecological systems, but at the cost of our competitors who still haven't got it.

Creativity in action: walking the Highline

If you were to visit the West Side of Manhattan back in 2000 you might well have been struck by the ugliness of a derelict railway line that snakes through the city and that's been closed for nearly twenty years. This rusting metal structure is hard to miss, as it's thirty feet up in the air. Originally built in the early 1930s to transport freight to factories and warehouses, those businesses have long since died out, and there are now repeated calls to demolish what is variously described as a health hazard and an urban ruin. Despite being barricaded off at street level, adolescents climb up onto it and make it even more dangerous and unsightly. It is an eyesore and depressing.

Then in 1999 two local residents formed Friends of the Highline with a view to preserving it and putting it to some public use. Eventually they persuaded the City of New York to sign on to the principle but no one really knew what this use might be. In 2003 an open design competition attracted thousands of proposals and out of these emerged the idea of a unique urban park that will thread its way through Manhattan. In 2006 construction began – the tracks were removed, a concrete base was laid and then wild grasses were seeded among the relined tracks.

In 2010 the first half mile opened to the public to a rapturous response. Now New Yorkers can climb the stairs and get away from the city below. Up here the pace of life is different and people come from miles to take a stroll. In one spot what was once just a bridge across a main road has been transformed into a glass fronted viewing platform looking down on the street below where you can sit and watch the cars drive on under your feet. Another spot now becomes an intimate covered arena for the performing arts. Such is the success that the rest of the still derelict Highline is now being developed along the same lines.

What was derelict and useless has been reconceived. But notice the structure remains the same. It's still a metal and concrete structure thirty feet up in the air snaking through Manhattan. Only now it serves a wholly new purpose. This is reframing in action. The result is a new kind of park. It is literally the first of its kind in the world and will almost certainly stimulate new thinking about derelict structures in other cities.

What these people share is the use of a clear and focused vision, something towards which they and others could focus their efforts. It's not a total fantasy – there has to be a believable element in it which sets out a difficult stretching but possibly achievable goal. And it isn't rigid – it can be revised and elaborated, with more detail added as the project emerges into reality.

Creativity in action: playing on the field of dreams

In the movie *Field of Dreams* (based on W.P. Kinsella's novel *Shoeless Joe*), Kevin Costner's character has a vision of creating a baseball field in the middle of the empty sprawling plains of Kansas. Among the many criticisms offered by others when he puts forward the idea is that no one in the area would want to watch it – there would be no audience. And how would he manage to attract big name players to help draw the crowds?

But his dream sustains him and in particular one encounter with the ghost of Shoeless Joe Jackson (a famous player from the past) gives the film a much misquoted but powerful line: 'if you build it, he will come.' The line originally referred to bringing the spirit of the game back in the form of a famous player from the past – but people widely use the phrase today as 'build it, and they will come' – the audience, other players, all the missing pieces of the dream. In other words the vision provides the focus for something which will gradually draw others into the idea as it takes shape.

Vision matters in innovation. Providing a clear stretching focus is at the heart of any successful start-up – and critical in the process of securing commitment and resources from others. Even if the vision becomes modified and adjusted in the face of experience – 'pivoting' – the emphasis on a core goal is critical to success. But it's equally important in the context of a large organization – aligning people's creative efforts around a clear shared focus. One of the most successful visions was that of John F. Kennedy, who galvanized NASA and thousands of companies working with it around the simply stated but stretching goal of 'putting a man on the moon and bringing him home safely within five years'.

Of course vision can be misused and is often a label for woolly unclear aspirations rather than a sharply focused and energizing goal. But well-formed visions provide enough detail that others can understand and adopt them, sharing them but also adding to their construction. Vision starts with a why and sets out the 'what?' and people can then mobilize their creativity around the 'how?' In many ways it is about storytelling – beginning with a simple sketch and then elaborating, refining, modifying – but keeping the core idea as a central 'boundary object' around which people can create.

> This is the dominant model in the film industry, for example, where the 'story-board' begins as an outline sketch for the film and is gradually elaborated and improved in a collective process. You can see this approach in action in the Pixar case study on the companion website. And you can try it out as an activity using the 'Entrepreneur's Storyboard', again on the companion website.

Visions matter as a mechanism for engaging the creative energies of others. Toyota's success in global markets across a number of sectors is based on replicating principles originally developed back in the 1930s around how to organize and manage the business. Central to their thinking is the idea of employee involvement in innovation – everyone is expected to contribute their creativity to help the company deal with its many challenges of growth and sustainability. The result is that the 'Toyota Way' enables a steady flow of millions of ideas each year from its employees – a wonderful resource, but only effective if these suggestions can be *aligned* towards a key goal. Otherwise they would be like a vivid firework display, sparkling and flashing in the sky but ultimately fading out. Toyota (and the many other organizations working with high involvement in innovation) manage this by providing clear visions to guide the idea generation and implementation process – something they call *hoshin kanri* and which might be translated as 'policy deployment'.

> You can read more about policy deployment as a tool and review some case examples on the companion website.

'Change management' is a challenge facing most organizations at some time in their lives and it refers to the adoption of *process* innovation – changes in the way the organization works. It might involve installing new technology, it might require changes in working practices. What we know about change management is that it is hard – and not always successful. People have a bias towards staying with what they know, they may find the change affects their skills, their social relationships inside the workplace, even their job itself. So there is a coiled spring of resistance to change in any organization – and when it triggers the results can be damaging. Resistance may not always be as violent as Ned Ludd and his 'Luddite' followers smashing textile machinery back in the Industrial Revolution, but it can and does slow or even divert progress. Research over decades suggests that simply ordering people to do something differently is not an effective strategy, and even 'selling' them the message in persuasive fashion may not work if there is an underlying concern not being addressed. The most successful strategy is to engage people, enable them to participate in shaping (even in small ways) the change – effectively getting them to 'buy in' to the vision.

You can find a discussion of change management as a 'deeper dive' on the companion website together with the case study of AMP as an example of participative design in practice.

What does research tell us about creating and sharing visions?

Using vision is not a new topic – back in 1954 Peter Drucker stressed the importance of goal setting for successful businesses [1]. Drawing on his own experience he introduced the concept of 'management by objectives', an approach which has become a standard part of any organization's management toolbox. Almost all studies, whether academic analyses or business cases, attribute success at least partially to the role of goal setting and visions. The trouble with this general acceptance is that there is a great deal of vague discussion of the topic, so in this section we will try to find some of the firmer bedrock below the surface froth.

Goals certainly matter. Drucker's ideas have become widely adopted, and research supports the view that giving people clear, difficult but attainable goals perform better than those who are given easy, non-specific goals, or no goals at all. Human resource management departments use this kind of thinking about motivation to design a wide variety of performance programmes within all kinds of organizations.

After reviewing over 400 studies over a thirty-five-year period, psychologists Edwin Locke and Gary Latham developed a widely accepted model of goal setting behaviour which is illustrated in Figure 6.1 [2].

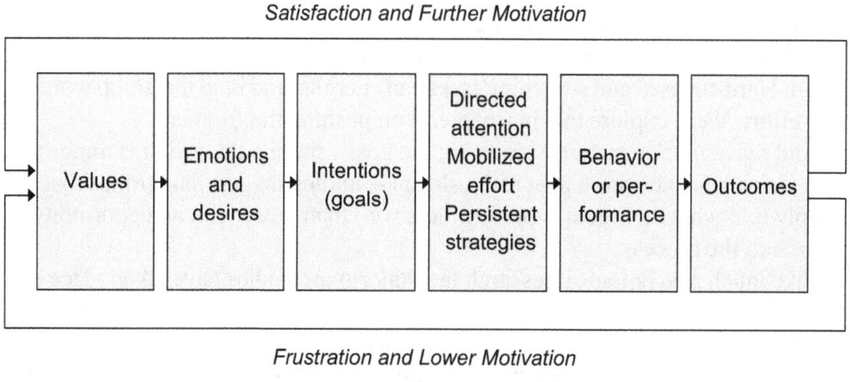

Satisfaction and Further Motivation

| Values | Emotions and desires | Intentions (goals) | Directed attention Mobilized effort Persistent strategies | Behavior or performance | Outcomes |

Frustration and Lower Motivation

Figure 6.1 Locke and Latham's goal setting model

In their view goals are what an individual or a group is consciously trying to achieve; they emerge from values and desires which create positive intentions – the goal. Goals motivate people to develop strategies to achieve them – and success provides positive feedback and further motivation. But failing to achieve can lead to reduced future motivation.

They suggest that goals perform four key functions [3]:

- Directing attention and efforts towards goal-relevant activities, in other word delivering focus;
- Energizing function and therefore producing effort;
- Increasing persistence;
- Affecting action indirectly by leading to the arousal, discovery and/or use of task-relevant knowledge and strategies.

We can see how this might have evolved as a survival mechanism both at an individual level and in the context of a group. Mobilizing one's efforts towards something which will be of value, using that to maintain effort when the going gets tough, aligning the contribution of others – these are all reinforcing characteristics which help achieve the goal.

Researchers have looked at how goal setting theory works at the level of teams, and their basic finding is that specific difficult group goals yield higher group performance than (1) nonspecific goals or (2) specific easy group goals [4]. In other words, stretching towards something which is sharply focused but also hard to achieve has the strongest effect.

Of course groups can often involve carrying 'passengers', people who ride on the efforts of others in a phenomenon called 'social loafing'. (We discuss this in more detail in Chapter 9.) But studies of goal setting in teams suggest that this effect is actually less than might have been expected; the sense of interdependence seems to counteract it, especially when the team is facing a challenging task. In other words, feeling a part of a team which depends on each other motivates people to give their best efforts.

Studies of individual goal setting suggest that as the task becomes more complex performance goes down – but this doesn't seem to be the case with group effort. Hard-focused and stretching tasks can energize and bind the group to maintain effort. We'll explore this in Chapter 9 on pushing the frontiers.

And *participation* matters – 'owning the goal', sharing the vision is important. The vision has to be more than just a slogan – studies suggest that groups that are simply told what their goal is perform less well than those with an opportunity to input into the process.

Like much psychological research the majority of studies have taken place in a laboratory setting so there are certain limitations – but these findings also seem to resonate with anecdotal evidence and experience in practice.

Of course groups are a collection of individuals and there is an important question about the alignment of individual goals with those of the group. How do individual goals influence group performance? A useful distinction is made by Deborah Crown and Joseph Rosse who talk about egocentric versus group-centric goal setting [5]. Egocentric individual goals focus on maximizing individual performance. They argue that these goals enhance commitment only to the individual performance and increase the possibility of competition among team members. Group-centric individual goals focus on how the individual can have a maximal contribution to the group performance. These goals should enhance commitment to the group performance and not only the individual performance. Therefore, co-operation among team members would be the ideal strategy to maximize performance. They found a positive effect for group-centric goals on team performance and a significant negative effect for egocentric goals on group performance.

Goals and group creativity

We are particularly concerned with creativity in groups, and this raises the question as to whether goals are beneficial for creative tasks in the same manner as for other performances? The answer, not surprisingly, is very much a 'yes' – as the research outlined in Table 6.1 shows.

The question is really about *how* goal setting is linked to creativity – and it appears that we need to look more closely at the type of goal. In particular there's a difference between performance goals and learning goals. The development of management by objectives builds on the idea of goal setting where the goal is set from outside and represents a performance which the individual or group should

Table 6.1 Studies of goals and group creativity

Researchers	Key findings
Amabile and Gryskiewicz (1987)	In an interview-based study with 120 R&D scientists, professional goal setting is perceived as a critical factor for fostering creativity.
Carson and Carson (1993)	Individuals showed higher creativity levels in an assigned task with assigned creativity goals than without.
Cardinal (2001)	Looked at the specificity of creativity goals and found an analogue to general goal setting research that specific goals enhance creative performance.
Kleingeld, van Mierlo and Arends (2011)	Goals have a positive effect on innovativeness on team level.
Shalley (1991, 1995)	Creativity goals have a positive effect on creative performance but performance goals do not enhance creativity.

achieve. Performance goals of this kind work well under the right conditions – as the research we described earlier confirms. In particular there is a strong case for setting what are called SMART performance goals.

Creativity in action: SMART goals

The idea of goal setting emerged during the 1950s following Peter Drucker's influential work on 'management by objectives'. This model began to raise questions about the nature of goals. Which ones were most effective at mobilizing people's effort?

In 1961 George Doran [6] wrote an article in the Management Review Journal which explored the importance of objectives and the difficulty of setting good ones. With the title 'There's a S.M.A.R.T. Way to Write Management's Goals and Objectives,' it suggested that goals should be:

- Specific – target a specific area for improvement;
- Measurable – quantify or at least suggest an indicator of progress;
- Assignable – specify who will do it;
- Realistic – state what results can realistically be achieved, given available resources;
- Time-related – specify when the result(s) can be achieved.

SMART goals have become widely used as an approach to management although more recent versions have changed the 'A' to 'achievable' – goals should not be too far out of reach since impossible targets lose their motivating effect.

SMART goals undoubtedly represent a powerful tool in organizational life, building as they do on the power of goal setting. But many tasks involving creativity do not fit neatly into the SMART framework. By their very nature they begin as fuzzy, ill-defined and uncertain – in many cases we don't even know what the problem is that we're trying to solve! As we have seen our creativity journey begins with a phase of problem *exploration*. And even when we have some idea of where we are going the road ahead is less a clear three-lane highway than a dense jungle through which we are going to have to hack our own particular path! Under these conditions the basic 'managed' principles of SMART goals begin to break down – we need something which retains their discipline but also allows for the high uncertainty involved in creativity.

There is also the challenge of persistence – the need to keep going even when the going gets tough. We saw this in the individual context in our chapter on willpower – and the same need for perseverance is present within groups working on creative tasks. Specific, difficult and complex goals are hard to achieve without persistence; groups need energy to keep going.

> You can find the example of Lockheed's famous Skunk Works on the companion website which illustrates powerfully the way in which a stretch goal – in this case design and build the fastest aeroplane in the world in less than six months – can trigger perseverance and motivation.

The evidence suggests that stretch goals are important – but they need to be perceived as achievable [7]. Too high a stretch and anxieties creep in with a negative impact on learning and therefore performance. It seems that the equation is not the higher the goal the higher the creativity. It is more a 'do-the-best-you-can' orientation which fosters creativity the most. The setting of a do-your-best goal is resulting in higher performance for creative tasks than the setting of a difficult and specific goal.

The SMART approach is good for performance goals, but sometimes the uncertainty and problem exploration characteristics of creative tasks means we need a modified approach. Building an impossible aeroplane isn't just a stretching target; there's a lot of risk, uncertainty, fuzzy front end about it. Putting on a 'wow' theatre performance in six weeks from now is not simply managing rehearsal schedules, it's about allowing space for exploration, creative conflict, changes in direction. Starting a new venture is more than a spreadsheet and a business plan, it's a learning journey. What creative tasks like these need is an approach which builds on SMART but also includes an element of *learning*.

Learning goals

In order to further understand the interaction of goals and performance, we refer to one of the shapers of modern psychology, Albert Bandura. In his research he was interested in how we achieve to acquire new behaviours, in other words how human beings learn. In his book *Social Foundations of Thought and Action: A Social Cognitive Theory* he proposed that individuals are self-organizing, proactive, self-reflecting, and self-regulating, in opposition to the behaviouristic conception that humans are mono-directionally influenced by environmental and other external factors. His concept of self-efficacy is essential to learn new material of any kind and to develop new skills or improve already acquired ones [8].

Creativity in action: self-efficacy [9]

One of the most influential concepts emerging from Bandura's work is 'self-efficacy'. He describes it as 'the conviction that one can successfully execute the behaviour required to produce the outcome'. Importantly self-efficacy is not concerned with the skills of an individual or group but rather

> with their judgments about what they can accomplish with those skills. Bandura makes an important distinction between self-confidence (which refers to firmness of belief without specifying its direction) and self-efficacy (which involves the setting a specific goal).
>
> This kind of self-belief is closely tied up with the type of goals people set for themselves and their commitment to achieving them. Research suggests that people with higher self-efficacy will set higher goals and are more committed to them and that they are better at finding suitable strategies to reach their goals. Importantly self-efficacy is something that can be learned [2].

Bandura distinguished between two different kinds of goal orientation: performance goal and learning goal orientation. They roughly correspond to internally set and externally set goals; a person with a learning goal is looking to develop their own competence by mastering something challenging. By contrast, a performance goal is linked to demonstrating competence in achieving some externally set target. As Fred Luthans and others have shown, a learning goal orientation is particularly relevant in situations which require people to be proactive, problem-solve, be creative and open to new ideas, and adapt to new and changing situations [10].

Some researchers suggest a third kind of goal, alongside performance and learning, which they describe as 'performance avoidance goal orientation'. This focuses on avoiding mistakes and negative evaluations (note the link to voice and speaking up-culture in our chapter about psychological safety) [11].

One of the important findings by Bandura and colleagues is that even when faced with failure individuals and groups view the situation as a learning opportunity. With a learning goal orientation failure is seen as useful feedback, not as a criticism; it suggests that the current strategies being used aren't working and so different approaches need to be tried [12–13]. It reinforces the need for renewed effort – in other words, it supports persistence.

This difference in goal orientation helps explain why there appear to be different results in studies around goal setting. Innovation is not about repeating already learned behaviour, but about conquering 'new land'; routine strategies will probably not work for creative tasks. For complex and creative tasks learning goals outperform performance goals. Gerard Seijts and Gary Latham found that the setting of specific learning goals, for example finding a certain number of different strategies to master the task, will be helpful [14].

Christina Shalley and Jill Perry-Smith conducted a study to find out more about the relationship between external evaluation and creative performance. Their work suggests that if individuals expected to learn something out of the evaluation on how to improve their performance, intrinsic motivation and creative performance increased [15]. Jing Zhou and colleagues showed the same effect with feedback. So-called informational feedback led to higher creative performance compared with controlling or disciplinary feedback. They found that feedback that increases developmental orientation and provides people with helpful information to learn, develop and improve is helpful for innovativeness [16–18].

The link to motivation is also important – 'keep going' is a key part of the creativity journey and without the inner motivation there's a temptation to give up. Teresa Amabile has looked in depth at motivation and its role in creativity and in particular found that *intrinsic motivation* – coming from the nature of the task itself and the activity around it – was far more important than external incentives or sanctions. In this context goals can be helpful – but the nature of those goals matters. It seems that learning goals are much more supporting for creative acts than strict and demanding outcome-oriented goals. She states that whereas goals are mostly helpful if they are in accordance with personal values and wishes, they can also extinguish intrinsic motivation and kill the creative impulse [19–21].

Other studies support this view – for example highlighting the link between evaluation (and goal setting is a kind of evaluation) and positive effects on intrinsic motivation and creative performance [22–23]. By producing a positive sense of challenge in the work and enabling a focus on the work itself, shared vision increases internal task motivation, which in turn is a key promoter of individual creativity [24].

And this leads us back to the idea that goal setting for creative performance need not be as specific and SMART as performance goals but rather needs to have an inspiring character – a vision.

So what is a vision?

Michael West defines vision as an 'idea of a valued outcome which represents a higher order goal and a motivating force at work' (p. 310, [25]). Teams with clearly defined visions which are shared among the team members and similarly valued are more likely to develop new methods of working because they are motivated and their efforts have focus and direction. The model that he and his team developed around supportive team climate for creativity included a component about vision; and it is not only one study which shows the importance of visions for creativity; their work has been replicated widely in different countries and fields of work [26]. Similar findings are reported by Tudor Rickards and colleagues drawing on the experience of studying multiple cohorts of managers working as creativity groups during their studies at Manchester Business School [27]. Jeffrey Pinto and John Prescott found in their study with 400 project teams that clearly stated visions enhance idea-generation and predicts successful innovation [28].

How do visions help? Essentially they provide the 'glue' which makes shared goals explicit and visible, allowing the group to focus on them and engage in practices like information sharing, constructive challenge and shared experimentation in order to reach them. For example, Yaping Gong and colleagues use the information exchange perspective: team goal orientation leads to a 'shared understanding of the extent to which a team emphasizes learning or performance goals, and, consequently, helps to facilitate group decision making, collaborative problem-solving, and intragroup coordination that maintain the group's emphasis on learning or performance goals' [29–30].

What's in a vision?

In their team climate inventory Neil Anderson and Michael West define vision for innovative teams as composed of four elements:

- Visionary nature
- Clarity
- Attainability
- Sharedness.

Visionary nature relies on one of the basic assumptions suggested by Edwin Locke and Gary Latham, that only a valued outcome by the team members will provide the motivation to go forward [25]. Visions need to be challenging and motivating – something which we will explore again in the chapter on pushing the frontiers. Kennedy's 'man on the moon' vision galvanized a large number of people to shared creative effort; it's no coincidence that Google uses the label 'moonshot' to describe similarly challenging and stretching projects.

You can find a link on the companion website to a TED Talk by Astro Teller talking about one of these 'moonshot' projects – the Loon programme—which aims to provide universally accessible internet via a network of balloons.

Jim Collins and Jerry Porras popularized the phrase 'big, hairy, audacious goals' (BHAG) in their 1994 book *Built to Last*, which reviewed practices in successful companies which had survived over the long term. They argue that BHAGs are more emotionally compelling:

> an audacious 10-to-30-year goal to progress towards an envisioned future . . . . . a true BHAG is clear and compelling, serves as unifying focal point of effort, and acts as a clear catalyst for team spirit. It has a clear finish line, so the organization can know when it has achieved the goal; people like to shoot for finish lines.
>
> [31]

Examples of such broad visionary goals would be Henry Ford's idea of democratizing the automobile or Dr Venkataswamy's dream of providing safe, low-cost eye care to the poor of India. But they can also operate at the level of the team, providing a challenging focus. Shigeo Shingo's efforts at Toyota to cut manufacturing times in half or Apple's 'pirates' developing a radical competitor in the difficult world of personal computers are good examples of building a focus and identity around a stretching challenge. And the examples of Lockheed's Skunk Works or Pixar's approach show how such visions can be repeatedly deployed as a tool to motivate creative teams.

You can read about these cases on the companion website.

Richard Leifer and colleagues carried out an extensive programme of research into radical innovation within US companies, defining 'radical' as having totally new performance features, offering performance improvements greater than five times what is currently available, or significant reduction in cost of over 30 per cent. 'Stretch' targets like these force the organization to find new ways of working and in particular give creative teams a clear vision around which to operate [32].

Clarity is the degree to which the vision is understandable. The danger with visionary goals is that they can be too vague, creating a sense of aspiration but not providing enough clarity to enable people to work towards them. Well-formed visions give enough specificity to help people see them and also some sense of what it would be like if they achieved them. In the Aravind Eye Care example the target was clear – eye surgery had to be provided at a tenth of the current costs ($30 per operation instead of $300) and safely. The challenge was how – but the team working on it had a clear focus for their efforts. Dr Devi Shetty – sometimes called 'the Henry Ford of heart surgery' – takes a similar approach in his ambitious vision for improved healthcare in India. He has slashed the costs of major operations like heart bypass while maintaining world class safety and quality levels, and he uses this approach to drive innovation within the network of hospitals which he founded. Again the targets are stretching but clear; the challenge to his teams is finding ways to realize them.

You can read more about Aravind and Dr Shetty (NHL case) on the companion website.

In this sense there is a close link to the SMART principles – well-constructed visions give some dimensions, such as what will be achieved by when. Structured approaches to developing shared visions can help here – for example the use of frameworks like the Entrepreneur's Storyboard or the Business Model Canvas – help to articulate the vision.

> You can explore these tools in the companion website.

Attainability refers to one of the basic principles of SMART goals that people have to believe that they are achievable even if difficult. In this sense a vision like 'feeding the world' is probably too broad to act as a motivating focus – but by narrowing the focus and being specific about a particular region the goal can be seen as achievable and act as a motivator. A valuable approach here is to break the broad vision down into smaller 'stepping stones' on the way to achieving it.

Research in this area has focused on the influence of 'proximal' and 'distal' goals – proximal are near-to-hand and achievable in the short term whereas distal goals are in the distance and may only be achievable in the long term. Bandura's concept of proximal goals were those short-term goals which provided individuals with more frequent feedback and specific information about performance which is not available when pursuing only distal goals. Groups can use the feedback to alter their strategies in trying to achieve the distal goal. This gives rise to approaches which emphasize 'small wins' during the life of a major project rather than a 'big bang' approach.

Gary Latham and Gerard Seijts, using a business game, found that do-your-best goals were more effective than distal goals, but when proximal outcome goals were set in addition to the distal outcome goal, self-efficacy and profits were significantly higher than in the do-your-best condition or in the condition where only a distal outcome goal had been set. In dynamic situations, it is important to actively search for feedback and react quickly to it to attain the goal; as Dietrich Dörner noted, performance errors on a dynamic task are often due to deficient decomposition of a distal goal into proximal goals. Proximal goals can increase what Michael Frese and colleagues call *error management*. Proximal feedback regarding errors can yield information for people about whether their picture of reality is aligned with what is required to attain their goal [33–35].

Sharedness emphasizes the team approach of the model. Only if the goals are accepted within the team and shared by the team members will the vision (goals) be effective. Here we see a close link to collaboration and the enhancement of collaboration that basically underlines the team character of this theory. It is not about individual goal setting but about the team.

The concept of mental models probably gives us an insight into the question how important this concept is and what skills or cognitive concepts have to be mastered in order to generate sharedness of vision. Team mental models are what researchers Susan Mohammed and Brad Dumville call 'a shared, organized understanding of knowledge about key elements in the relevant environment' (p. 97–98, [36]). They further proposed subdomains of team mental models about information sharing, group learning and cognitive consensus. Many studies show the relationship between mental models and performance [37–38]. As teams encounter frequent issues and problems in innovative projects, higher teamwork quality can enhance the team's ability to find solutions to problems. Through collaborative interaction, team members can freely exchange ideas and interpretations and develop a more common understanding of problems, thus enhancing the probability of finding reasonable solutions [39]. Furthermore, higher teamwork quality also implies that the team members are interacting frequently to monitor their progress on achieving the goals. Thus, higher teamwork quality not only ensures that teams are aware of their progress but also aids them in planning project milestones and deadlines.

As Ikujiro Nonaka and Ryoko Toyama found, shared vision may be especially important for integrating knowledge in groups, where participants are highly dissimilar and come from different backgrounds, giving a direction to knowledge creation, stimulating the intellectual passion of individuals and encouraging them to create knowledge [40].

It's important to see vision not as something set in stone but rather as a living thing, elaborated and embedded through a process of sharing, discussion and so forth. The participation theme from earlier comes in here – we talk about people buying into the vision, meaning they invest their energies and commitment. But they also can shape it and in the process it becomes their vision, not someone else's. In turn that process elaborates and refines the vision.

A useful tool, not only for articulating but also sharing visions – is the Business Model Canvas. In its various forms this provides a template on which people can collaborate to develop and refine a vision – the 'canvas' metaphor is very relevant. Other tools serve a similar purpose – for example LEGO Serious Play is an approach which effectively invites people to create 'sculptures' – three dimensional representations of a future vision and then allows them to explore by playing with these, rearranging them and developing a coherent underlying narrative. Storytelling is another approach which is increasingly used to provide a coherent picture of the future and allow others to contribute and adapt the narrative [41].

You can find examples of these tools and cases which describe their application in organizations like Amazon, Procter and Gamble, Nokia and Shell on the companion website.

Why is creating and sharing visions important for creativity?

Let's summarize the key points emerging from our quick tour of the research landscape around shared vision.

- Goals matter to individuals and to groups – they sustain, energize, provide motivation and so forth.
- It's important to distinguish different types of goals – especially between those which are externally set (performance goals) and those which are internally set (learning goals).

- It seems that learning goals are much more supporting for creative acts than strict and demanding outcome-oriented goals.
- SMART provides a powerful framework for thinking about how to set performance goals, but we probably need a SMART Plus focus for goal setting around creativity which allows for more of a learning goals/inner-directed orientation.
- This can be achieved through the use of a shared vision – the 'idea of a valued outcome which represents a higher order goal and a motivating force at work'.
- Effective vision needs four key things – stretching vision, clarity, attainability and sharedness.

In practice we can see these principles in the world of innovation. They set stretch goals – high-profile challenges around which teams can focus to deliver creative solutions. Table 6.2 gives some examples of such 'sprint' projects drawn from a variety of settings, which underline the importance of this capability.

Table 6.2 Stretch targets and innovation

Project	Stretching characteristics	How they achieved it (and links to more details on website)
Rethinking the flight simulator business – a major international company looking to compete in an increasingly competitive marketplace by radically rethinking their approach to design and manufacture of what is, in effect, the front end of an airliner.	Cut time to design and build a simulator from three years to one, and costs by 50%.	Build a 'group mind', taking all the key people with insights from across the company (including not only designers and software engineers but logistics, stores, sales, etc.) away to a hotel for three days. Then break them into small cross-functional teams tasked with challenging every aspect of the design and build cycle with the core goal in mind. Shared multiple brainstorms and a mixture of convergence, sharing new ideas and then elaborating them further.
German city utilities provider making the transition from public service provider to private sector player in an increasingly competitive industry. (You can read more on this case as SWK on the companion website.)	Turn a public sector utility from a public service to an innovative player – faster, flexible, more customer-focused, more competitive.	A series of workshops building temporary teams drawn from across the organization. Trained in simple creativity tools and tasked with developing novel solutions which addressed one or more of the key vision targets. Managing director presented the challenge at the outset and returned to hear their presentations the following afternoon.

Project	Stretching characteristics	How they achieved it (and links to more details on website)
Lockheed's Skunk Works (You can read this case on the companion website.)	Originally set up to design and build a jet aircraft in 180 days, under conditions of high secrecy and with very limited resources.	Dedicated team managed in very different, highly autonomous style working on challenging existing approaches.
Crisis-driven innovation in humanitarian innovation (You can read these cases on the companion website.)	Rapid response to social innovation challenges under conditions of limited resources and urgent time pressure.	Working with users in context, adopting challenging and entrepreneurial frameworks to quickly mobilize creative responses, often recombining existing solutions in new ways.
Aravind Eye System/ NHL Hospitals/Lifespring Hospitals	Bring safe, low-cost health care to the poorest people of India.	Entrepreneurial creativity especially using recombinant innovation approaches.

Creativity in action: Leicester's flying foxes

The BBC's main sports programme for football is called 'Match of the Day' (MOTD) and has been presented for many years by Gary Lineker, a former England player with a great reputation for individual skills. The edition broadcast on 13th August 2016 was interesting – while his two co-presenters were dressed in smart casual outfits Gary was only wearing his underpants! The reason for this was a promise he had rashly made at the start of the preceding season when bottom of the Premier League club, Leicester City, started their first match. Lineker had once played for the Foxes (Leicester City's nickname) in his early days and would have loved to see them do well, but the overwhelming consensus was that they were outclassed and unlikely to stay in the top flight. Lineker reckoned their chances so slim that he promised to present the MOTD show in his underpants if they won the league.

By the end of the 2015–2016 season Leicester had become a fairy-tale success story, capturing the imagination of millions of fans around the world. Some of their supporters had placed bets that the club would win the League and the bookmakers happily accepted their money, offering odds of 5,000 to 1 or better. Those fans became wealthy overnight but far more important was the sense of pride in the achievement of the underdogs.

Their success was not a one-match win or a flash of star performance from an individual player. The entire squad cost less than a single top team player in clubs like Arsenal, Chelsea or Manchester United and the manager, Claudio Ranieri, had been written off by many. Yet through teamwork and perseverance week after week, over nine months they achieved their stretch goal.

Importantly it was also a matter of taking each match as a challenge – a proximal goal – and building on each success with the confidence to approach the next.

But it's not just putting the team together and giving them a stretching task. The skill lies in getting them to perform well towards achieving it, not to fall apart in the process. It's a long haul and requires a balance between creative conflict and focused effort – and the real value comes in teams which can repeat this trick – something we will explore further in Chapter 9.

Challenging goals are one thing, but giving a sense of their being achievable is another, and here organizations use proximal goals – stepping stones – as a key methodology. For example the broad vision of 'zero defects' in a quality programme is very much a distant goal but helps keep focus while the proximal goals of specific projects can be achieved on the way to delivering that broad vision. This is the principle of *hoshin kanri* – 'policy deployment' – which we mentioned earlier. Organizations using tools like scenario thinking to explore novel futures couple the target vision they create with 'roadmapping' and 'back-casting' tools to help set proximal stepping-stone goals for the journey towards those futures. And in the 'lean start-up' approach to entrepreneurship the emphasis is placed on 'minimum viable product' – develop and test a working prototype and learn from that – essentially an incremental stepping-stone approach to achieving the broader, bigger vision of the new venture.

So far we've established that building shared vision is an important competence for enabling creativity at group level. The question is one of how we can best develop it – and that's the focus of the next section.

What is the skill set around creating and sharing visions?

Creating and sharing a vision is the first group level competence we introduce. As in the individual competence chapters we want to give you an overview of what the competence is all about. Figure 6.2 below indicates the key skills underpinning it.

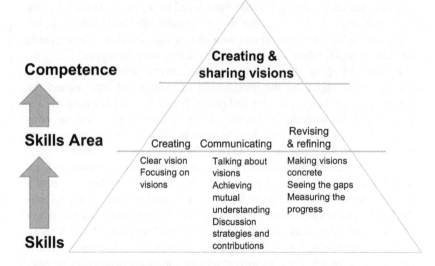

Figure 6.2 Competence creating and sharing visions

Programming the GPS for the creativity journey – what's your position?

To help you explore this group competence, we offer two complementary approaches. First, similar to the individual competences, we developed a self-check questionnaire to help you assess yourself. Additionally, to evaluate your team, we developed a team questionnaire. Both questionnaires are based on the research we described in the chapter.

Creating and sharing a vision involves developing a shared picture which has meaning for the team members. The skills described in this section are not just about generating a vision or a goal but about communicating it, sharing it and finding a common understanding of it.

Creatively successful teams are solution-oriented and driven to reach the goal together. In a team setting it is not about an individual reaching the goal – the whole team has to do so in order to be successful. So, measuring only your progress does not make sense. You have to find ways to measure the team progress, see the contributions of the individual team members to it.

It's also important to avoid the 'blame game' when things go wrong – and a key part of this is having shared approaches to how the team will deal with the surprises, roadblocks and pitfalls on their journey.

Next we offer you a skills self-check on creating and sharing a vision. It will help you think about your own approach, your strengths and weaknesses, and where you might wish to develop skills further. We suggest you rate yourself with a five-point rating scale:

1 = Not like me at all
2 = Not much like me
3 = I cannot decide if I am good or bad at it, just doing OK
4 = Describes me to a good extent (but not exactly)
5 = Describes me exactly

And (as we described in earlier chapters) try to avoid the central tendency and try to give some specific examples from your past behaviour to help you decide where to score yourself (Table 6.3).

Team check

Next we offer you a team-level skills check on creating and sharing a vision in your team (Table 6.4) which is strongly influenced by Anderson and West as well as Hoegl and Parboteeah [26, 42–43]. We suggest you rate your team with a five-point rating scale:

1 = Not like us (my team) / I do not agree at all
2 = Not much like us / I disagree to a certain extent

3 = I cannot decide if we are good or bad at it, just doing OK / I neither agree nor disagree

4 = Describes us to a good extent (but not exactly) / I agree somewhat

5 = Describes us exactly / I completely agree

Table 6.3 Self-check creating and sharing visions

#	Core behavioural skills	Your score (1–5)	For instance write at least one example of your own
1	I have a clear idea of the future state of our projects and assignments.		
2	I often talk with my colleagues and team members about our vision and ensure that everybody understands it.		
3	I am able to cascade down a vision or strategy into specific goals.		
4	I discuss my visions and goals with others to achieve a mutual understanding.		
5	I see clearly the gaps between the current state and the desired state and find actions/ strategies to reduce them.		
6	I discuss the gaps with my colleagues.		
7	I discuss strategies and contributions for each team member.		
8	I can focus my attention and energy on the activities related to achieving our vision and goals.		
9	I encourage my colleagues and team members to focus their attention and energy on the activities related to achieving our goals.		
10	I measure our mutual progress, not just mine.		

Table 6.4 Team-check creating and sharing visions

#	Team behaviours	Score (1–5)	For instance write at least one example
1	The team vision and goals are transparent for all team members.		
2	Team members participate in formulating a compelling vision.		
3	The team has a mutual understanding about the vision and goals.		
4	The vision is energizing for all team members.		
5	The shared vision is a cornerstone of the team's goal setting process.		
6	The team goals are considered worthwhile by all team members.		
7	The team members are committed to the goals.		
8	The team finds concrete actions closing the gap between current state and goal.		
9	The team members are motivated to contribute to achieve the vision and the goals.		
10	The team members measure the mutual progress towards reaching the goals.		

You can use this 'fitness check' in a number of ways. You can try and fill it in on your own, guessing at what the others might say. Or you can try to get them involved in completing it – which is likely to give a much more helpful picture. There are several ways you might do this – for example:

Do it as an anonymous team check. Hand out the team check to every team member, let them fill in the questionnaire, find a way to gather the results in an anonymous way (so it is not possible to reconstruct which answer is by whom), and then discuss the results openly in a team meeting.

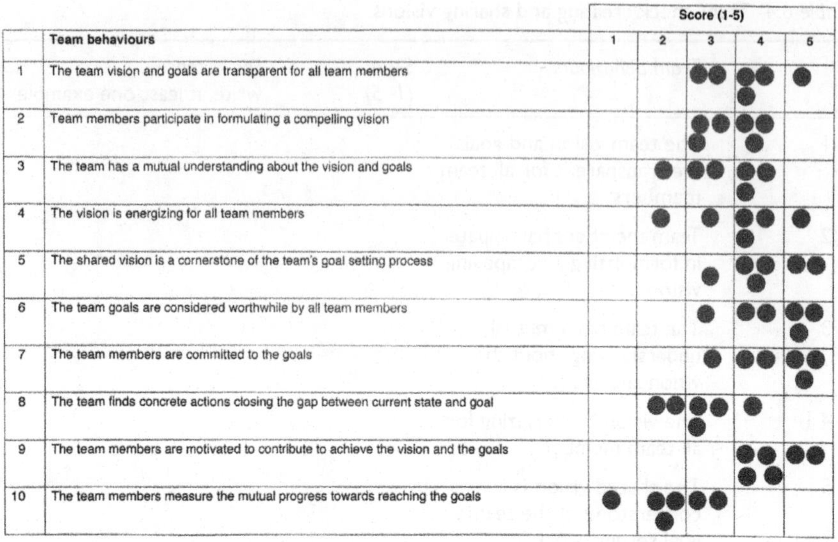

Figure 6.3 Example of a team rating poster

Rate publicly and discuss in a team meeting. A variation of the procedure is rating together in a team meeting with sticky dots, then look at the results and discuss what is your general opinion in the team and what to do with it.

Start with the discussion right away. Put up a poster with the team check on the wall or project it on the wall and call in a team meeting. Every team member should be able to familiarize himself/herself with the items. All questions concerning understanding should be discussed together and the team should find a common understanding. Then each item is discussed in the team, one after the other. It helps if examples about experiences within the team are discussed before the rating. At the end the team decides on a rating.

All three approaches work – which one you use is linked in part to the level of psychological safety the team feels it needs to explore these issues. The first procedure is the safest, but as you go through the challenge as well as the potential learning increases.

Now think about your team – how far are these statements a reflection of your experience?

For a template of a team rating poster go to the companion website.

Working out at the gym – how to train your skills in creating and sharing a visions

Skills and competencies that are needed in a group context can be trained as well. One does not need to have a fixed training group; any group will do. But we will also describe some exercises, recipes and procedures you can train alone quasi as a preparation to your group creative experiences.

Make it SMART

We describe SMART goals as a framework in the chapter, and this approach is still helpful to develop the craft of goal setting.

Visualize feedback

If you do not know where you are, then it is hard to take the next step. So it's helpful to have some idea of the overall map and goal but also of progress towards it; it's here that using different ways to visualize and give feedback about progress is helpful. To take a simple example, if the goal is to cut down thirty trees in a day, people have no way to tell if they are on target unless they know how many trees have been cut. This gets even harder when you work in a team across the globe; you do not see the progress of the others. Studies show that when people find they are below target, they normally increase their effort or try a new strategy [44]. So visualizing your current status in respect of moving towards the goal is a much more helpful strategy than simply setting the goal.

Use proximal goals

Closely linked to this is the idea of stepping stones or mileposts, targets and sub-goals on the way to the major task. As one memorable phrase has it, the best way to eat an elephant is one spoonful at a time! Breaking the big challenge down is helpful partly in terms of motivation – there is a sense of achievement and movement towards the bigger goal – but it is also valuable in terms of learning and adapting the journey towards the goal. In our later chapter we look at the idea of 'agile innovation' and the 'lean start-up' – approaches which involve a series of short cycles and proximal goals as ways of helping guide the journey as well as reaching the final goal. In similar fashion, large-scale efforts trying to mobilize creativity across many different people – such as in a company-wide quality or service improvement programme – can benefit from breaking the big targets down into smaller, achievable chunks.

This is the idea behind policy deployment, and you can find out more on this and read some example cases on the companion website.

Back to the future

Visions are all about the future, and the great thing is that anything can happen 'out there'. So creating visions using tools which help create pictures of the future – for example scenarios – is a powerful approach. But getting to there from here requires a degree of 'roadmapping' – how will we make the journey? And we can use techniques like 'back-casting' – working our way back from some future point where we have achieved the vision to today and asking how we got there.

> You can find descriptions of these tools – scenarios, roadmapping and back-casting – on the companion website.

Use vision building tools

There are many powerful tools to help you move from a vague vision to put some shape around it, and make it available to others. For example think of creating a vision as storytelling – and develop and embellish the story as you start to tell it. It's a journey from now towards somewhere, with various challenges to be overcome on the way. As you begin to write it, so you can elaborate and expand it; importantly as you begin to tell it, so others can add their ideas and help develop it. It doesn't have to be a written story – it could be a film idea or a piece of theatre – the important point is to use some kind of framework to capture and develop it.

> On the companion website there are several tools to help including the Entrepreneur's Storyboard.

Learn to dream

Goal setting is extremely valuable if it comes to application, training and implementation, but for creativity a little more is needed – a vision. Something that draws you into the future, a picture (in your mind) that is so tempting that you will do almost anything to accomplish it. That is a true vision. But many people have a problem coming up with an attractive vision. Richard Boyatzis, a psychologist, developed a useful exercise – the 27 dream challenge [45]. It's very simple – collect those activities that you have been dreaming of doing in the next ten years (professionally as well as privately).

Dreams mobilize positive energies and show us how our ideal self and/or our ideal future can look like. Number a sheet of paper 1 through 27. List all of the things you want to do or experience before you die. Don't worry about priorities or practicalities. Just write down whatever comes to your mind. Be as specific as you can (travelling is too unspecific, write down either where to or how you want to travel). If you need more than 27 lines, go ahead, add more. When you are done with this exercise, then and only then are you 'allowed' to think about what would be the first thing you want to accomplish, what do you want to start doing, then go ahead and start planning or just do nothing. It is not about the implementation so much as an exercise in finding dreams and visions of the future.

Celebrate achievements

An important part of creating, sharing and accomplishing visions is self-efficacy and the need to recognize success in order to know what you are able to do. The field of positive psychology offers an exercise that enhances self-efficacy for others. It is not meant to be done for yourself but to help others; nevertheless it has benefits for you as well since it enhances your positive feelings. The exercise is called active constructive response (ACR) and works in the following way [46]. Take five minutes to give your full attention to the success story of a colleague (the technique works just as well with spouses, friends and family members). Get into a helpful questioning mode and listen attentively. Do not talk about your own successes or that you wish you have had the same experience. It is only about the other person, her/his experience, their feelings towards this success, their reflection about their contributions to this success (self-efficacy) and probably their future expectations. All these subtopics are worth exploring, and in this exercise it is your job not only to listen to the success but to steer the person through their experienced success with questions. Typical questions might include:

* What did you experience? (You can even ask about concrete actions like where have you been? who was there? and so forth.)
* How did you feel? What were your emotions?
* What did you think contributed to your success?

Feed-forward

Goal setting is first and foremost a discrepancy-creating process. Motivation requires feed-forward control in addition to feedback. After people attain the goal they have been pursuing, they generally set a higher goal for themselves. This adoption of higher goals creates rather than reduces motivation discrepancies to be mastered. 'Self motivation thus involves a dual cyclic process of disequilibratory discrepancy production followed by equilibratory reduction' [47].

The exercise goes as following: (1) Ask yourself a question, for example about what skill you want to develop. (2) Ask at least three people what they would recommend to do in order to succeed and write down their answer. Do not comment, and at the end (after probably three to five minutes) say thank you. (3) After you have asked three to five people, sit down and read the answers you got. (4) Select the answers you like (do not judge before that moment) and decide what to do.

Use your team

Discuss in your team what are your current competencies to be successful in this job and what do you want to learn or have to learn to have a higher chance in succeeding. Talk about possible exploring strategies and ideas for how to gather new knowledge or new know-how.

End of chapter summary

- It all starts with a vision. Goals and visions are steering and focusing our actions. There is a close link to intrinsic motivation and willpower.
- Goals perform four functions:

  - Directing attention and efforts towards goal-relevant activities, in other words delivering focus;
  - Energizing function and therefore producing effort;
  - Increasing persistence;
  - Affecting action indirectly by leading to the arousal, discovery, and/or use of task-relevant knowledge and strategies.

- Visions consist of four elements:

  - Stretching nature
  - Clarity
  - Attainability
  - Sharedness.

- Goals and visions are important for creativity, but learning and do-your-best goals are better than pure performance goals. Almost in contrast to that, research shows that visions are better if they have a stretching nature.
- The skills related to the competence of creating and sharing a vision is creating, communicating and refining (measuring) visions and goals.

References

[1]   Drucker, P. (1954). *The principles of management.* New York, NY: Harper-Collins.
[2]   Locke, E.A., & Latham, G.P. (2002). Building a practically useful theory of goal setting and task motivation. *American Psychologist, 57,* 705–717.

[3]   Wood, R. E., & Locke, E. A. (1990). Goal-setting and strategy effects on complex tasks. *Research in Organizational Behavior, 12,* 73–109.

[4]   Kleingeld, A., van Mierlo, H., & Arends, L. (2011). The effect of goal setting on group performance: A meta-analysis. *Journal of Applied Psychology, 96,* 1289.

[5]   Crown, D. F., & Rosse, J. G. (1995). Yours, mine, and ours: Facilitating group productivity through the integration of individual and group goals. *Organizational Behavior and Human Decision Processes, 64,* 138–150.

[6]   Doran, G. T. (1981). There's a S.M.A.R.T. way to write management's goals and objectives. *Management Review, 70,* 35–36.

[7]   Earley, P. C., Connolly, T., & Ekegren, G. (1989). Goals, strategy development, and task performance: Some limits on the efficacy of goal setting. *Journal of Applied Psychology, 74,* 24–33.

[8]   Bandura, A. (1986). *Social foundations of thought and action: A social cognitive theory.* Englewood Cliffs, NJ: Prentice-Hall.

[9]   Bandura, A. (1977). Self-efficacy: Toward a unifying theory of behavioral change. *Psychological Review, 84,* 191.

[10] Luthans, F. (2011). *Organizational behavior* (12th ed.). New York, NY: McGraw-Hill.

[11] Gong, Y., Kim, T.-Y., Lee, D.-R., & Zhu, J. (2013). A multilevel model of team goal orientation, information exchange, and creativity. *Academy of Management Journal, 56,* 827–851.

[12] Bandura, M., & Dweck, C. S. (1985). *The relationship of conceptions of intelligence and achievement goals to achievement-related cognition, affect and behavior.* Unpublished manuscript, Harvard University.

[13] Elliott, E. S., & Dweck, C. S. (1988). Goals: An approach to motivation and achievement. *Journal of Personality and Social Psychology, 54,* 5.

[14] Seijts, G. H., & Latham, G. P. (2001). The effect of distal learning, outcome, and proximal goals on a moderately complex task. *Journal of Organizational Behavior, 22,* 291–307.

[15] Shalley, C. E., & Perry-Smith, J. E. (2001). Effects of social-psychological factors on creative performance: The role of informational and controlling expected evaluation and modeling experience. *Organizational Behavior and Human Decision Processes, 84,* 1–22.

[16] Zhou, J., & Oldham, G. R. (2001). Enhancing creative performance: Effects of expected developmental assessment strategies and creative personality. *Journal of Creative Behavior, 35,* 151–167.

[17] Zhou, J. (1998). Feedback valence, feedback style, task autonomy, and achievement orientation: Interactive effects on creative performance. *Journal of Applied Psychology, 83,* 261–276.

[18] Zhou, J. (2003). When the presence of creative coworkers is related to creativity: Role of supervisor close monitoring, developmental feedback, and creative personality. *Journal of Applied Psychology, 88,* 413.

[19] Amabile, T. M. (1979). Effects of external evaluation on artistic creativity. *Journal of Personality and Social Psychology, 37,* 221–233.

[20] Amabile, T. M., Goldfarb, P., & Brackfield, S. C. (1990). Social influences on creativity: Evaluation, coaction, and surveillance. *Creativity Research Journal, 3,* 6–21.

[21] Shalley, C. E., & Oldham, G. R. (1985). Effects of goal difficulty and expected external evaluation on intrinsic motivation: A laboratory study. *Academy of Management Journal, 28,* 628–640.

[22] Harackiewicz, J. M., & Elliot, A. J. (1993). Achievement goals and intrinsic motivation. *Journal of Personality and Social Psychology, 65,* 904–915.

[23]   Shalley, C.E. (1995). Effects of coaction, expected evaluation, and goal setting on creativity and productivity. *Academy of Management Journal, 38*, 483–503.

[24]   Amabile, T.M. (1988). From individual creativity to organizational innovation. In K. Gronhaug & G. Kaufmann (Eds.), *Innovation: A cross disciplinary perspective* (139–166). Oslo: Norwegian University Press.

[25]   West, M.A. (1990). The social psychology of innovation in groups. In M. A. West &.J. L. Farr (Eds.), *Innovation and creativity at work: Psychological and organizational strategies* (4–36). Chichester: Wiley.

[26]   Anderson, N.R., & West, M.A. (1998). Measuring climate for work group innovation: development and validation of the team climate inventory. *Journal of Organizational Behavior, 19*, 235–258.

[27]   Rickards, T., Chen, M.-H., & Moger, S. (2001). Development of a self-report instrument for exploring team factor, leadership and performance relationships. *British Journal of Management, 12*, 243–250.

[28]   Pinto, J.K., & Prescott, J.E. (1988). Variations in critical success factors over the stages in the project life cycle. *Journal of Management, 14*, 5–18.

[29]   Team learning goal was significantly correlated to team creativity. Avoidance goal had a negative relationship with team creativity. But also performance goal had a positive correlation. Martin Hoegl and K. Praveen Parboteeah (2003) found a positive relationship between goal setting and performance. They looked additionally at teamwork quality, meaning a high degree of collaboration.

Bunderson, J.S., & Sutcliffe, K.M. (2003). Management team learning orientation and business unit performance. *Journal of Applied Psychology, 88*, 552–560.

Hoegl, M., & Parboteeah, K.P. (2003). Goal setting and team performance in innovative projects: On the moderating role of teamwork quality. *Small Group Research, 34*, 3–19.

[30]   Gong, Y., Kim, T.-Y., Lee, D.-R., & Zhu, J. (2013). A multilevel model of team goal orientation, information exchange, and creativity. *Academy of Management Journal, 56*, 827–851.

[31]   Collins, J., & Porras, J. (1994). *Built to last: Successful habits of visionary companies.* New York, NY: Random House.

[32]   Leifer, R., McDermott, C., O'Conner, G., Peters, L., Rice, M., & Veryzer, R. (2000). *Radical innovation.* Boston, MA: Harvard Business School Press.

[33]   Latham, G.P., & Seijts, G.H. (1999). The effects of proximal and distal goals on performance on a moderately complex task. *Journal of Organizational Behavior, 20*, 421–429.

[34]   Dietrich, D. (1991). *Die Logik des Misslingens.* Reinbek bei Hamburg: Rowohlt.

[35]   Van Dyck, C., Frese, M., Baer, M., & Sonnentag, S. (2005). Organizational error management culture and its impact on performance: A two-study replication. *Journal of Applied Psychology, 90*, 1228–1240.

[36]   Mohammed, S., & Dumville, B.C. (2001). Team mental models in a team knowledge framework: Expanding theory and measurement across disciplinary boundaries. *Journal of Organizational Behavior, 22*, 89–106.

[37]   Lim, B.-C., & Klein, K.J. (2006). Team mental models and team performance: A field study of the effects of team mental model similarity and accuracy. *Journal of Organizational Behavior, 27*, 403–418.

[38]   Mathieu, J.E., Heffner, T.S., Goodwin, G.F., Salas, E., & Cannon-Bowers, J.A. (2000). The influence of shared mental models on team process and performance. *Journal of Applied Psychology, 85*, 273–283.

[39]   Sicotte, H., & Langley, A. (2000). Integration mechanisms and R&D project performance. *Journal of Engineering and Technology Management, 17*, 1–37.

[40] Nonaka, I., & Toyama, R. (2005). The theory of the knowledge-creating firm: Subjectivity, objectivity and synthesis. *Industrial and Corporate Change*, *14*, 419–436.

[41] Beckman, S., & Barry, M. (2009). Design and innovation through storytelling. *International Journal of Innovation Science*, *1*, 151–160.

[42] Anderson, N., & West, M.A. (1994). *Team climate inventory: Manual and user's guide*. Windsor: ASE.

[43] Hoegl, M., & Parboteeah, K.P. (2003). Goal setting and team performance in innovative projects: On the moderating role of teamwork quality. *Small Group Research*, *34*, 3–19.

[44] Matsui, T., Okada, A., & Inoshita, O. (1983). Mechanism of feedback affecting task performance. *Organizational Behavior & Human Performance*, *31*, 114–122.

[45] Boyatzis, R., & McKee, A. (2013). *Resonant leadership: Renewing yourself and connecting with others through mindfulness, hope and compaction*. Boston: Harvard Business Press.

[46] Seligman, M.E.P. (2012). *Flourish: A visionary new understanding of happiness and well-being*. New York, NY: Simon & Schuster.

[47] Bandura, A. (1989). Self-regulation of motivation and action through internal standards and goal systems. In L.A. Pervin (Ed.), *Goal concepts in personality and social psychology* (19–85). London: Psychology Press.

## Chapter 7

Practising psychological safety

Chapter objectives

By the end of this chapter you will:

- Understand the role which psychological safety plays in creativity;
- Recognize the key skills associated with feeling psychologically safe in a team environment;
- Develop awareness of tools and techniques to help being able to take interpersonal risks in a team setting;
- Reflect on and be able to develop your own skills and those of the team around psychological safety.

Introduction

Try this. Get hold of a group of people, mostly strangers, and have them gather at the opposite side of a large room. Now run very fast towards them and, just before you reach them, leap off the ground and let yourself fly through the air. Sounds a crazy thing to do and one which is not too healthy if they fail to catch you – yet it is a typical warm up exercise in the world of theatre. Groups of actors gather together to try and create a theatrical experience which will be memorable, drawing an audience into a journey of imagination. And in order to innovate in this fashion they need some core skills around building trust – a sense of support for each other as they take risks and explore new ways of delivering that experience. Flying through the air and hoping someone will catch you is a powerful way of developing a sense of support – and it underlines a key element in our understanding of what makes for effective interpersonal creativity. We need a sense of *trust* or to be more precise a sense of *psychological safety*.

> You can find a link on the companion website to a TED Talk by Amy Edmondson about psychological safety.

In 2016 Charles Duhigg published an article in the *New York Times* describing an internal project at Google exploring what makes teams successful. The project was named Aristotle, and they looked at data from 180 teams scattered throughout the country and areas of working. To cut a long story short, in the end they settled on group norms as being the key factor – not inspirational leaders or careful team selection. And the most important of these norms was psychological safety; it was all about being heard by the team, speaking up and having a sensitivity towards one another's feelings [1].

> You can find a link on the companion website to a video by Charles Duhigg about the Google study Aristotle.

In this chapter we will look at this question of psychological safety, something that is the result of actual behaviour of team members leading to better creative results [2]. As Edmondson and colleagues point out, based on their extensive study of psychological safety, it is a group-level phenomenon [3–5]. It cannot work if only one team member is experiencing it. Team members must hold similar perceptions of it. And in practice what it means is that people in the group feel OK about taking risks, speaking up, acting proactively. A similar concept in the area of innovation research exists – Anderson and West call it 'participative safety' [6–8].

> ## Creative activity: barriers to psychological safety
>
> Imagine a situation in which you are part of a team working on a creative project. You have plenty of ideas – but what might stop you speaking out? Maybe some of your answers relate to anxieties – fear of looking foolish, fear of saying the 'wrong thing' and so forth. These are all examples where we need to feel OK before we will contribute fully – in other words, we need a sense of psychological safety.
>
> Write down what stopped you to speak up for your ideas in this kind of group situation.

What is psychological safety?

Amy Edmondson defines team psychological safety as 'a shared belief that the team is safe for interpersonal risk taking', going on to describe it as 'a sense of confidence that the team will not embarrass, reject, or punish someone for speaking up. This confidence stems from mutual respect and trust among team members' [9]. It gives individuals a feeling of safety and makes them more capable of changing while learning new behaviours and overcoming defensive routines.

William Kahn looked at individuals in different fields of work in order to see how psychological safety influences engagement at work [10]. His qualitative data shows the effect of speaking up and engaging oneself (today also often referred to as 'voice') if psychological safety is present among colleagues. Psychological safety is the confidence to do so because of the belief that there is no risk of embarrassment, rejection or depreciation of oneself. Kahn agrees with Edmondson that this confidence arises from mutual support and trust among the team members.

Creative activity: your team experiences

First, think about your own experiences with teams and about examples of teams you have read or heard about: What makes a team a good or a bad team? What are the building blocks? What are the differences between these teams?

Second, think about how these building blocks of good teams relate to being a more creative team.

Psychological safety is a shared belief by team members based on an appraisal of the work environment, and acting upon that cognitive appraisal with the effect of creating a team climate [11]. Anderson and West describe this climate as

> active involvement in group interactions wherein the predominant interpersonal atmosphere is one of non-threatening trust and support. For example, it is argued that participative safety exists where all members of a work group feel able to propose new ideas and problem solutions in a non-judgemental climate.
>
> [12]

Research note: trust and psychological safety

Trust is a person's willingness to be vulnerable towards another person and as a consequence to take the risk to get hurt [13]. McAllister referred to the emotional bonds between individuals as affect-based trust [14]. The main difference between psychological safety and trust is the focus of the belief: while psychological safety is a group norm belief, trust is a belief about the other person [4]. Team psychological safety involves but goes beyond interpersonal trust. It describes a team climate characterized by interpersonal trust and mutual respect in which people are comfortable being themselves characterized by the absence or presence of a blend of trust, respect for each other's competence and caring about each other as people.

Edmondson argues that the basic process of psychological safety is information exchange and that trust is a core element in creating psychological safety, but that they are conceptually distinct from one another [9].

What does research tell us about psychological safety?

The reverse is also true – without psychological safety people feel anxious and threatened, and these emotions can reduce cognitive and behavioural flexibility and responsiveness. This phenomenon is described over and over again and different terms were found for this effect: 'threat rigidity' (or the 'frightened rabbit' effect) [15], learning inhibitions [16], saving face as a reaction to threat [17]. In organizations where people feel threatened the willingness to speak up, engage in problem-solving or take initiative for innovation is fairly small [18–22].

Generally speaking, psychological safety enables people to use their full potential. It leads to various behavioural outcomes (see Figure 7.1). Organizations and work environments differ in their need for psychological safety – the more resources are scarce and the more uncertainty is in a work environment or task the more psychological safety takes effects. So interestingly enough psychological safety seems to be most important when we are on an innovative journey – high task uncertainty and never enough resources.

Figure 7.1 draws on an extensive overview article by Edmondson and Lei but also other research around psychological safety and tries to show the main effects of it [2]:

- First, psychological safety has consistently been shown to play a role in enabling performance. Implementation success, quality improvement and team performance in general are only a few outcomes named here. But it also fosters creative outcomes like divergent thinking or experimenting. If we include studies about trust (based on the concept of psychological safety) then we also see a connection to the outcomes of enhancing negotiation effectiveness or problem-solving as well as constructive conflict (read more about this in the chapter about striving for excellent ideas). Behaviour linked to creative performance is for example speaking up in team settings, contribution during idea generation, supporting communication among team members, and

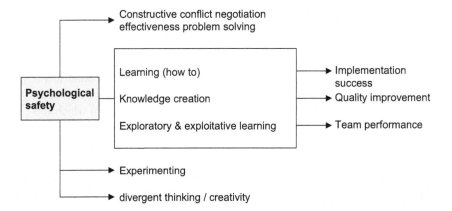

Figure 7.1 Effects of psychological learning

enhancing learning (discussing errors, sharing and seeking information, and reflecting on alternative viewpoints in the team).

- Second, psychological safety enables learning and learning processes. 'Fear-less' learning behaviour is associated with distinct behaviours: asking for help, admitting an error and seeking feedback. All three ways of interacting could lead to losing face in an unsafe environment and therefore only with a climate of psychological safety will this behaviour be supported [23–24]. Edgar Schein argued in line with these results that psychological safety also reduces learning anxiety (a state occurring when people are presented with data that contradict their expectations or hopes). With psychological safety, he reasons, individuals are free to focus on collective goals and problem prevention rather than on self-protection [25].
- Third, team members speak up at work if they experience psychological safety. Speaking up, or voice, is defined as upward-directed communication and it provides an important mechanism for team members to challenge the status quo and offer new ideas [26–27]. This is of particular significance in the context of 'shop-floor' problem-solving teams where their relative status in the organization can act as an inhibitor to their contribution of ideas – a theme we'll return to in a later chapter. William Kahn's work supports this, suggesting that with psychological safety people are willing to engage themselves physically, cognitively, and emotionally in their work. Losing face or protecting one's status is no longer needed. He focuses especially on the fact that psychological safety gives team members the belief that they will not be ridiculed and be given the benefit of the doubt [10].
- Fourth, probably most interesting for innovation, is the direct effect of enhancing experimenting as behaviour and divergent thinking in general (see more in the next section).

Research note: psychological safety and team cohesiveness

It's important not to confuse psychological safety in the group with team cohesiveness. As we will see in the next chapter on task orientation, cohesiveness can reduce the team's ability to challenge and to take risks. Instead psychological safety is about giving the sense of trust and support which enables group members to explore. Various research studies point to the same conclusion – effective creative teams need both constructive conflict and challenge but also the psychological safety context within which this can take place without damaging the group or its motivation.

One last word for those who believe that accountability is neglected because of psychological safety. Amy Edmondson explained this well in one of her talks: accountability and psychological safety are not two poles of one dimension but rather two different dimensions opening up a room for different working zones.

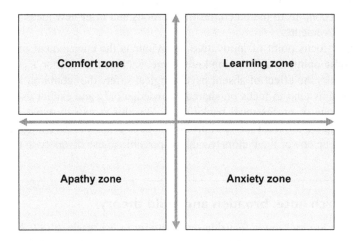

Figure 7.2 Psychological safety zones

The comfort zone is where psychological safety is high but accountability is low. Here people feel like at a nice little chat but will not develop or innovate because everything is nice as it is. The anxiety zone has the opposite values: high on accountability and low on psychological safety. We cited enough research showing the outcome of this kind of working environment. Being low on both dimensions is called the apathy zone, because neither do you have any personal connections and good feelings in the team but you also have no emphasis on accomplishments. The learning zone is the contrast: high on psychological safety and high on accountability. Here people thrive, they move forward with a safety net due to psychological safety and they engage more in exploitative and explorative behaviour.

Why is practising psychological safety important for creativity?

In essence psychological safety makes it OK for people within the group to take risks and to engage in learning behaviour. Under these conditions team members will develop new ideas and solutions rather than maintaining the status quo. Anderson and West introduced participative safety as one dimension of their team climate model and showed extensively (in different settings and countries) that psychological safety is a group process leading to innovation and creativity [7–8, 12, 28–31]. Team members are more likely to propose new ideas and innovative problem solutions due to their lack of anxiety about negative judgement. Psychological safety facilitates team innovation involving frequent dialogical interaction and widespread participation in the group, conducted in a positive, supportive and interpersonally safe environment [32]. The more people can participate in decision-making through interaction and information sharing, the more likely they are to commit to the outcomes of decisions and offer new ideas about possible improvements.

Another focus point of innovative behaviour is the engagement into exploring different opinions and sharing knowledge. Kathleen O'Connor, a professor at Cornell, calls the effect of absent psychological safety the 'common knowledge effect'. Teams tend to focus on shared knowledge only and cannot use diversity of knowledge or professional background. But this is exactly what innovation needs: using the different views of problem and/or solutions. Psychological safety is found to be one of the factors to make it possible to use diversity in teams [2].

Research note: broaden and build theory

Barbara Fredrickson is focusing on positivity in her research [33–34]. The broaden and build theory hypothesizes that positive emotions broaden the scope of attention and thought-action repertoires (see Figure 7.3). Thus, unlike negative emotions, which promote and support specific action, positive emotions prompt individuals to pursue a wider range of thoughts and actions than is typical. Over the long run, positive emotions can promote the discovery and development of people's strengths and resources and therefore resources (e.g. physical, social, intellectual and psychological resources) can be built. These resources are durable; they outlast the transient emotional states that led to their acquisition. Consequently, they can function as reserves that can be accessed in times of need.

This has also effects for creativity. People with positive emotions show patterns of thought that are notably unusual, flexible and inclusive, creative, integrative, open to information and efficient [35–36]. Isen has suggested that positive affect produces a 'broad, flexible cognitive organization and ability to integrate diverse material' [37].

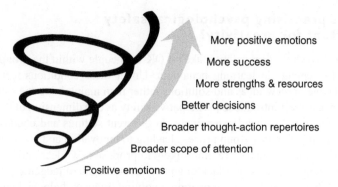

More positive emotions
More success
More strengths & resources
Better decisions
Broader thought-action repertoires
Broader scope of attention
Positive emotions

Figure 7.3 Fredrickson's broaden and build theory

To summarize, psychological safety is important because it enables a context within which:

- Behaviours linked to creative performance can be fostered – for example, speaking up in team settings, contribution during idea generation, supporting communication among team members, and enhancing learning (discussing errors, sharing and seeking information, and reflecting on alternative viewpoints in the team.
- Learning processes can operate – 'fear-less' learning behaviour is associated with distinct behaviours: asking for help, admitting an error and seeking feedback.
- Speaking up – using 'voice' – is enabled allowing for challenge within organizational contexts.
- Constructive conflict can take place without risk of team fragmentation, loss of motivation or other negative effects.

There are many practical situations where building this kind of climate is important to innovation – for example:

- Enabling an optimum level constructive conflict within 'front end' innovation teams where there is high uncertainty and a need for open-ended exploration;
- Facilitating start-up entrepreneurial teams to build trust and share risks under conditions of high uncertain, high ambiguity and resource constraint;
- Supporting participation of shop-floor employees in innovation – for example through quality circles and *kaizen* groups.

The practical takeaway from the literature on psychological safety is that this positive interpersonal climate, which is conducive to learning and performance under uncertainty, does not emerge naturally. It needs building and reinforcing, and that's the focus of the next section.

What is the skill set around practising psychological safety?

In this section we give you some help to find out where you and your team stand in terms of your competence around psychological safety. Here we give a short description of the competence itself and then we follow with a list of ten skills that are needed to master the different aspects of psychological safety. In the questionnaire you can check for yourself where you are. This self-check gives a hint of what elements of psychological safety you can further develop and what elements are already a strength. If you are interested where your team is at and what are areas of improvement and areas of strength, then fill in the team check. The competence description and the given skills are rooted in the research we described in the chapter.

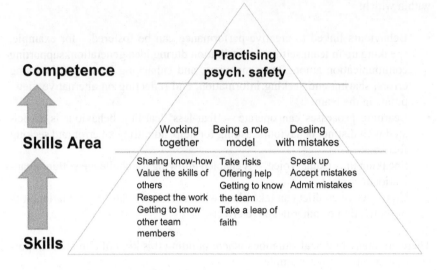

Figure 7.4 Competence practising psychological safety

Programming the GPS for the creativity journey – what's your position?

Psychological safety is about feeling safe in a team environment to take inter-personal risks [36]. As a single person one acts as a role model for psychological safety, either enabling or limiting it. Team members respect each other, sharing know-how and being prepared to admit errors. It depends on building a sense of mutual trust and provides a platform on which it is safe to engage in 'constructive conflict' – something which we'll see in the next chapter is a key resource in creative teams.

Next we offer you a skill self-check on psychological safety (Table 7.1). We suggest you rate yourself with a five-point rating scale:

1 = Not like me at all
2 = Not much like me
3 = I cannot decide if I am good or bad at it, just doing OK
4 = Describes me to a good extent (but not exactly)
5 = Describes me exactly

And again please think about the central tendency and try to come up with some specific examples of how you behave relative to the skill areas as described in Table 7.1.

Table 7.1 Self-check psychological safety

#	Core behavioural skills	Your score (1–5)	For instance write at least one example of your own
1	I give my team members a leap of faith.		
2	I take risks in my team (and I am a role model).		
3	I respect the work of other team members.		
4	I'm ready to admit when I'm wrong or when I have made an error.		
5	I speak up in the presence of others and encourage others to do so.		
6	I try to get to know other team members to build up a strong relationship.		
7	I'm happy to share my know-how with others in the team.		
8	I'm happy to offer help to others and to ask for it when needed.		
9	I accept that mistakes are made and do not hold them against my fellow team members.		
10	I value and try to use the (unique) skills and talents of the other team members.		

Team check

Next we offer you a team-level skill check on psychological safety in your team that is strongly influenced by Edmondson [9]. We suggest you rate your team with a five-point rating scale:

1 = Not like us (my team) / I do not agree at all
2 = Not much like us / I disagree to a certain extent
3 = I cannot decide if we are good or bad at it, just doing OK / I neither agree nor disagree

4 = Describes us to a good extent (but not exactly) / I agree somewhat
5 = Describes us exactly / I completely agree

Now think about your team – how far are these statements a reflection of your experience (Table 7.2)?

For a template of a team rating poster go to the companion website.

Table 7.2 Team-check psychological safety

#	Team behaviours	Score (1–5)	For instance write at least one example
1	It is safe to take a risk on this team.		
2	It is easy to ask other team members for help or to get them to accept it from other team members.		
3	Members of this team are able to bring up problems and tough issues without raising objections.		
4	Mistakes made by team members are not held against them.		
5	No one on this team would deliberately act in a way that undermines the efforts of another team member.		
6	Team members accept differences and value distinct talents of team members.		
7	Team members are eager to share information about what does and does not work.		
8	There are good relationships between the team members.		
9	On this team, it is easy to speak up.		
10	There's a high level of trust in this group.		

Working out at the gym – how to train your skills in psychological safety

In his work reviewing successful teams at Google in the 'Aristotle' project Charles Duhigg developed a number of checklists and guidelines for managers. We would like to complement that perspective with looking at some of the tools and techniques which can help develop psychological safety from the standpoint of the individual and the team.

Use the clock

One of the simplest tools is to ensure that people get equal amounts of 'air time'. Most groups have a mixture of people who will speak up easily and those who prefer to stay back; the risk is that the voices of the latter group may not always be heard. So a useful team rule is to find ways of ensuring everyone gets the chance to speak and is encouraged to do so by the others.

Short, frequent feedback

Another simple but useful tool is to have short feedback sessions after every meeting. Typical and useful questions to focus on might be:

- Did everybody have enough speaking time?
- Did everybody say what they wanted to or is there something not addressed? Was somebody behaving differently?
- Is there anything we as a team can do in order to help somebody perform better?

The purpose of the sessions is to be aware of the shared and supportive environment which the team needs and is able to create.

What's good for a couple is good for a team

Another exercise draws on the work of John and Julie Gottman, who made detailed studies of what a good marriage is made of. In several longitudinal studies he found patterns for good marriages and those for marriages that are likely to fail [38]. While we are not concerned with marital issues here, there are many elements of his approach which are helpful in the context of developing psychological safety.

John Gottman and his colleagues propose a ratio of positivity to negativity during conflict situations of 5:1 (positive behaviour is classified as, for example, listening to the needs of the other; negative behaviour is, for example, ignoring the other or just saying no). It is not about the individual person's ratio but about the ratio of the couple. The researchers found they could predict with an accuracy of 90% whether couples would stay married or not due to that ratio.

Marcial Losada and Barbara Fredrickson applied a similar approach in the context of business meetings and suggested a ratio correlated with business success of around 3:1 [39]. Whether success can be reduced to a simple ratio is less important than the underlying idea of developing a positive and psychologically safe environment through the use of positive communication.

Practise 'intelligent failure'

As we've seen throughout the book the idea of failure is intimately linked with creativity and innovation. We need to experiment and by their nature experiments fail – but offer rich opportunities to learn from them. Unfortunately many teams have a culture in which it is difficult to own up to mistakes and so important learning opportunities are lost; even worse, the same mistakes get repeated. Every good project management handbook uses some form of wrap-up/review meeting at which lessons for improvement are supposed to be captured. And a key element in 'agile innovation' is the idea of a 'double loop learning' opportunity to help review and reset the goals [40].

One important aspect of such formalized sessions is that they enhance psychological safety. Well-managed reviews can help move the agenda away from blaming individuals to identifying underlying messages and lessons. But they don't happen by accident – there needs to be a style of exploratory questioning which draws out the mistakes and failures in ways which are non-threatening and which allow for psychological safety. So positive reinforcement (along the lines of 'thanks for standing up. I think it is worthwhile to discuss what we can do to make this better or not to happen again') becomes a key approach to practice.

Be curious and focus on learning

Linked to this is the approach which Amy Edmondson recommends, one which accepts fallibility. She offers three tips to enhance psychological safety:

- Frame the work as a learning problem, not as an execution problem.
- Be a model of curiosity and ask a lot of questions.
- Acknowledge your own fallibility.

You can find links to Amy Edmonson's work via the companion website.

Build relationship maps

Another useful approach draws on techniques around what is often called 'sensitivity training' – how to make groups more effective through developing a better mutual understanding and awareness. Amy Edmondson's work places emphasis on being able to 'read' others and understand how they are feeling, what they are thinking and so forth as a way of developing the understanding which leads to greater psychological safety.

One useful tool here is to build a relationship map – effectively a framework through which you can understand the others in your team. Here are some questions you can ask in order to get to know each other better in a team and to understand more about each other:

- What do you like about your job?
- What project did you like in the last two years?
- What are your strengths for this field of work?
- What was your best day at the job?
- What was your worst day?
- What puts you under pressure?
- What would you do if you haven't followed your current career path?
- What are your plans for the next five years?
- What would you love to do?

Appreciative inquiry

This organizational development method seeks to engage stakeholders in self-determined change. The model was created by David Cooperrider and Suresh Srivastva [41], and proposed as a method to create new ideas, images, and theories that would lead to social innovations. A useful definition is:

> Appreciative Inquiry is about the co-evolutionary search for the best in people, their organizations, and the relevant world around them. In its broadest focus, it involves systematic discovery of what gives 'life' to a living system when it is most alive, most effective, and most constructively capable in economic, ecological, and human terms. AI involves, in a central way, the art and practice of asking questions that strengthen a system's capacity to apprehend, anticipate, and heighten positive potential. It centrally involves the mobilization of inquiry through the crafting of the 'unconditional positive question' often-involving hundreds or sometimes thousands of people. In AI, the arduous task of intervention gives way to the speed of imagination and innovation; instead of negation, criticism, and spiraling diagnosis, there is discovery, dream, and design.
>
> (p. 3, [42])

> You can read more about the technique on the companion website.

Practice developing trust

Trusting each other is at the heart of psychological safety, as we tried to indicate in the introduction to this chapter. In many fields learning the skills of trusting others is part of the curriculum – for example in drama school. There are several exercises and games where you can explore and practice developing trust via team projects – for example building towers, devising new machines to stop eggs breaking and so forth. While they may have an element of fun, they are also powerful vehicles for learning.

> You can find some examples of teambuilding games on the companion website.

End of chapter summary

- Psychological safety is the shared belief that the team is safe for interpersonal risk-taking.
- It has effects on a variety of outputs as team performance, implementation success and quality improvements as well as on constructive conflicts and creativity.
- In particular it has a positive effect on learning and learning behaviour of teams. Psychological safety increases exploring and experimenting of team members.
- Another behaviour connected to psychological safe team is speaking up or 'voice'. A positive safe environment is one in which team members openly voice their opinions and address mistakes and feel safe to admit to mistakes of their own.
- High psychological safety is linked to highly creative teams where team members engage with each other, exchange know-how, ask for help, address possible mistakes or threats to reach the vision, and respect each other.

References

[1]   Duhigg, C. (2016). *Smarter faster better.* New York, NY: Penguin Random House.

[2] Edmondson, A. C., & Lei, Z. (2014). Psychological safety: The history, renaissance, and future of an interpersonal construct. *Annual Review of Organizational Psychology and Organizational Behavior, 1*, 23–43.

[3] Edmondson, A. C. (2002). The local and variegated nature of learning in organizations: A group-level perspective. *Organization Science, 13*, 128–146.

[4] Edmondson, A. C. (2003). Speaking up in the operating room: How team leaders promote learning in interdisciplinary action teams. *Journal of Management Studies, 40*, 1419–1452.

[5] Edmondson, A. C., Higgins, M., Singer, S., & Weiner, J. (2016). Understanding psychological safety in health care and education organizations: A comparative perspective. *Research in Human Development, 13*, 65–83.

[6] Anderson, N., & West, M. A. (1996). The Team Climate Inventory: Development of the TCI and its applications in teambuilding for innovativeness. *European Journal of Work and Organizational Psychology, 5*, 53–66.

[7] West, M. A. (1990). The social psychology of innovation in groups. In M. A. West & J. L. Farr (Eds.), *Innovation and creativity at work: Psychological and organizational strategies.* Chichester, UK: Wiley.

[8] West, M. A., & Anderson, N. R. (1992). Innovation, cultural values, and the management of change in British hospitals. *Work and Stress, 6*, 293–310.

[9] Edmondson, A. (1999). Psychological safety and learning behavior in work teams. *Administrative Science Quarterly, 44*, 350–383.

[10] Kahn, W. A. (1990). Psychological conditions of personal engagement and disengagement at work. *Academy of Management Journal, 33*, 692–724.

[11] Kessel, M., Kratzer, J., & Schultz, C. (2012). Psychological safety, knowledge sharing, and creative performance in healthcare teams. *Creativity and Innovation Management, 21*, 147–157.

[12] Anderson, N. R., & West, M. A. (1998). Measuring climate for work group innovation: Development and validation of the Team Climate Inventory. *Journal of Organizational Behavior, 19*, 235–258.

[13] Mayer, R. C., Davis, J. H., & Schoorman, F. D. (1995). An integrative model of organizational trust. *Academy of Management Review, 20*, 709–734.

[14] McAllister, D. J. (1995). Affect- and cognition-based trust as foundations for interpersonal cooperation in organizations. *Academy of Management Journal, 38*, 24–59.

[15] Staw, B. M., Sandelands, L. E., & Dutton, J. E. (1981). Threat-rigidity effects in organizational behavior: A multilevel analysis. *Administrative Science Quarterly, 26*, 501–524.

[16] Argyris, C. (1982). The executive mind and double-loop learning. *Organizational Dynamics, 11*, 5–22.

[17] Brown, R. (1990). Politeness theory: Exemplar and exemplary. In I. Rock (Ed.), *The legacy of Solomon Asch: Essays in cognition and social psychology* (23–37). Hillsdale, NJ: Erlbaum.

[18] Dutton, J. (1993). The making of organizational opportunities: An interpretive pathway to organizational change. In L. L. Cummings & B. M. Staw (Eds.), *Research in organizational behavior* (Vol. 15, 195–226). Greenwich, CT: JAI Press.

[19] MacDuffie, J. P. (1997). The road to 'root cause': Shop-floor problem-solving at three auto assembly plants. *Management Science, 43*, 479–502.

[20] Detert, J. R., & Burris, E. R. (2007). Leadership behavior and employee voice: Is the door really open? *Academy of Management Journal, 50*, 869–884.

[21]   Liang, J., Farh, C.I., & Farh, J.L. (2012). Psychological antecedents of promotive and prohibitive voice: A two-wave examination. *Academy of Management Journal*, *55*, 71–92.

[22]   Baer, M., & Frese, M. (2003). Innovation is not enough: Climates for initiative and psychological safety, process innovations, and firm performance. *Journal of Organizational Behavior*, *24*, 45–68.

[23]   Michael, D.N. (1976). *On learning to plan & planning to learn*. San Francisco: Jossey-Bass.

[24]   Lee, F. (1997). When the going gets tough, do the tough ask for help? Help seeking and power motivation in organizations. *Organizational Behavior and Human Decision Processes*, *72*, 336–363.

[25]   Schein, E.H. (1993). On dialogue, culture, and organizational learning. *Organizational Dynamics*, *22*, 40–51.

[26]   Premeaux, S.F., & Bedeian, A.G. (2003). Breaking the silence: The moderating effects of self-monitoring in predicting speaking up in the workplace. *Journal of Management Studies*, *40*, 1537–1562.

[27]   Van Dyne, L., & LePine, J.A. (1998). Helping and voice extra-role behaviors: Evidence of construct and predictive validity. *Academy of Management Journal*, *41*, 108–119.

[28]   Anderson, N.R., & West, M.A. (1994). *The Team Climate Inventory (TCI) and group innovation: A psychometric test on a Swedish sample of work groups*. Windsor, UK: ASE/NFER-Nelson Press.

[29]   Burningham, C., & West, M.A. (1995). Individual, climate, and group interaction processes as predictors of work team innovation. *Small Group Research*, *26*, 106–117.

[30]   West, M.A. (1997). *Developing creativity in organizations*. Leicester, UK: The British Psychological Society.

[31]   West, M.A., & Anderson, N.R. (1996). Innovation in top management teams. *Journal of Applied Psychology*, *81*, 680–693.

[32]   Prince, G.M. (1970). *The practice of creativity*. New York, NY: Harper and Row.

[33]   Fredrickson, B.L. (2001). The role of positive emotions in positive psychology: The broaden-and-build theory of positive emotions. *American Psychologist*, *56*, 218.

[34]   Fredrickson, B.L., & Branigan, C. (2005). Positive emotions broaden the scope of attention and thought-action repertoires. *Cognition & Emotion*, *19*, 313–332.

[35]   Isen, A.M., Johnson, M.M., Mertz, E., & Robinson, G.F. (1985). The influence of positive affect on the unusualness of word associations. *Journal of Personality and Social Psychology*, *48*, 1413.

[36]   Isen, A.M. (2001). An influence of positive affect on decision making in complex situations: Theoretical issues with practical implications. *Journal of Consumer Psychology*, *11*, 75–85.

[37]   Isen, A.M. (1990). The influence of positive and negative affect on cognitive organization: Some implications for development. In N. Stein, B. Leventhal & T. Trabasso (Eds.), *Psychological and biological approaches to emotion* (75–94). Hillsdale, NJ: Erlbaum.

[38]   Gottman, J.M. (1994). *What predicts divorce?: The relationship between marital processes and marital outcomes*. Hillsdale, NJ: Lawrence Erlbaum.

[39]   Fredrickson, B.L., & Losada, M.F. (2005). Positive affect and the complex dynamics of human flourishing. *American Psychologist*, *60*, 678.

[40]   Argyris, C. (1982). *Reasoning, learning, and action: Individual and organisational*. San Francisco: Jossey Bass.

[41] Cooperrider, D.L., & Srivastva, S. (1987). Appreciative inquiry in organizational life. In R. W. Woodman & W. A. Pasmore (Eds.), *Research In organizational change and development* (Vol. 1, 129–169). Stamford, CT: JAI Press.
[42] Cooperrider, D.L., & Whitney, D. (2001). A positive revolution in change. In D.L. Cooperrider, P. Sorenson, D. Whitney, & T. Yeager (Eds.), *Appreciative inquiry: An emerging direction for organization development* (9–29). Champaign, IL: Stipes.

Chapter 8

Supporting ideas

Chapter objectives

By the end of this chapter you will:

- Understand the role which support for ideas plays in creativity;
- Recognize the key skills associated with support in a team environment searching for ideas;
- Develop awareness of tools and techniques to help being able to successfully support ideas;
- Reflect on and be able to develop your own skills and those of the team around supporting idea-generation.

Introduction

Imagine this. You're on stage at a comedy club doing an improvisation routine with two actors you've never met before. The performance is based on the audience shouting out the names of people and things and you have to weave them into the story you are creating together. It's not simply a story – the audience is expecting you to keep the flow going and to be funny as well. You glance across at the woman who is currently speaking and she smiles broadly at you and suddenly adopts the pose of a patient speaking confidentially to her doctor about her embarrassing illness, throwing you the line 'of course, I know you understand, Doctor, now tell me what to do!'

You have several options. You can freeze and look blindly at her, panic in your eyes as you are aware of the audience expecting you to say something funny to keep the flow of the sketch going. That kills the moment, leaving everyone disappointed and your colleague angry at you for leaving her stranded inside her role. Or you bluster and splutter something about not knowing what she is talking about – again putting her back on the spot so that she has to find a credible way out of the situation she has created. Or you can accept the scenario she has just thrown at you, try and climb inside the personality of the doctor she has just cast you as, and find a funny way of taking the conversation forward.

Welcome to the world of shared creativity. This is the kind of situation which happens all the time in improvisational theatre – someone tosses you an idea and instead of blocking it, or analyzing it, or finding reasons why it won't work, you accept it, adapt it and take it forward. It's not confined to theatre – the same thing happens in music (watch any band taking an instrumental break and they are doing the same thing, tossing phrases around and catching them, modifying them, weaving new ideas into them). Become a fly on the wall at an advertising agency and watch how they come up with new ideas for marketing campaigns – the same free-flowing toss and catch of ideas. Sit in a product development meeting, join a process improvement team on the factory floor, huddle together in a coffee shop trying to work out the details of your great new idea for a start-up social venture. These are all versions of the same scenario – coming up with and developing good ideas. And they emerge through a process of team creativity which is high on the dimension of support.

Coming up with an idea is a tricky thing – but launching it into the big wide world is a second major challenge. It's risky – there are so many ways in which the fragile green shoots of an idea can be damaged as they poke their heads out of the ground for the first time. And it's unpredictable – other people can be destructively critical, they can ignore the idea, they can reject it, or they can support and nourish it, helping it to grow. So, as we explained in the last chapter there needs to be psychological safety among the team members.

Here's another example. Recently, one of us was part of a start-up team. In former discussions we had discussed our vision, unique selling proposition (USP), and possible market opportunities. We were quite happy about this. While discussing our new business model we started to have more and more trust in each other as people and in our competences to do this together and be successful. (To be fair, we knew each other quite intimately before, having worked together in the same company for over 15 years. So there was no question about our level of psychological safety.) We were sitting in this room together and our goal for the next two hours was to find a name for the business. We were looking for something that would reflect our core business idea and the USP of the new company, something that we could use internationally (at least in German- and English-speaking countries) and not an abbreviation of our names. Easy?

No – despite the conditions of trust and psychological safety we were still stuck. We were looking into blank faces. This is where you start to think about another group process important for innovation – the supporting of ideas.

Michael West defines support as 'the expectation, approval and practical support of attempts to introduce new and improved ways of doing things' [1]. It's something which can make a powerful difference to creativity within teams – as this definition suggests, even the expectation that an idea won't find support can be enough to stop its creator expressing it. And the reverse is true; where creativity is concerned teams can often be greater than the sum of their parts. As Anna-Maja Nisula and Aino Kianto suggest, 'When individuals get help and support from others in developing and implementing their ideas, this enables them to be more innovative. This seems likely to be true in temporary and informal contexts as well as in more stable situations' [2].

It's a property of the team and the interpersonal relationships between members. It's easy to slip into thinking that providing support is somehow a role for management, especially within larger organizations. But what about start-ups where no real hierarchy is established, what about teams working with high autonomy, like our improv theatre troupe? Even in situations where the manager plays a key role in preparing teams for action, he or she still spends much of the time on the sidelines while the team plays out their game on the centre of the pitch. That's not to say that there isn't an important role of management for helping and enabling support, creating the conditions within which creative behaviour in teams can flourish. In this chapter we'll focus particularly on team member behaviours and skills team members needed to support innovation but we will explore the role of leadership (and the many forms it can take) in Chapter 10 (managing creativity).

> You can explore a number of team-based activities which highlight the importance of support on the companion website.

Creativity in action: putting the trust into Pixar

We've already seen that organizations with a track record of creativity don't get there by accident. Anyone might get lucky once, but being able to repeat the trick depends on putting key behaviours in place and reinforcing them so that they become 'the way we do things around here'. Pixar's continuing success in pushing the boundaries of animated and CGI filmmaking provides a good example – and one of the key lessons they learned was to create a group which was high on support – the 'brain trust'.

As Ed Catmull, CEO, explains in his book Creativity Inc., the origin of this lay in the experience of making Toy Story:

> During a crisis that occurred while making that film, a special relationship developed among John, Andrew, Lee, and Joe, who had remarkable and complementary skills. Since they trusted one another, they could have very intense and heated discussions; they always knew that the passion was about the story and wasn't personal. Over time, as other people from inside and outside joined our directors' ranks, the brain trust expanded to what it is today: a community of master filmmakers who come together when needed to help each other.

So what is supporting ideas?

Activity: your own experiences with team and supporting ideas

Think about your last team experiences about generating or implementing ideas. This could be at work or school, in a sports team or an organizational committee. Write down your best and your worst experiences concerning supporting ideas.

When did you experience it? Who was supporting you (one person, the whole team, part of the team)? How were you supported? How did it feel and what were your conclusions?

When we talk about support the first behaviour that comes to mind is verbal support – acknowledging the birth of a 'good' idea. But support goes a long way beyond that, including, for example:

- Building and further shaping the idea, helping develop it;
- Providing physical evidence of idea support – the pat on the back, the group 'whoop!' of shared celebration;
- Giving resources to help the idea develop – time, energy, physical resources;
- Social recognition – it is the public acknowledgement of ideas and how important and meaningful they are;
- Constructive criticism and feedback – one of the worst fates a new idea can suffer is unconditional acceptance. As we've seen, good ideas are the product of many iterations to refine and elaborate them and other group members can provide valuable and focused input to this process. Effective creative teams are not simply 'yes' teams! For this read through our next chapter about pushing the frontier.

Creativity in action: improving the climate for creativity

The consultancy ?Whatif! specializes in Creative Problem-Solving for and with clients. They make use of many techniques linked to brainstorming and have a simple framework using the metaphor of helping nurture early shoots of ideas.

They need plenty of SUN:

S = Support, encourage;
U = Understand, listen to the ideas;
N = Nurture, help them to grow.

And avoid too much RAIN:

R = React, respond directly and judge the ideas rather than listen to them;
A = Assume, bringing your preconceptions and your interpretation too quickly;
I = Insist on your viewpoint, be closed in your mind to other ways of seeing the problem;
N = Negative, closing down and shutting out possible new directions, saying 'no' to the idea in its early undeveloped form.

What does research tell us about supporting ideas?

It's a truism to say that teams are more than just a group of people thrown together. Think about your own experience – the whole is often less than the sum of the parts. While groups ought to be a positive environment for enabling creativity, this isn't always the case, as Table 8.1 suggests. There's a 'dark' side to bringing together different people and expecting them to contribute effectively.

The challenge of understanding what goes into effective group performance has been explored in many research studies and we have learned a great deal about what is often termed 'group dynamics'.

For a 'deeper dive' around team working for innovation see the companion website.

One of the famous models which is widely used to capture our understanding comes from Bruce Tuckman, who suggested that the process of building an effective team from a group of individuals involves four stages – forming, storming, norming and performing (see Figure 8.1) [3]. This rather simplistic view has the advantage of being easy to remember – and it's not a bad representation

Table 8.1 Advantages and disadvantages of group-level creativity

Advantages	Disadvantages
Diversity – more different ideas	'Groupthink' – social pressures to conform
Volume of ideas – 'many hands make light work'	Lack of focus – 'too many cooks spoil the broth'
Elaboration – multiple resources to explore around the problem	Group dynamics and hierarchy
Rich variety of prior experience	Political behaviour, people following different agendas

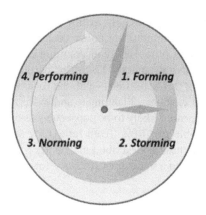

Figure 8.1 Tuckman's team development model

of what goes on. As we have already seen, effective creative teams need psychological safety, they need to trust each other, but they need actual support in order to develop and implement ideas. In our next chapter you will see that learning to 'fight' is another competence teams need to develop, starting in the storming phase with experiencing conflicts about performance norms and how to handle interpersonal conflicts and being able to use them constructively as a performing team.

Next to Tuckman's model there is a wealth of research around group dynamics, and we can draw upon this to help understand the importance of support. In particular:

• Support for innovation is identified as an antecedent of both team innovation [4] and individual innovation [5–6]. In common with studies at the team level, previous research has consistently found that a climate supportive of innovation is conducive to organizational-level innovation [7].
• Innovation literature suggests that innovation is more likely to occur in contexts (whether organizational or group) in which there is support for innovation or innovative attempts are rewarded rather than punished [8–9].
• Physical support is shown to be important for innovation [10–11]. (We'll come back to this point in Chapter 10.)
• Mihaly Csikszentmihalyi emphasizes the importance of social recognition of creative work [12].

As we have seen, teams learn and embed behaviours which help them play an effective role in creativity – they develop norms, ways of working which help them. But to do this requires a capacity for reflection – reviewing and improving on what they do.

Reflexivity

Michael West describes team reflexivity as 'the extent to which group members overtly reflect upon, and communicate about the group's objectives, strategies (e.g. decision-making) and processes (e.g. communication), and adapt them to current or anticipated circumstances' [1]. We're particularly interested in this chapter in the first part of this definition – with the focus on reflection rather than the planning and action elements. Planning – and even more so, acting – are of course important but are more likely to be consequences of reflexivity rather than an integral and inseparable part of it. Team reflexivity is a look into the mirror, very similar to self-awareness as described in Chapter 5.

Its importance emerges in a number of studies – for example:

• Michael West and Claudia Sacramento:

Reflexivity can lead to radical change in the status quo and sometimes the creative destruction of existing processes. For example, one plastics packaging production team which we studied succeeded in removing management controls on intervention so they were able to discuss product specifications, pricing and delivery dates directly with customers. Productivity and quality improved, and the time from customers placing their orders to delivery dropped by a factor of three.

[13]

• Pascale Widmer, Michaéla Schippers and Michael West cite several studies showing that reflexivity is a significant predictor of senior managers' ratings of the effectiveness and creativity of teams [14].
• Reflexivity had a significant influence on both product innovativeness and on new product performance [15].
• A study among 145 software development teams found further proof of the positive relationship between reflexivity and effectiveness as rated by team members [16].
• A study among thirty-two organizational teams performing complex, ill-defined tasks showed a moderating effect of reflexivity on the relationship between minority dissent and team innovation and effectiveness. Results showed more innovation and greater effectiveness in teams with low levels of minority dissent, but only when there was a high level of team reflexivity [17].

Since team reflexivity is a process that takes place between team members rather than within one person, it is worth taking a closer look at what is needed to enable it. Research by Amy Edmondson found that psychological safety is an important element for team reflexivity [18]. She looked at the management of errors within health care teams (see more in Chapter 9). Reflecting about the errors in order to learn from them and improve processes only happened under conditions of high perceived psychological safety. She also looked at the Hubble telescope development project and found similar results. European research on error management broadly supports Edmondson's interpretations [19–20]. Teams benefit from taking time out from working to reflect on their work habits, objectives, team processes and outcomes.

Sharing and building on ideas

At the heart of a supportive creative team are ways on enabling a free flow of ideas, both in terms of originating them and then refining and elaborating them. So it is worth looking at what research can tell us about support mechanisms and behaviours around this theme.

One of the most widely used approaches to team creativity is brainstorming. Its origins lie in the work of Alex Osborn, an advertising executive who was interested in the ways in which groups came up with ideas – and the difficulties they encountered. In particular he suggested that the early stage criticism of half-formed ideas was destructive and that allowing a period of non-evaluation (simply letting the ideas flow) might be of value. His approach developed the idea of postponing judgment and explored ways of generating large numbers of ideas from which good ones would emerge ('quantity breeds quality').

You can find a description of brainstorming as a tool on the companion website.

Looking at brainstorming is helpful here because it offers a kind of laboratory within which we can see the effect of group processes and the role of support.

Alex Osborn described the technique in his book *Applied Imagination* and set out certain behavioural rules for participants [21]. The most important are:

- Bring all ideas forward, whatever comes to mind;
- No criticism and no evaluation of outspoken ideas;
- Use ideas of others to further elaborate on them.

His ideas were picked up on and diffused rapidly, and many writers and researchers have elaborated on the basic models; brainstorming also forms a key part of the 'Creative Problem-Solving' (CPS) approach. Their interest stems from the fact that brainstorming appears to offer a helpful structured approach to group idea generation, offering both high volume and high quality of ideas [22–23]. But almost from the outset there has been criticism of the approach and a debate as to whether group brainstorming really is helpful [24].

> You can find a detailed description of CPS on the companion website.

One important test for the effectiveness of brainstorming lies in research on nominal as opposed to real groups. Nominal groups are collections of individuals who do not interact as a group; in this condition individuals write down their ideas in a group without discussing it with other members of this group. In group brainstorming people sit and talk together, sharing the ideas. In both conditions all collected ideas are then used as the group brainstorming result. Despite its widespread popularity most scientific research shows rather weak results for brainstorming as a way of enhancing production and quality of ideas. Nominal group brainstorming shows better research in laboratory research than real group brainstorming. Groups often generated only half as many ideas as similar numbers of solitary performers and no higher quality of ideas emerged [25–27]. In one of the few real-life research studies Marvin Dunnette and colleagues presented problems to groups of four (in total forty-eight research scientists and forty-eight advertising personnel) in a mining and manufacturing company [28]. In the individual conditions more ideas than in the group condition were produced and had the same quality of ideas. Interesting is the fact that individual brainstorming was even better when it was preceded by a group participation [29]. But also with this effect they are contradictory results [30].

So what's the problem? Why is group brainstorming apparently less effective, despite the apparent logic of Osborn's claims? Several explanations have been researched and there seems to be a consensus that it is various elements of social influence which are the problem. For example, people with a tendency to anxiety may feel inhibited in social situations like brainstorming or where there is a fear of evaluation [31–34].

Another factor might be social loafing (which we encountered in the chapter on creating and sharing visions). However research suggests that even when individual performance is measured the effect is still there speaking strongly against a social loafing effect in brainstorming sessions [27, 32, 35–37].

Paul Paulus and Mary Dzindolet suggest that low performance could have become a performance standard for the groups [32, 34, 37]. But norms are not made in one go. Other researchers reason that groups suppress dissenting opinions very fast and therefore do not outperform individuals in brainstorming [38]. Summarizing, we can see three main explanatory processes: evaluation apprehension, social comparison and production blocking [39].

We want to look a little bit more into the cognitive explanation of production blocking. Production blocking describes the effect that while someone is uttering an idea the other person is listening and can no longer think about her/his own ideas, therefore the production of ideas is blocked [33, 39]. Bernard Nijstad and colleagues conducted three experiments to look more closely at the decrease of

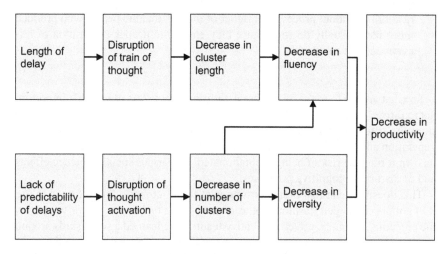

Figure 8.2 SIAM model

productivity in group brainstorming sessions. In the first experiment they looked at the effect of length of delay. The longer the person had to wait to bring in her/his idea, the more production of ideas suffered, but more interesting for understanding the mechanisms of brainstorming is the result that the train of thoughts were disturbed and the length of semantic clusters decreased [40].

In Chapter 2 we looked at the importance of associative thinking in creativity – the way the brain makes connections between different elements. One theory has explored the idea of 'semantic networks', arguing that the longer the gap between connections the more divergent the underlying thinking. Conversely short gaps between semantic nodes are associated with convergent thinking.

In a second experiment they varied the predictability of delays, so sometimes there was a short delay, then there was a long one or no delay at all. Here different effects could be found from the first experiment. Here the number of semantic clusters decreased, leading to a decrease in diversity. These experiments are very promising and show a model (see Figure 8.2) that is helpful for improving brainstorming and can with further development explain the differing results.

Another stream of research has explored further the cognitive approach, especially looking to rebut the assumption that idea generation is just a random cognitive process [41–42]. Various experiments have shown that creative idea generation is linked to the expert knowledge ('deep domain knowledge') held by participants and that

> manipulations that increase the quantity of ideas will probably only enhance the quality of ideas if these manipulations encourage deeper exploration of relevant domain knowledge. This suggests that the high correlation between

quantity and quality usually observed in brainstorming studies is not the result of a random process, but rather of the fact that the people who produce more ideas usually do so because they engage in deeper exploration of relevant content categories.

[43]

So what are we to make of this brainstorming debate? As always it's important not to throw the baby out with the bathwater. On the plus side we know that brainstorming offers a useful structure, a framework of 'rules' which can guide the generation and elaboration of ideas within a group. But we also know that used on its own it runs the risk of being 'contaminated' by various social influence effects and of disrupting cognitive processes.

This doesn't mean that brainstorming is at fault but rather that we need to use it in a more 'managed' fashion, not as a stand-alone technique. As we've seen in the preceding chapters, effective creative teams have learned a set of skills around psychological safety – so they can create conditions which can mitigate the problems of social influence. And we will see that understanding and deploying competences around striving for excellent ideas, including 'constructive controversy', is also helpful.

It's also important to remember that much of the research on creativity in groups has been done under laboratory conditions, and often this involves relatively inexperienced students doing tasks for the first time. In the world of practice creative teams are often experienced and have learned and improved the ways in which they work – including how they approach and 'manage' a brainstorming session. We've given several examples – Pixar, Lockheed's Skunk Works, IDEO – these and many others suggest that there is what might be termed a 'maturity effect', with effective creative teams learning to use tools like brainstorming to good effect.

> You can read more about these experienced teams – and watch a video of IDEO in action – on the companion website.

Scott Isaksen reviewed over fifty studies looking at brainstorming and found more support for brainstorming than not. This has maybe to do with some ways that have to be followed besides the regular brainstorming rules in order to make brainstorming effective. Here are some of them, and all of them are research-based:

- Use experienced facilitators or moderators who can help guide the process of brainstorming and ensure the negative influences are minimized [44].
- Train the group in the brainstorming rules.
- Take five-minute breaks in the brainstorming sessions to enhance reflexivity.

This supports the view of many practitioners that the rules and the enforcement of the rules are the most important aspect of the technique and separates brainstorming from mere idea-generation in a group. All of this suggests that brainstorming – as a framework for generating and elaborating ideas – can work. But it depends on a context which is supportive and learning that requires the kind of reflexivity discussed in this section.

Why is supporting ideas important for creativity?

Let's summarize the key points we've been trying to make in this chapter:

- Support matters – it makes a difference, the context within which creative teams can operate.
- It emerges through reflection and development; it's an equivalent of self-awareness.
- It's something which experienced teams learn and develop – we can think of a 'maturity model' for problem-solving teams.

Developing skills around being a supportive team member are important. For example in the world of theatre and film the typical model is that a temporary team comes together and works intensively for a short time to create something. Doing this well is not simply a matter of technical skills; it requires additional behavioural skills enabling team players to quickly form a high-performance team. This might well include elements of creative conflict, but the skill set also allows for resolving those conflicts so that they do not disrupt the work of the group. For many actors these skills are honed in drama school through a series of exercises designed to develop an understanding of support and how it can be built as a team resource.

You can find a video interview with actor and theatre director Piers Ibbotson talking about this skill set on the companion website.

The same pattern is increasingly true of project teams in other kinds of organizations, where the skills of working together and co-creating depend on developing a supportive context. It is rarely the case that teams are hand-picked, so the skills involved in moving quickly from Tuckman's forming stage to the performing stage are particularly relevant, especially if the team involves a diverse set of skills and backgrounds.

And in the context of a start-up venture, building a team which can quickly perform, underpinned by the kind of trust and idea shaping described in the chapter, is of critical importance because resources and time are scarce.

What is the skill set around supporting ideas?

In this section we'll try to help you locate where you stand in relation to navigating the creativity journey. We'll begin with a short description of the competence itself and then go on to list ten skills that are needed to master the different aspects of supporting ideas. In the questionnaire you can check for yourself where you are. This self-check gives a hint which elements you can further develop and what elements are already a strength. The competence description and the given skills are rooted in the research we described in the chapter as well as the Creative Behaviour in Teams (CbiT) approach [45].

Programming the GPS for the creativity journey – what's your position?

The competence supporting ideas includes two modes of support: ideally (mostly via communications) and physically. In our self and team checks we focus mostly on the communication side of support: sharing your own ideas and asking others explicitly for their ideas. It is about mutual exchange of ideas but also about helping this exchange take place. Another quite different facet of this competence is reflection about what's going on in the team creative process in order to become better. Giving and receiving feedback is an important part of it.

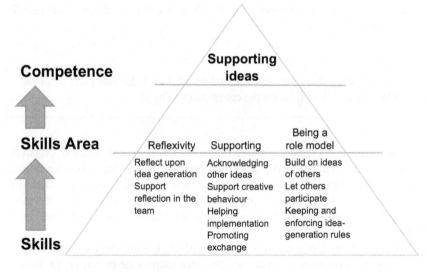

Figure 8.3 Competence supporting ideas

Next we offer you a skill self-check on supporting ideas (Table 8.2). We suggest you rate yourself with a five-point rating scale:

1 = Not like me at all
2 = Not much like me
3 = I cannot decide if I am good or bad at it, just doing OK
4 = Describes me to a good extent (but not exactly)
5 = Describes me exactly

And again please think about the central tendency and come up with some examples of your previous behaviour before just believing you are good or bad at these skills.

Table 8.2 Self-check supporting ideas

#	Core behavioural skills	Your score (1–5)	For instance write at least one example of your own
1	I promote the mutual exchange of ideas.		
2	I build on the ideas of others.		
3	I let others participate in my ideas.		
4	I do not criticize the ideas of others during idea generation.		
5	If needed, I moderate our process of moving forward to foster support for ideas.		
6	I actively help to implement our ideas.		
7	I actively support creativity and make it clear that it is a desirable behaviour.		
8	I reflect upon our way of approaching idea generation and implementation.		
9	I support team reflection.		
10	I acknowledge other team members for their ideas.		

Team check

Next we offer you a team-level skill check on supporting ideas (Table 8.3) that is among other research based on Anderson and West's Team Climate Inventory (TCI) scale [4]. We suggest you rate your team with a five-point rating scale:

1 = Not like us (my team) / I do not agree at all
2 = Not much like us / I disagree to a certain extent
3 = I cannot decide if we are good or bad at it, just doing OK / I neither agree nor
    disagree
4 = Describes us to a good extent (but not exactly) / I agree somewhat
5 = Describes us exactly / I completely agree

Table 8.3 Team-check supporting ideas

#	Team behaviours	score (1–5)	for instance write at least one example
1	Team members engage in mutual exchange of ideas.		
2	Team members interact to develop new ideas together.		
3	Team members assist each other in developing new ideas.		
4	Team members help each other to implement new ideas.		
5	Team members provide and share resources to help in the application of new ideas.		
6	Team members provide practical support for new ideas and their application.		
7	In this team the time needed to develop new ideas is taken.		
8	Ideas are seen as property of the team, not of individual team members.		
9	Team members engage in team reflection to become better in creative settings.		
10	Reflection is seen as a necessary way to improve creative output.		

Now think about your team – how far are these statements a reflection of your experience?

For a template of a team rating poster go to the companion website.

Going to the gym – how to train your skills in supporting ideas

These skills are best trained in a team setting. But whether it is your creative working team or other team settings you use for training practices, that is, of course, up to you.

Enhancing reflexivity

It sounds obvious, but one of the most powerful tools is simply to ask the group to reflect on the task and the ways in which they are working on it – their interactions, their roles, their process. Research has shown that this is valuable; in an experiment testing this simple intervention [46] the results confirmed groups in the reflexivity condition clearly performed better. So try to incorporate some kind of team and task review into the project. Part of the review will be about group processes and is likely to contribute to enhancing psychological safety; part of the review will be about the tasks and enhance support for innovation.

You can find some creativity team exercises which encourage reflection, including the use of observers to help reflect back to the rest of the group, on the companion website.

Sharing know-how

Another simple intervention is to share implicit knowledge about the creative task. It is often difficult to articulate 'tacit' knowledge but doing so can be helpful in terms of team development [47]. A suggested process would be:

1   Immediately after the task, ask every team member to reflect upon the task that just happened for three to five minutes.
2   All team members share their thoughts in turn, with someone acting to record their input on a flip chart.

3   Now start a discussion about what was helpful for the team and what was maybe not so helpful.
4   Try to develop recommendations for improving the next time the group works on a similar task.

Brainstorming by the rules

Although creativity is often about challenging and even breaking rules in the context of brainstorming, it is worth reverting to a disciplined approach. Osborn's original idea was not simply to let people shout out ideas but rather to bring a degree of structure and process to the context of group problem-solving. So it's worth reminding ourselves of the key 'rules' – and then trying to observe this discipline. The main principles are:

*   Defer judgement
*   Go for quantity
*   Build on ideas of others
*   List every idea
*   One conversation at a time.

Improving your brainstorming

Once you have the core discipline then there is scope for variations on the theme, deploying the idea in different ways to enhance creativity. Some examples of variants include:

*   Brainwriting. In a first step, everybody writes down his/her ideas; then, the team members share their ideas, and in a last step ideas are clustered or complemented. There is less interference and people can in the beginning concentrate on what's in their mind.
*   Incubation between brainstorming: rather than having one brainstorming session of forty-five minutes, do short sessions of ten minutes each with intervals of five to ten minutes.
*   Another helpful method is to break down the general challenge into several narrow topics and give people prior to the brainstorming session some reflection time. This can increase the originality of the ideas and the number in total.

Learning to look

Creativity in a team is a process you can watch and observe. Become a good observer by looking at different phases of the creative process in a team, watch out for the different levels of teamwork (each individual vs. the whole team and its dynamic), and pay attention to verbal and non-verbal interactions of the team members.

You can find some activities/games on the companion website which set up creative tasks and also include an explicit role and process for observers – see the New Product Development game and other teambuilding exercises.

Another technique to help develop observation and reflection skills is the 'fish-bowl'. This requires a minimum of six people and the first step is to split into two subgroups, A and B.

Subgroup A sits in the middle in a circle and discusses a predetermined topic. Subgroup B stands or sits outside of the circle and observes the discussion without interfering. It is best to assign for each member of subgroup A an individual observer from subgroup B. Then formulate the appropriate topic for a ten- to fifteen-minute discussion. Since reflexivity is an important part of establishing psychological safety, it is useful to start with topics addressing different aspects of psychological safety for the particular team. Two of the best topics we have encountered are: What does psychological safety mean *for us*? And what can we do in our team to establish psychological safety (the more concrete the answers the better)? It's important to emphasize that this exercise is about the discussion process of the subgroup rather than the results (although it is still valuable to get to some results). It's also helpful to capture and display the results on some shared medium – a flipchart for example – rather than as notes in a notebook.

After the discussion time, somebody from subgroup A should present the results as a summary. Then comes the feedback round; each assigned observer from subgroup B gets together with their counterpart from subgroup A and gives them feedback about what strengths and competencies they have observed and what they did in order to enhance psychological safety. After the five-minute feedback session you can exchange the roles of subgroups A and B and do it all over again with a second question that helps to continue the discussion. We recommend a shared feedback session at the end that also enables the entire team to discuss their opinions regarding psychological safety and ask the team members about conclusions.

End of chapter summary

*   Supporting ideas is one of the four group competences we describe in this book. We describe the skills that each team member can acquire in order to support idea generation and implementation from within the team.
*   Two main elements make up the building blocks for supporting ideas: sharing and building on ideas and reflexivity. Many studies show the effectiveness of both elements for creativity.

- Reflexivity on the team level has close links to the competence self-awareness on the individual level.
- Sharing and building on ideas can happen in many forms, for example building and further shaping an idea, providing physical evidence of idea support, giving resources to help the idea develop and social recognition.
- Brainstorming is an approach developed to enable the support of many different ideas. Besides the early positive findings, there is also research showing detrimental effects of brainstorming concerning quantity and quality of ideas. Enforcing the rules, brainwriting, and using 'incubation' time are guidelines to help improve idea generation sessions.

References

[1]   West, M.A. (1990). The social psychology of innovation in groups. In M.A. West & J.L. Farr (Eds.), *Innovation and creativity at work: Psychological and organizational strategies*. Chichester, UK: Wiley.

[2]   Nisula, A.-M., & Kianto, A. (2016). The antecedents of individual innovative behaviour in temporary group innovation. *Creativity and Innovation Management, 25*, 431–444.

[3]   Tuckman, B.W. (1965). Developmental sequence in small groups. *Psychological Bulletin, 63*, 384–399.

[4]   Anderson, N.R., & West, M.A. (1998). Measuring climate for work group innovation: Development and validation of the team climate inventory. *Journal of Organizational Behavior, 19*, 235–258.

[5]   Pirola-Merlo, A., & Mann, L. (2004). The relationship between individual creativity and team creativity: Aggregating across people and time. *Journal of Organizational Behavior, 25*, 235–257.

[6]   Yuan, F., & Woodman, R.W. (2010). Innovative behavior in the workplace: The role of performance and image outcome expectations. *Academy of Management Journal, 53*, 323–342.

[7]   Patterson, M.G., West, M.A., Shackleton, V.J., Dawson, J.F., Lawthom, R., Maitlis, S., . . . Wallace, A.M. (2005). Validating the organizational climate measure: Links to managerial practices, productivity and innovation. *Journal of Organizational Behavior, 26*, 379–408.

[8]   Amabile, T.M. (1983). *The social psychology of creativity*. New York, NY: Springer.

[9]   Kanter, R.M. (1983). *The change masters: Corporate entrepreneurs at work*. London: Allen & Unwin.

[10]   Mumford, M.D., & Gustafson, S.B. (1988). Creativity syndrome: Integration, application, and innovation. *Psychological Bulletin, 103*, 27–43.

[11]   Abbey, A., & Dickson, J.W. (1983). R&D work climate and innovation in semiconductors. *Academy of Management Review, 26*, 362–368.

[12]   Csikszentmihalyi, M. (2014). *Flow and the foundations of positive psychology: The collected works of Mihaly Csikszentmihalyi*. Dordrecht: Springer.

[13]   West, M., & Sacramento, C. (2012). Creativity and innovation: The role of team and organizational climate. In M.D. Mumford (Ed.), *Handbook of organizational creativity* (359–385). London, UK: Academic Press.

[14] Widmer, P. S., Schippers, M. C., & West, M. A. (2009). Recent developments in reflexivity research: A review. *Psychology of Everyday Activity*, *2*, 2–11.

[15] Lee, M. D. (2008). Three case studies in the Bayesian analysis of cognitive models. *Psychonomic Bulletin & Review*, *15*, 1–15.

[16] Surprisingly, however, in their study team reflexivity was not related with higher efficiency as measured by self-rating questionnaires. They explain this unexpected result by the fact that engaging in reflexive actions involves additional time and other costs (such as training of reflexive behaviour, altering work strategies etc.). The thought that reflexivity might have a downside in terms of resource consumption is interesting, indeed, and points to the fact that reflexivity might be more helpful in certain circumstances, such as detrimental performance and/ or adverse working conditions, as discussed before. The predominance of studies highlighting the positive effect of reflexivity on performance, however, indicate that this downsize is usually offset by its gains in terms of effectiveness benefits.

Hoegl, M., & Parboteeah, P. (2006). Autonomy and teamwork in innovative projects. *Human Resource Management*, *45*, 67–79.

[17] In a more recent study, De Dreu (2007) found positive direct effects of reflexivity on team effectiveness as rated by supervisors and on learning. Moreover, reflexivity had a moderating function insofar as it was a necessary condition to foster positive effects of team interdependence: Outcome interdependent teams engaged in more information sharing, learned more, and had higher levels of team effectiveness, but only if task reflexivity was high.

De Dreu, C.K.W. (2007). Cooperative outcome interdependence, task reflexivity and team effectiveness: A motivated information processing approach. *Journal of Applied Psychology*, *92*, 628–638.

De Dreu, C.K.W. (2010). Social conflict: The emergence and consequences of struggle and negotiation. In S. T. Fiske, D. T. Gilbert, & G. Lindzey (Eds.), *Handbook of social psychology* (5th ed.). New York, NY: Wiley.

[18] Edmondson, A. C., & Lei, Z. (2014). Psychological safety: The history, renaissance, and future of an interpersonal construct. *Annual Review of Organizational Psychology and Organizational Behavior*, *1*, 23–43.

[19] Edmondson, A. C. (1996). Learning from mistakes is easier said than done: Group and organizational influences on the detection and correction of human error. *Journal of Applied Behavioral Science*, *32*, 5–28.

[20] Edmondson, A. (1999). Psychological safety and learning behavior in work teams. *Administrative Science Quarterly*, *44*, 350–383.

[21] Osborn, A. (1953). *Applied imagination: Principles and procedures of creative problem solving*. New York, NY: Scribner.

[22] Prince, G. M. (1970). *The practice of creativity*. New York, NY: Harper and Row.

[23] Rawlinson, J. G. (1981). *Creative thinking and brainstorming*. Farnborough, Hants: Gower.

[24] Taylor, D. W., Berry, P. C., & Block, C. H. (1958). Does group participation when using brainstorming facilitate or inhibit creative thinking? *Administrative Science Quarterly*, *6*, 22–47.

[25] Diehl, M., & Stroebe, W. (1987). Productivity loss in brainstorming groups: Toward the solution of a riddle. *Journal of Personality and Social Psychology*, *53*, 497–509.

[26] Larey, T., & Paulus, P. (1999). Group preference and convergent tendencies in small groups: A content analysis of group brainstorming performance. *Creativity Research Journal, 12*, 175–184.

[27] Mullen, B., Johnson, C., & Salas, E. (1991). Productivity loss in brainstorming groups: A meta-analytic integration. *Basic and Applied Social Psychology, 12*, 3–23.

[28] Dunnette, M. D., Campbell, J., & Jaastad, K. (1963). The effect of group participation on brainstorming effectiveness for two industrial samples. *Journal of Applied Psychology, 47*, 30–37.

[29] Bouchard, T. J., Jr., & Hare, M. (1970). Size, performance, and potential in brainstorming groups. *Journal of Applied Psychology, 54*, 51–55.

[30] Paulus, P. B., Larey, T. S., & Ortega, A. H. (1995). Performance and perceptions of brainstormers in an organizational setting. *Basic and Applied Social Psychology, 17*, 249–265.

[31] Paulus, P. B., Larey, T. S., & Dzindolet, M. T. (2002). Creativity in groups and teams. In M. E. Turner (Ed.), *Groups at work: Theory and research* (319–338). New York, NY: Psychology Press.

[32] Camacho, L. M., & Paulus, P. B. (1995). The role of social anxiousness in group brainstorming. *Journal of Personality and Social Psychology, 68*, 1071.

[33] Diehl, M., & Stroebe, W. (1991). Productivity loss in idea-generating groups: Tracking down the blocking effect. *Journal of Personality and Social Psychology, 61*, 392–403.

[34] Larey, T. S., & Paulus, P. B. (1999). Group preference and convergent tendencies in small groups: A content analysis of group brainstorming performance. *Creativity Research Journal, 12*, 175–184.

[35] Karau, S. J., & Williams, K. D. (1993). Social loafing: A meta-analytic review and theoretical integration. *Journal of Personality and Social Psychology, 65*, 681–706.

[36] Kerr, N. L., & Bruun, S. (1983). The dispensability of member effort and group motivation losses: Free rider effects. *Journal of Personality and Social Psychology, 44*, 78–79.

[37] Paulus, P. B., & Dzindolet, M. T. (1993). Social influence processes in group brainstorming. *Journal of Personality and Social Psychology, 64*, 575–586.

[38] Hackman, J. R., & Morris, C. G. (1975). Group tasks, group interaction process, and group performance effectiveness: A review and proposed integration. *Advances in Experimental Social Psychology, 8*, 45–99.

[39] Diehl, M., & Stroebe, W. (1987). Productivity loss in brainstorming groups: Toward the solution of a riddle. *Journal of Personality and Social Psychology, 53*, 497–509.

[40] Nijstad, B. A., Stroebe, W., & Lodewijkx, H.F.M. (2003). Production blocking and idea generation: Does blocking interfere with cognitive processes? *Journal of Experimental Social Psychology, 39*, 531–548.

[41] Rietzschel, E. F., Nijstad, B. A., & Stroebe, W. (2007). Relative accessibility of domain knowledge and creativity: The effects of knowledge activation on the quantity and originality of generated ideas. *Journal of Experimental Social Psychology, 43*, 933–946.

[42] Nijstad, B. A., & De Dreu, C. K. (2002). Creativity and group innovation. *Applied Psychology, 51*, 400–406.

[43] Stroebe, W., Nijstad, B. A., & Rietzschel, E. F. (2010). Chapter four-beyond productivity loss in brainstorming groups: The evolution of a question. *Advances in Experimental Social Psychology, 43*, 157–203.

[44]   Oxley, N. L., Dzindolet, M. T., & Paulus, P. B. (1996). The effects of facilitators on the performance of brainstorming groups. *Journal of Social Behavior and Personality*, *11*, 633.

[45]   Goller, I. (2011). *Creativity in an organisational context: Innovation capability in R&D departments.* Doctoral dissertation, ETH Zürich.

[46]   Gurtner, A., Tschan, F., Semmer, N. K., & Nägele, Ch. (2007). Getting groups to develop good strategies: Effects of reflexivity interventions on team process, team performance, and shared mental models. *Organizational Behavior and Human Decision Processes*, *102*, 127–142.

[47]   Muller, A., Herbig, B., & Petrovic, K. (2008). The explication of implicit team knowledge and its supporting effect on team processes and technical innovations: An action regulation perspective on team reflexivity. *Small Group Research*, *40*, 28–51.

Chapter 9

Pushing the frontiers

Chapter objectives

By the end of this chapter you will:

*   Understand the role which constructive conflict and stretching for good ideas plays in creativity;
*   Recognize the key skills associated with pushing the frontiers in creativity;
*   Develop awareness of tools and techniques to help fight for ideas;
*   Reflect on and be able to develop your own skills and those of the team around pushing beyond the first ideas.

Introduction

> Excellent firms don't believe in excellence – only in constant improvement and constant change.
>
> —Tom Peters

Imagine yourself just after your plane has crashed in the Arabian desert. You and several others have survived and the plane, although wrecked, affords you a little shelter. The radio is out and you have only limited water and food – what do you do? It's a classic movie script and one which quickly brings into play the creativity of the group – not to mention the tensions and conflicts around which solutions might be followed and how to make them happen. In this particular version the impossible target towards which the group stretches is to fashion a new flying machine out of the wreckage and somehow persuade it to fly far enough and long enough to bring them back to civilization. And the novel describes the challenges the group faces around coming up with ideas, arguing and even fighting over which solution to adopt, coping with the despair of trying something which fails, motivating themselves to try again along a new line – and all the while stretching for an impossible goal – to rescue themselves.

> You can read the story 'The Flight of the Phoenix' by Elleston Trevor [1] and also watch a movie of the same name.

Sounds fanciful, the stuff of gripping but unrealistic fiction. Then how about this challenge? You are part of a team working in the aerospace industry and you've just been tasked with the objective of coming up with a brand new plane which will travel faster than anything else currently in the skies. Oh, and you have to do so against a loudly ticking clock, with very limited resources and without some of the key information you need (which is top secret and held by your big competitor).

Here's another. You work in a large automotive company facing major competitive pressures – you haven't got enough money to buy the latest machinery, you're desperately short on key skills and your materials costs are crippling you because you have to import so much. If you could sell more cars then things might improve – but your market is small and varied; the only way your company can survive is by being more flexible, producing many different models to meet the needs of different customers. The trouble is that every time you change from making one car design to the next you have to stop everything and reset the machines – especially the giant body ogresses that squash out the panels – so that knocks your productivity hard on the head. Your boss has just met with you and asked that you reduce the set-up time for these presses from the one day it currently takes to less than half a day!

A third challenge. You're part of a theatre company about to put on a performance of *Hamlet* and you have six weeks before the curtain goes up. You're working with a group of actors you have never met before; you have no scenery, costumes or set design; and the play has been performed all around the world by thousands of other groups going back over a period of 400 years. How do you come up with something which is original, exciting, memorable and challenging? How do you create a new experience of a well-established play?

These are all real examples and they highlight the need to develop capability around key aspects of team creativity:

- Striving towards a stretching goal;
- Decision making among diverse viewpoints;
- Managing creative conflict;
- Motivating under crisis conditions;
- Coping with failure and setback – mobilizing persistence.

The 'impossible aeroplane' trick is one which Lockheed Martin have been repeating for over 70 years using their famous 'skunk works' approach. Hand-picked teams work in a very distinctive way separated from the rest of the 'normal' organization to deal with stretching challenges (like making an aeroplane invisible to radar – the basis of today's stealth technology).

You can read more about the Skunk Works approach and examples on the companion website.

Shigeo Shingo was Toyota's Chief Engineer and developed a powerful approach to reducing set-up time not just for body presses but also for a wide range of factory equipment. Where it once took as much as a day to reset equipment, it can now be done in minutes; his approach has been borrowed by many other sectors looking to change things over fast – hospital operating theatres, aircraft terminals and even Formula 1 motor racing pit stops. He achieved the original goal of cutting the set-up time from a day to half a day by working with a specialist team over several months. When he finally and proudly presented the results of their efforts to Taichi Ohno, the chief executive, the response was 'Very good. Now go and cut the time in half again!'

You can read more about Shingo and setup time reduction on the companion website.

The challenge to any performing arts group is to come up with something with impact, something perceived as innovative by the audience, and to do so in a short period of writing and rehearsal, often bringing a group of strangers together for the first time to do so; and in performing Shakespeare there is the additional constraint that there are only a small number of well-known scripts to use. Yet there are still magical performances to be found not only in big cities and with big name companies like the Royal Shakespeare Company, but also in small theatres and venues around the world. The secret of success is down to shared creativity and a key factor in energizing this is the stretching urgent task which the team faces.

You can watch a video interview exploring this theme with Piers Ibbotson, former director with the Royal Shakespeare Company, on the companion website.

Let's look at the last world championship in soccer. Who won? Was it the team with the best individual players? Then it should have been Argentina with Lionel Messi, voted the world's best footballer in 2014. But in fact it was the German team that won the World Cup. Most observers talk about the way they played together, used their skills and tried not to outdo each other, how they worked as a *team*. And this was not only about psychological safety and a good team spirit. They were fighting to be good, striving for excellence.

You can find an example on the companion website of the approach taken by the design consultancy IDEO in their team-based competences around solving problems – and especially a video demonstrating its application over a five-day challenge in front of the TV cameras.

Another part of this challenge is perseverance. We saw in Chapter 4 that this matters at an individual level and the same is true of the group. They need to sustain themselves even when the going gets tough (as it inevitably will). And they also have to counter the effects of other group members wanting to give up – there have to be norms within the group around challenging and pushing each other forward.

Larry Leifer of the d.school at Stanford talks about the need to look for the 'wow-ideas'. This is what happens when we do not stop after the first round of brainstorming but when we go on and 'fight' for the best ideas. He points out that it is rare to find an innovation success story in which the best solution emerged after the first round of ideas. In reality – as we have been arguing throughout the book – it involves a long and sometimes arduous journey.

Think about the example of James Dyson, which we described earlier in our chapter on willpower. It is full of 'not just there yet' moments. This is where pushing the frontiers comes into the picture. What perseverance is for the individual, a shared sense in striving for excellent ideas is for teams. It is about the ability of a team to use the diverse information within a team, to fight for the best solution during decision-making (e.g. deciding which idea to follow-up) and the general norm in a team to search and struggle for the best idea rather than accept an easy solution or try to maintain a happy harmonious atmosphere.

So what's behind this? The competence around pushing the frontiers consists of two main areas:

* Stretching search for excellent ideas (refining, elaborating, and improving – making it wow);
* Constructive challenge in decision-making.

Creativity in action: picturing creativity

Pixar is one of the most successful film production companies. But their ability to repeat the trick isn't an accident – they have learned this competence and honed and refined it over the years. As Ed Catmull, founder and president of Pixar, explains:

> What's equally tough, of course, is getting talented people to work effectively with one another. That takes trust and respect, which we as managers can't mandate; they must be earned over time. What we can do is construct an environment that nurtures trusting and respectful relationships and unleashes everyone's creativity. If we get that right, the result is a vibrant community where talented people are loyal to one another and their collective work, everyone feels that they are part of something extraordinary, and their passion and accomplishments make the community a magnet for talented people coming out of schools or working at other places.

You can explore more of the Pixar case on the companion website.

What does research tell us about pushing the frontiers?

As we saw in the introduction to this section, there is a helpful model developed by Neil Anderson and Michael West which sees four factors as being of key significance in creative team performance – shared vision, group support, psychological safety, and our current focus, task orientation. Teams with a high task orientation and one which involves stretching towards some notion of 'excellence' do well. But it's important to note that this is not about 'happy teams = successful teams' – rather it is the internal struggles and their constructive resolution which matters. Teams with a high score on harmonic social contacts are rarely able to produce great outcomes [2].

Dean Tjosvold and colleagues describe a similar concept which they call 'constructive controversy'. In other words the team push themselves towards a shared challenging target and they push each other to go further; importantly they also have ways of working which help them get there without falling apart! [3].

Finding stretch goals is not hard – today's turbulent environment means that there are plenty to go around and survival is often dependent on achieving them! The issue is not the goal but how to motivate the team to work effectively towards it – and this isn't just a matter of picking people. For a start we need to confront some of the negative factors in group work – what are the forces in group behaviour which can militate against such focused stretch behaviour?

Why groups are often not creative

Several forces within groups act against shared creativity:

- Social loafing
- Negative norms
- Groupthink

- Conformity pressures
- Minority influence
- Choice shift.

Social loafing

A well-documented group effect is social loafing. This effect has been studied by a number of researchers; it suggests that we can hide within a group and act as a passenger, letting others do the work and take the strain [4–6]. A French professor of agricultural engineering, Max Ringelmann, began exploring this phenomenon in the late nineteenth century and published an influential study in 1913. His work involved the simple idea of getting individuals and groups of various sizes to pull on a rope and he measured how hard they pulled. As Figure 9.1 shows, the more people in the group the less work they did! [4].

Many other researchers began to explore the concept and used different versions of the experiment. In particular Bibb Latané and his team showed that the decreased performance of groups was not a result of poor co-ordination but emerged because of individuals reducing their efforts. His team's experiments involved blindfolding students and giving them headphones which blocked out all external noise. They were then asked to shout as loudly as possible; when they believed they were alone they shouted louder than when they believed they

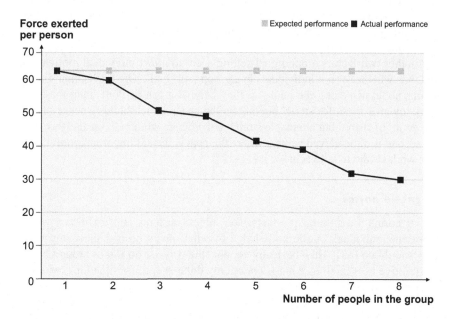

Figure 9.1 Social loafing

were part of a group. By the time the group size reached six individuals were only shouting at one-third of their capacity! The same effect emerged if they were asked to clap or make sounds in other ways; the researchers concluded that 'If the individual inputs are not identifiable the person may work less hard. Thus if the person is dividing up the work to be performed or the amount of reward he expects to receive, he will work less hard in groups' [5].

The effect seems to emerge regardless of culture and appears in a variety of tasks. One area where it becomes of particular significance is in the growing world of online communities where virtual collaboration is involved. 'Free riding' is an alternative name for the experience where some members take advantage of the group's efforts without putting something back. Linus Dahlander made a fascinating study of the shared creativity around development of music software in the online community around 'Propellerhead' and noted the free riding effect but also the ways in which the community acted to 'police' this, effectively excommunicating those who didn't contribute. As he put it, the group norm emerged around the idea that 'you have to give to get' [7].

At the heart of social loafing is a belief that 'my individual effort won't matter to the group' – so ways of countering this depend on mobilizing a different belief. One way is to set up a sense of competition – everyone's effort matters. Everybody has to fight in order to survive and therefore nobody can get a free ride. Problem solved. But researchers Johnson and Johnson reviewed over 500 studies looking at this effect and found that the more complex the task the better co-operation is as a strategy than competition. Meaning that we need a different solution to foster innovation than just competitive environments [8]. Other studies suggest that when people think the task is important they do less loafing [9]. And when the group is important to the members, they identify strongly with it and they work harder [10].

Another two factors around goal setting seem to affect individual motivation, and thus whether or not individuals in a group will 'loaf'. The first is their expectations about achieving the goal – if they believe it can be done, then they will work towards it. So for stretching targets the group which builds a sense of 'we can do it,' of shared but attainable stretch will engage more individual effort. And the second is of perceived value – where the goal is seen as important, individuals will work harder to help achieve it [11–12].

Negative norms

Social norms are cultural products like values, customs and traditions, which represent individuals' basic knowledge of what others do and think and what they should do [13]. They basically set out 'the way we do things around here'. Descriptive norms tell us what is commonly done in specific situations, whereas injunctive norms give us information about what should be done [14]. Norms can be endorsed by small groups, such as a team or an office, but also by cultures or societies. They can guide behaviour in a certain situation or environment [15].

As social beings, individuals learn when and where it is appropriate or not to say certain things, to use certain words, to discuss certain topics or wear certain clothes [13–15].

Negative norms for creativity are those around accepting the status quo – 'it's good enough, why change?,' 'if it ain't broke, don't fix it' and so forth. And their flip side is a positive group culture with norms which support innovating. Michael West and his colleagues give a good example of such group norms at work in a UK manufacturing organization [16]:

> The main production team on the shop floor had complained about the storage of dirty materials, and was given time off from production, and a budget to design and build a suitable storage extension for the factory. They completed the task under time and budget, and thereafter began to suggest many more innovations in work processes and structures. The team, as a result of their good experience, developed clear norms for valuing and discovering innovation. In effect, the team was provided with the conditions to be innovative and, once empowered, proactively fostered innovative team norms.

What you can read in this example is that successful behaviour leads to behavioural norms. Norms in themselves are not competences but the ability to reflect about them; to remind one another to go for it can be described as competence important for creativity and innovation.

Groupthink

In 1972 Irving Janis published an article describing patterns about how group decisions were made – particularly the ones which went badly wrong [17]. His analysis of foreign policy disasters included the poor decision by the United States to invade the Bay of Pigs. His analysis suggested that there was a strong motivation to make decisions in a way that enhances the team cohesiveness regardless of the cost for effectiveness or quality of decisions. He gave this phenomenon the memorable label 'groupthink' – and it has been found in a wide variety of other situations where decision making comes under stress.

One of the tragic examples in the world of innovation was the Challenger Space Shuttle disaster back in 1986. The team involved in the launch were under enormous pressure to succeed and as a result didn't speak up to challenge the decision to launch, even though they knew of, and were worried about, a problem with the O-ring seals in the engine. The failure of that seal led to fuel leakage and the subsequent explosion [18].

Sadly this was not an isolated example; almost fifty years earlier the novelist Nevil Shute was working in the aircraft industry at a time when there was intense international rivalry and therefore strong pressure from outside to succeed. Developing the new generation of passenger carrying airships – the R100 and the R101 – put great stress on the teams involved so that, again, they felt unable to speak up and challenge when they had technical concerns. In 1930 the R101 crashed into a hillside killing all those on board [19]. As he commented, 'it was impossible for them to admit mistakes without incurring discredit far exceeding their deserts, for everybody makes mistakes from time to time. Surely no engineers were ever placed in so unhappy a position'

Groupthink emerges when there is a strong external pressure to succeed, but a climate within the group which does not allow for challenge or questioning. Group cohesiveness is very strong which tends to stifle individual concerns for the greater harmony of the group. Peer pressure can also reinforce this – the underlying sense being that 'if you disagree you can always leave the team'.

Countering the tendency towards groupthink depends on being able to challenge, on diversity of information and opinion and on developing internal group norms which allow for and encourage constructive challenge.

Strain for consensus

A similar effect is called *strain for consensus*. The outcome of this effect is comparable to groupthink and conformity pressures – poor group decisions are made.

This could be because of a desire for consensus or to put it differently, not enough open dissent in a team [20]. Another explanation focuses on the pressure to be aligned, for example a moral pressure to be with the team, that leads to premature closure [17]. So, strain for consensus could be seen as a cluster of all effects to behave according to a majority or a felt pressure towards one opinion in a team.

Conformity pressures or the power of majority

Back in 1956 researcher Solomon Asch devised a simple experiment in which he asked participants to compare the length of lines. They were invited to compare the reference line in the Figure 9.2 with three others (A, B, C) and decide which has the same length. Try it yourself.

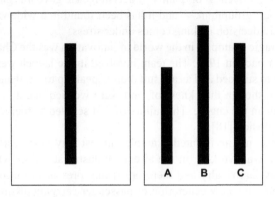

Figure 9.2 Input for conformity pressure experiments

Working on your own you would almost certainly say that 'C' is the closest. But if you were doing this as part of a group and all the other members in your group had already said it was 'B' there is a strong chance that you would also say 'B'. In eighteen trials carried out in his experiment, typically two-thirds of participants gave this answer!

Solomon Asch developed a variety of elegant versions of his experiment involving shapes and colours, but the same effect emerged. We tend to agree with other people even if they are wrong, just because they are the majority [21].

One argument against the experiments of Solomon Asch was the trivial character of the tasks given. Robert Baron and colleagues changed the perceived importance of the task and the task difficulty in an experiment. Results showed that there is an interaction between task difficulty and importance. If the task was simple, less conformity was found than if the task was perceived to be important. But with difficult tasks it was the complementary effect; the more difficult the task and the importance of the task, the more conformity [22].

Conformity pressures are also found in organizations. Elizabeth Morrison and Frances Milliken termed this 'organizational silence', the way individuals feel the need to stay silent in the face of a majority with a differing opinion [23]. Two main explanations are given in the literature. It seems that most people just accept that they are wrong if confronted with a differing majority. Most people take on the majority position whether it is right or wrong [24], meaning that there is no reflection or verification of the position itself but only a consideration of majority ratio.

The other one shows again the link to psychological safety: the fear of speaking up or not enough psychological safety. We explored the theme of psychological safety in an earlier chapter and showed its importance for allowing risk-taking and stretching behaviour within the group.

Minority influence

Serge Moscovici felt that Solomon Asch's theory had a limitation – it isn't always the case that the majority view in a group prevails. Sometimes it is the *minority* which can act as an irritant and eventually change the mind of the rest of the group. He gave examples like the Suffragette movement in England and the Civil Rights campaign in the United States, where minority views changed the mainstream over time. Where majority influence is driven by a desire to fit in and conform, minority influence works on individuals reviewing information and changing their minds – 'conversion' in Moscovici's theory – and then influencing others to change theirs [25–31].

Four factors appear to affect the ability of minorities to influence the group:

- Size of minority. One person is likely to be judged as an eccentric; two people can be very successful in influencing the majority [22, 29, 32], especially if the second person is falling in with the first 'eccentric'. The famous film *12 Angry Men* offers a good example of minority influence at work, where the jury is gradually led to changing its mind by the persuasion and argument of one of the jurors.

- Size of majority. There seems to be a magic number for the effect of conformity in groups – three. Conformity of majority starts to emerge with this number of group members; before that there is no real conformity, and beyond four to five group members the increase is just marginal [33].
- Behavioural style of the minority. The most important among others is the consistency of the opinion of a minority. The more consistent it is, the more influential it will become. In order to have influence, minorities must be perceived as consistent over time – flexible and reasonable but still consistent [34].
- Characteristics of minorities. The more similar a minority is perceived the more influence it has, and the more different it is the less influence it gets. So called in-group minorities (same characteristics, e.g. being heterosexual in a discussion about gay rights) are more likely to be successful whereas outgroups are more likely to be discriminated against [27].

Creative activity

Identify minority groups you have either interaction with, belong to or at least know something about. In order to get a view on your minority/majority bias, answer the following questions:

- What are the views of these minority groups? How do you react towards them?
- How much do you know about the 'why' of the opinion of each group? How much thought have you given the viewpoints?
- If you are disagreeing/agreeing: how much do the effects described have an influence on your decision?
- Would you change your opinion described even so slightly in different social settings?

Choice shift (group polarization)

In 1961 James Stoner, in an unpublished master's thesis, put forward the idea of what he called 'risky shift' [35]. The essence of risky shift is that a group's decisions become riskier than the average of the individuals within the group. That is groups are more likely to push each other to take bigger risks. However there is a converse effect which is when the group becomes more cautious than the individuals within it – termed 'cautious shift'. So psychologists talk about 'choice shift' as a term to describe how the group can behave differently to the sum of the individuals within it.

Choice shift really is an example of *group polarization* where attitudes become more extreme in groups [36]. Teams with members who have shared beliefs and attitudes tend to have more extreme decisions when they start out with differing opinions on a certain subject. These discussions often lead to a consensus, due to their shared overall beliefs, but the shared decision is more extreme than the opinions before the discussion, and moreover every team member becomes more extreme in his/her opinions at the end of the discussion process. So if team members are generally anti–European Union and discuss this subject with other like-minded people, they will become more anti–European Union after this discussion [37–39].

There are several explanations for this phenomenon. Two primary mechanisms are social comparison and persuasive arguments. Social comparison theory, or normative influence, states that group polarization occurs as a result of individuals' desire to gain acceptance and be perceived in a favourable way by their group [37]. To achieve this, people take a position that is similar to everyone else's but a little more extreme. Studies have demonstrated that normative influence is especially likely with judgments, a group goal of harmony, person-oriented group members, and public responses.

Persuasive arguments theory, or informational influence, states that while a group member's initial opinion is determined by the balance of pro and con arguments, shifts in opinion following discussions occur only when the persuasive arguments are novel to them. When familiar arguments are presented by others, an individual hears more reasons that strengthen one's own judgment. Informational influence is more likely with intellective issues, a group goal of making correct decisions, task-oriented group members and private responses.

So what does a team searching for excellent ideas look like?

Many researchers point to the importance of dissent, conflict and controversy within the group as a requirement to enable creativity [17, 32, 37–38, 40–48]. Effective teams are not always nice teams; being friendly and supportive may not be enough. Dean Tjosvold's concept of 'constructive controversy' is important here. It is characterized by full exploration of opposing opinions and a focus on analysis of task-related issues. Team members are focusing on solving the task and not so much on who is right or wrong. It is the awareness that point of views may differ but without the judgment of good or bad. Other researchers are using the term 'task conflict', 'task orientation' or 'information conflict' as opposed to conflicts of relationship and process conflicts.

For example, the most effective self-managing teams in a manufacturing plant that Steve Alper and Dean Tjosvold studied were those which had compatible goals and promoted constructive controversy [49]. Members of teams which promoted interdependent conflict management (people co-operated to work through their differences), compared to teams with win/lose conflict (where team members tended to engage in a power struggle when they had different views and interests), felt confident that they could deal with differences. These teams were rated by their managers as more productive and innovative.

Conflict and psychological safety

Constructive controversy depends on having a cooperative group climate. So, psychological safety is a prerequisite for pushing the frontiers in creative tasks. Dean Tjosvold and colleagues describe the circumstances when constructive controversy is likely to happen as a co-operative team context. Shared goals and psychological safety are important shapers of this team environment. Studies show that only in a psychological safe environment task conflicts lead to higher performance and learning behaviour [50–51].

This is in line with Allen Amason's definition of functional versus dysfunctional conflicts [52]. Functional conflicts are about information or task-related aspects, allowing the exploration of opposing perspectives and a more complete analysis of the evidence. Dysfunctional conflicts are about interpersonal and emotional aspects. Functional conflicts are linked to a cooperative environment in order to have positive influence. In other words it's not conflict which is bad but having the wrong kind of conflict.

As Figure 9.3 shows, the evidence suggests that there is a 'sweet spot' at which effective creative groups can work. Too little conflict and the group is a nice place to be but doesn't challenge itself. Too much, and the resulting interactions can cause the group to explode and the efforts to dissipate in different directions [53–55].

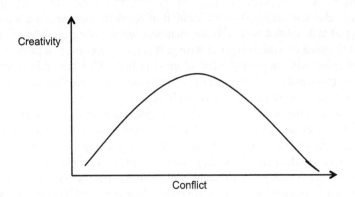

Figure 9.3 'Sweet spot'

Creativity in action: bashing brainstorming

For many decades brainstorming was seen as a powerful tool for group creativity. Suspending judgment, allowing wild ideas, hitchhiking on the back of other people's suggestions – all positive effects associated with Alex Osborn's pioneering method.

But gradually a backlash has emerged which challenges the fundamental behind this. In particular, evidence emerged which suggests that the 'no criticism' rule simply meant a stream of ideas without much practical value. Instead the argument goes, there is a need for healthy and robust criticism and challenge to ensure better ideas.

The reality is that these views support the 'constructive controversy' model – too little challenge but also too much can result in ineffective creative performance.

For a 'deeper dive' in this area see Chapter 8.

Why is pushing the frontiers important for creativity?

Innovation is rarely a solo act. Most of the value-creating activities in organizations, whether public or private sector, take place in teams. Teams can be agents of extraordinary performance – melding their different skills and talents into something more than the sum of the parts. As we've seen throughout this section of the book, teams don't just happen – they build and develop key competences. And an important dimension is around stretching and struggling for excellence, or as we called it pushing the frontiers. In particular these teams have:

• A shared commitment to excel;
• Ways of working together which enable this.

Effective teams walk a tightrope between group effects which act towards conformity (groupthink, consensus, etc.) and destructive conflict where too much diversity, minority views and so forth pull the team apart.

Constructive conflict or task orientation leads to innovation by encouraging discussions among team members. Alternative views are considered and discussed in detail. Individuals are ready to go an extra mile to fight for the best idea side by side with their team members.

Being able to mobilize these skills is becoming increasingly important since many innovation teams are set up for relatively short focused sprints of activity. Whether it is getting a start-up going as soon as possible, putting a new product on the market or energizing change in a larger organization, there is growing emphasis on sprint teams, scrum approaches, and other versions of an agile, team-based approach. In many cases these are temporary teams – bringing relative strangers together for short bursts of focused energy. And in environments like music and theatre where this is the norm, part of the skill set trained at drama school is the ability to hit the ground running, to quickly enter into a team and manage a process of sometimes stormy interaction, stretching towards a highly creative outcome.

Charles (Boss) Kettering and the Barn Gang [56]

Driving a car in the early twentieth century was hard work. To be more specific, starting a car was hard work – a long way from today's instant ignition, back then cars needed hand cranking, which meant someone having to stand in front of the car and turn a handle. One night Thomas Watson (later to become head of IBM) got off the train in Dayton, Ohio, and was met by two men, Charles Kettering and Henry Leland, who offered him a lift. Watson knew Kettering and his reputation as somewhat absent-minded, and so when Kettering sat in the driver's seat and adjusted the controls Watson assumed he had forgotten that he needed to get out and crank the engine first. To his astonishment Kettering simply pushed a button and the car started. He had just experience the first live demonstration of the electrical ignition switch.

This was only one in a long series of inventions which Kettering came up with. Born on August 29, 1876, he studied mechanical and electrical engineering and supported himself through college by working as an installer for the Star Telephone Company in Ashland, Ohio. He took his theoretical and practical knowledge with him to the National Cash Register Company and began to have a major impact as an inventive engineer. The 'impossible' task of making the world's first electric cash register (previously the drawer mechanism was hand operated) was only one of the many innovations he brought to that company. Eventually he left, keen to set up his own business and explore opportunities in the newly growing car industry; with his friend Edward Deeds he started the Dayton Engineering Laboratories Company (DELCO for short).

Working at DELCO and later with General Motors, which bought the company, Kettering produced a stream of important innovations including automotive lighting and ignition systems, lacquer finishes for cars, antilock fuels and leaded gasoline. His work found application in other sectors – for example he is credited with introducing Freon (essentially the world's first fluorocarbon) to the world of refrigeration – now a problem but at that time a key enabler in the expansion of the industry into the domestic world.

Like Thomas Edison, Kettering was not only a gifted engineer but also recognized the need for a team and many of these inventions came from a group who became known as 'the Barn Gang'. Kettering brought in a wide variety of skills and background disciplines – a diverse group of craftsmen and engineers who were united in their love of a challenge. As he once observed, 'development work is always slightly organized chaos!' and the Barn Gang typified this. Working long and late was typical – as one of the Gang put it, 'Say! Quit at five-o-clock? Boy, we didn't know there was any five-o-clock! All we knew was light and dark!' The creative buzz was fuelled in part by music – but the team only had one record to play on their old gramophone, so many of the major innovations which revolutionized the car industry were born to the repeated sounds of 'When we were young, Maggie' played over and over and over again!

What is the skill set around pushing the frontiers?

In this section we give you some help to find out where you and your team stand relative to the competence around pushing the frontiers. We first give a short description of the competence itself and then follow it by identifying ten skills that are important in pushing the frontiers. If you are interested where your team is at and what are areas of improvement and areas of strength then fill in the team check. The competence description and the given skills are rooted in the research we described in the chapter.

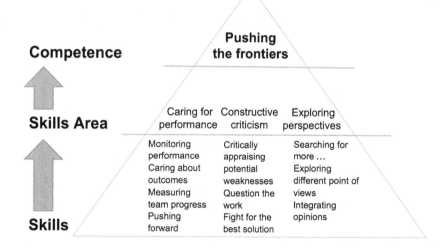

Figure 9.4 Competence pushing the frontiers

Programming the GPS for the creativity journey – what's your position?

There are two main areas of this competence: searching for excellent ideas and constructive decision-making. Searching for excellent ideas is about refining, elaborating and improving ideas, be it one's own ideas or others. It is the commitment not to stop before there is an excellent idea. This has similarities with the 'willpower' competence we saw in the individual section but pushing the frontiers is also about the commitment to high standards (not just going on).

The second facet of pushing the frontiers is about constructive decision-making. This involves the idea of not always agreeing but instead enabling 'constructive conflict'. It is about fighting together for the best ideas and not against each other in a team.

Table 9.1 Self-check pushing the frontiers

#	Core behavioural skills	Your score (1–5)	For instance write at least one example of your own
1	I monitor the work in our team to achieve a high standard of work.		
2	I question the work in our team in order to become better.		
3	I search for more information and ideas on our problem.		
4	I critically appraise potential weaknesses in what we are doing in order to achieve the best possible outcome.		
5	I care about the outcome of our work.		
6	I measure our progress, not just mine.		
7	I explore different points of view.		
8	I fight for the best solution without hurting fellow team members personally.		
9	I try to integrate different opinions.		
10	I push for the best idea with all my abilities.		

Here we offer you a skill self-check on psychological safety (Table 9.1). We suggest you rate yourself with a five-point rating scale:

1 = Not like me at all
2 = Not much like me
3 = I cannot decide if I am good or bad at it, just doing OK
4 = Describes me to a good extent (but not exactly)
5 = Describes me exactly

To help you fill this in remember the 'central tendency' and try to score yourself more clearly, and also use specific examples to help you reflect on how you actually behave.

Team check

Next we offer you a team-level skill check on pushing the frontiers (Table 9.2) that is based on research by Neil Anderson and Michael West as well as Dean Tjosvold [2, 47]. We suggest you rate your team with a five-point rating scale:

1 = Not like us (my team) / I do not agree at all
2 = Not much like us / I disagree to a certain extent
3 = I cannot decide if we are good or bad at it, just doing OK / I neither agree nor disagree
4 = Describes us to a good extent (but not exactly) / I agree somewhat
5 = Describes us exactly / I completely agree

Now think about your team – how far are these statements a reflection of your experience?

Table 9.2 Team-check pushing the frontiers

#	Team behaviours	Your score (1–5)	for instance write at least one example of your own
1	The performance in the team is constantly monitored to achieve a high standard of work.		
2	Team members question the basis of what the team is doing without being reproached.		
3	Team members share a high concern to achieve the highest standards of performance.		
4	Team members appraise potential weaknesses to achieve the best possible outcome.		

(Continued)

Table 9.2 (Continued)

#	Team behaviours	Your score (1–5)	for instance write at least one example of your own
5	Team members are committed to a high standard of work and outcome.		
6	Success and failure is assigned to the team as a whole.		
7	Different opinions are thoroughly explored in the team.		
8	Constructive conflict is the way to move forward for team members.		
9	Team members integrate different opinions.		
10	The complete team is stretching in order to get to a 'wow' idea.		

For a template of a team rating poster go to the companion website.

Working out at the gym – how to train the skills around pushing the frontiers

Pushing the frontiers is a competence set with several facets. All these facets can be trained, but in the training one can see that these facets are not independent but rather linked and entwined with other competences already described. Some of the suggestions by Dean Tjosvold (the 'father' of constructive conflict), like reflecting upon work methods or having clear outcome criteria, we included in other chapters [44]. Here we add some other ideas about approaches to training the competence around pushing the frontiers.

Reviewing your attitude to conflict

As we've tried to show, conflict is not always a bad thing, and constructive challenging can help refine a good idea into a great one. But for many of us the idea of conflict is something we try to avoid – so it's worth reflecting a little on our views and seeing if we can challenge them. Try this simple task. Write down ten things, adjectives, persons, or situations you associate with conflict. Only after you have completed your list, rate the statements either as positive, negative or neutral. How many positive, negative or neutral associations do you count on your list? If you are already have more positive than neutral and negative, you have the mindset for constructive conflicts. If not, look for five reasons why conflict could be positive for you. See how this changes your mindset.

Yes, and . . . thinking

Another simple tool, this requires a positive approach to ideas, seeking to find something good about them while also being able to express constructive challenge and criticism. Instead of simply closing down an idea by saying something like 'that would never work,' try prefacing the response with 'yes, and' and then reinterpret your criticism in terms of some positive action/addition to the idea which will embrace your concern and help refine the idea.

Six thinking hats

Edward de Bono developed this technique which helps groups understand the different modes of thinking which we need to help progress creative ideas. The idea is that we wear different metaphorical hats – a green one when we are open to any suggestion or idea, generating all sorts of possibilities, and a black hat when we are making judgments and critically evaluating. White hats are associated with bringing facts to the discussion and red hats with feelings and emotional responses. Yellow hats are when we look for the positive aspects, and blue hats are used when we are reflecting on and trying to manage the overall group process of being creative.

The principle behind this technique is to develop skills within the group in being flexible in their thinking patterns.

You can find more about this technique on the companion website.

Devil's advocate

Back in the fourteenth century the Catholic Church established a role called the Advocatus Diaboli (Devil's Advocate), which sought to bring a challenging perspective to the discussions of who might be canonized. This formal position is a powerful way of channelling constructive criticism; in the context of a creative team it gives someone the licence to be challenging without the negative emotional tensions which might otherwise be set up. Organizations make use of different approaches based on this – for example in many projects there is a 'red team', whose task is to challenge and constructively criticize the efforts of the 'blue team', who are the creative originators of ideas.

Playing the devil's advocate needs conviction on the side of the role owner. Research found that the more 'natural' the role is taken on, the better the results for constructive conflict [17, 57]. Equally good results can be gained if the role is accepted by everyone in the team as an important element of creative discussions.

> On the companion website you can explore a group technique called advocacy teams that relies on this principle to encourage constructive conflict.

Giving feedback regularly

Feedback that enhances constructive conflict is a special case relevant to creative team development and follows a simple but powerful rule – be hard on the problem but nice to the people! It's all about reflecting on the way the team behaves and encouraging review of those behaviours which help support and stretch the idea without giving negative impacts or damaging psychological safety.

In order to do this it's important to formulate the feedback in the following way: first, describe the context/the situation where the behaviour took place, then describe the actual behaviour, and then describe the effect of this behaviour.

This way of giving feedback leads to concrete and non-threatening feedback. It's important to avoid any generalizations or accusations, otherwise there is a risk of creating a sense of being challenged and criticized on the part of the recipient of the feedback.

Feedback also has another role. It is there for making clear the contribution of each team member and therefore to support high performance norms. Feedback sessions among team members or a team review helps to enforce and monitor performance standards, but it also helps to reveal the contributions of each team member to the success of the team.

Learning negotiation skills

Negotiation is a means of getting what we want from others and is part of our everyday lives. However, it is not easy to do, and often there is a trade-off between getting what we want by hard negotiating and getting along with people by soft negotiating. A way to combine both was developed at the Harvard Negotiation Project and is called 'principled negotiation'. It recommends looking for mutual gains whenever possible, and when the interests conflict, to insist that the result be based on some fair standards independent of the will of either side. The method proposes four principles of negotiating:

• First, negotiators should separate the people from the problem. The basic approach is to deal with the people as human beings, recognizing their viewpoints and emotions.

- Second, it is important to focus on interests, not positions. For example, if there is a conflict between two people about having the office window open or closed, these are the positions. The underlying interests causing these positions might be to get some fresh air versus to avoid the draft. Only when the interests are considered is it possible to reach agreement, because different interests like needs, desires, concerns and fears define the problem.
- Third, negotiators need to invent various options for mutual gain. Since judgment hinders imagination, you need to separate the creative act of developing options from selecting among them.
- Fourth, insisting on using objective criteria and procedures that are independent of the parties' will is crucial for a fair solution. The solution should be based on fair standards that are defined in advance, such as efficiency, costs, originality or assumed time to market.

Preparing for idea conflicts

Given that constructive controversy is an important team skill it's worth thinking about your individual preparations for entering into this arena. Rather than just advancing your idea and hoping it will be able to speak for itself, prepare yourself for it, develop sample arguments for your idea or solution, think about the benefits of the idea, and gather facts and figures that support it. But also do the opposite: try to find the counterarguments, the risks that go along with your idea and the possible downside of it. Try to be as passionate as possible in every step.

Decision making 101

List as many facts, information and theories regarding the ideas and in this process clarify as you can. The more transparent the ideas the better they are for decision making. In a cooperative decision team members evaluate the idea against the transparent criteria and only then decide. The following questions are good for that:

- What are the pros and cons?
- What are possible consequences of a decision?
- What are possible effects on people involved?
- What are possible risks of this decision?
- What beliefs are behind every decision?

End of chapter summary

- Pushing the frontiers in creativity starts with high performance norms or the will to excel. Team members develop a shared commitment to go (at least) one extra step in order to get the best creative solution.

- In this chapter we explore why groups so often lack the competence to push the frontiers. Social loafing, negative norms, groupthink, conformity pressures, minority influence, and choice shift are described and explained.
- These group effects are the basis for the insight of how to develop then needed skills. Constructive conflict/criticism and exploring different perspectives are the two 'answers' in creative settings.
- For this competence divergent and convergent processes are working hand in hand, for example exploring different perspectives and opinions is followed by an integration of these different point of view.
- The link to psychological safety as a provider of a safer team environment can be clearly seen and shows the interdependency of the team competencies.

References

[1]   Trevor, E. (1964). *The flight of the phoenix.* New York, NY: Harper and Row.
[2]   Anderson, N. R., & West, M. A. (1998). Measuring climate for work group innovation: Development and validation of the team climate inventory. *Journal of Organizational Behavior, 19,* 235–258.
[3]   Tjosvold, D., Wedley, W. C., & Field, R. H. (1986). Constructive controversy, the Vroom-Yetton model, and managerial decision-making. *Journal of Occupational Behaviour, 7,* 125–138.
[4]   Ringelmann, M. (1913). Recherches sur les moteurs animés. Travail de l'homme. *Annales de l'Institut National Agronomique, 2,* 1–40.
[5]   Latané, B., Williams, K. D., & Harkins, S. (1979). Many hands make light the work: The causes and consequences of social loafing. *Journal of Personality and Social Psychology, 37,* 822–832.
[6]   Ingham, A. G., Levinger, G., Graves, J. and Peckham, V. (1974). The Ringelmann Effect: Studies of group size and group performance. *Journal of Experimental Social Psychology, 10,* 371–384.
[7]   Dahlander, L., & Wallin, M. (2006). A man on the inside: Unlocking communities as complementary assets. *Research Policy, 35,* 1243–1259.
[8]   Johnson, D. W., & Johnson, F. P. (1997). *Joining together: Group theory and group skills* (6th ed.). Boston: Allyn & Bacon.
[9]   Zaccaro, S. J. (1984). Social loafing: The role of task attractiveness. *Personality and Social Psychology Bulletin, 10,* 99–106.
[10] Worchel, S., Rothgerber, H., Day, E. A., Hart, D., & Butemeyer, J. (1998). Social identity and individual productivity within groups. *British Journal of Social Psychology, 37,* 389–413.
[11] Karau, S. J., & Williams, K. D. (1993). Social loafing: A meta-analytic review and theoretical integration. *Journal of Personality and Social Psychology, 65,* 681–706.
[12] Karau, S. J., & Williams, K. D. (2001). Understanding individual motivation in groups: The collective effort model. In M. E. Turner (Ed.), *Groups at work: Theory and research* (113–141). Mahwah, NJ: Erlbaum.
[13] Sherif, M. (1936). *The psychology of social norms.* Oxford: Harper.
[14] Cialdini, R. B., Reno, R. R., & Kallgren, C. A. (1990). A focus theory of normative conduct: Recycling the concept of norms to reduce littering in public places. *Journal of Personality and Social Psychology, 58,* 1015–1026.
[15] Aarts, H., & Dijksterhuis, A. (2003). The silence of the library: Environment, situational norm, and social behavior. *Journal of Personality and Social Psychology, 84,* 18–28.

[16]   West, M.A., & Sacramento, C.A. (2006). Flourishing in teams: Developing creativity and innovation. *Creative Management and Development* (3rd ed., 25–44). London: SAGE.

[17]   Janis, Irving L. (1982). *Groupthink: Psychological studies of policy decisions and fiascoes* (2nd ed.). New York, NY: Houghton Mifflin.

[18]   Rogers, W. (1986). Report of the Presidential Commission of Enquiry into the Washington D.C. U.S. Government.

[19]   Shute, N. (1954). *Slide rule*. London: Heinemann.

[20]   Nemeth, C.J., & Nemeth-Brown, B. (2003). Better than individuals? The potential benefits of dissent and diversity for group creativity. In P. Paulus & B. Nijstad (Eds.), *Group Creativity*. Oxford: Oxford University Press. See more at *http://psychology. berkeley.edu/people/charlan-j-nemeth#sthash.AAXggnal.dpuf*

[21]   Asch, S.E. (1956). Studies of independence and conformity: I. A minority of one against a unanimous majority. *Psychological Monographs, 70*, 1–70.

[22]   Baron, R.S., Vandello, J.A., & Brunsman, B. (1996). The forgotten variable in conformity research: Impact of task importance on social influence. *Journal of Personality and Social Psychology, 71*, 915.

[23]   Morrison, E.W., & Milliken, F.J. (2000). Organizational silence: A barrier to change and development in a pluralistic world. *Academy of Management Review, 25*, 706–725.

[24]   Nemeth, C.J., & Wachtler, J. (1983). Creative problem solving as a result of majority vs minority influence. *European Journal of Social Psychology, 13*, 45–55.

[25]   Moscovici, S., & Lage, E. (1976). Studies in social influence III: Majority versus minority influence in a group. *European Journal of Social Psychology, 6*, 149–174.

[26]   Moscovici, S., Lage, E., & Naffrechoux, M. (1969). Influence of a consistent minority on the response of a majority in a color perception task. *Sociometry, 32*, 365–379.

[27]   Maass, A., & Clark, R.D. (1984). Hidden impact of minorities: Fifteen years of minority influence research. *Psychological Bulletin, 95*, 428–450.

[28]   Nemeth, C.J. (1986). The differential contributions of majority and minority influence. *Psychological Review, 93*, 23–32.

[29]   Nemeth, C., & Chiles, C. (1988). Modeling courage: The role of dissent in fostering independence. *European Journal of Social Psychology, 18*, 275–280.

[30]   Nemeth, C.J., & Kwan, J.L. (1987). Minority influence, divergent thinking and detection of correct solutions. *Journal of Applied Social Psychology, 17*, 788–799.

[31]   Nemeth, C., & Owens, P. (1996). Making work groups more effective: The value of minority dissent. In M.A. West (Ed.), *The handbook of work psychology* (125–141). Chichester: Wiley.

[32]   Allen, V.L., & Levine, J.M. (1969). Consensus and conformity. *Journal of Experimental Social Psychology, 5*, 389–399.

[33]   Latané, B., & Wolf, S. (1981). The social impact of majorities and minorities. *Psychological Review, 88*, 438–453.

[34]   Moscovici, S., & Nemeth, C. (1974). Social influence: II. Minority influence. In Charlan Nemeth (Ed.), *Social psychology: Classic and contemporary integrations* (328). Chicago: Rand McNally.

[35]   Stoner, J.A.F. (1961). *A comparison of individual and group decisions involving risk*. Doctoral dissertation, Massachusetts Institute of Technology.

[36]   Moscovici, S., & Zavalloni, M. (1969). The group as a polarizer of attitudes. *Journal of Personality and Social Psychology, 12*, 125.

[37]   Isenberg, D.J. (1986). Group polarization: A critical review and meta-analysis. *Journal of Personality and Social Psychology, 50*, 1141.

[38]   Moscovici, S., & Doise, W. (1974). Decision making in groups. In Charlan Nemeth (Ed.), *Social psychology: Classic and contemporary integrations* (328). Chicago: Rand McNally.

[39]   Myers, D.G., & Lamm, H. (1976). The group polarization phenomenon. *Psychological Bulletin, 83*, 602–627.

[40]   Mumford, M.D., & Gustafson, S.B. (1988). Creativity syndrome: Integration, application, and innovation. *Psychological Bulletin, 103*, 27–43.

[41]   Tjosvold, D. (1998). Cooperative and competitive goal approach to conflict: Accomplishments and challenges. *Applied Psychology, 47*, 285–313.

[42]   De Dreu, C.K.W. (1997). Productive conflict: The importance of conflict management and conflict issue. In C.K.W. De Dreu & E. Van de Vliert (Eds.), *Using conflict in organizations* (9–22). London: Sage.

[43]   Jehn, K.A. (1997). A qualitative analysis of conflict types and dimensions in organizational groups. *Administrative Science Quarterly, 42*, 530–557.

[44]   Tjosvold, D. (1982). Effects of approach to controversy on superiors' incorporation of subordinates' information in decision making. *Journal of Applied Psychology, 67*, 189–193.

[45]   Tjosvold, D., & Field, R.H.G. (1983). Effects of social context on consensus and majority vote decision making. *Academy of Management Journal, 26*, 500–506.

[46]   Tjosvold, D., Wedley, W.C., & Field, R.H.G. (1986). Constructive controversy, the Vroom-Yetton model, and managerial decision making. *Journal of Occupational Behaviour, 7*, 125–138.

[47]   Tjosvold, D. (1993). *Learning to manage conflict: Getting people to work together productively*. New York, NY: Lexington Books.

[48]   Jarzabkowski, P., & Searle, R.H. (2004). Harnessing diversity and collective action in the top management team. *Long Range Planning, 37*, 399–419.

[49]   Alper, S., Tjosvold, D., & Law, K.S. (2000). Conflict management, efficacy, and performance in organizational teams. *Personnel Psychology, 53*, 625–642.

[50]   Mu, S., & Gnyawali, D.R. (2003). Developing synergistic knowledge in student groups. *Journal of Higher Education, 74*, 689–711.

[51]   De Dreu, C.K.W., & West, M.A. (2001). Minority dissent and team innovation: The importance of participation in decision making. *Journal of Applied Psychology, 86*, 1191–1201.

[52]   Amason, A.C. (1996). Distinguishing the effects of functional and dysfunctional conflict on strategic decision making: Resolving a paradox for top management teams. *Academy of Management Journal, 39*, 123–148.

[53]   Hülsheger, U.R., Anderson, N., & Salgado, J.F. (2009). Team-level predictors of innovation at work: A comprehensive meta-analysis spanning three decades of research. *Journal of Applied Psychology, 94*(5), 1128–1145.

[54]   Task conflict correlated at only .07 and relationship conflict correlated marginally negatively at only −.09 with innovation, suggesting that team conflict may be either unrelated or related in a curvilinear manner to team innovativeness (Jehn, Rispens, & Thatcher, 2010).

Jehn, K.A., Rispens, S., & Thatcher, S.M. (2010). The effects of conflict asymmetry on work group and individual outcomes. *Academy of Management Journal, 53*, 596–616.

[55]   Farh, J.L., Lee, C., & Farh, C.I. (2010). Task conflict and team creativity: A question of how much and when. *Journal of Applied Psychology, 95*, 1173–1180.

[56]   Boyd, T. (2002). *Charles F. Kettering: A biography*. New York, NY: Beard Books.

[57]   Leonard, D., & Swap, W. (1999). *When sparks fly: Igniting creativity in groups*. Boston, MA: Harvard Business School Press.

Section 4

## Chapter 10

Creating the context

Chapter objectives

By the end of this chapter you will:

- Know about the different aspects contributing to a creative environment;
- Understand that for most aspects of a creative environment competences play a key role in implementing and sustaining them;
- Develop awareness of what it means to build a creative environment;
- Being able to reflect on what kind of creative environment you need and want.

So far we've looked at the idea of creativity and its importance in many areas. And we've seen that it is a natural capability, something anyone can apply. We've also learned from research and practice about some of the ways in which creativity can be developed. It's a complex capability made up of several competences, and the good news is that it is possible to build and strengthen these. Using the metaphor of a gym there are various tools and techniques to help us work on the different muscle groups which will help us build our 'creativity fitness'.

We've also seen that creativity can have 'emergent properties' – when we practice it in the company of others the results can be greater than the sum of the parts. Shared problem-solving is a powerful approach which almost certainly emerged very early on in our evolution when it made sense to work together to deal with a dangerous and uncertain world. 'Two heads are better than one' isn't just an old saying; it probably has been behind our survival through fast and creative adaptation. While it is possible to sport the odd lone genius, most of today's innovation landscape is made up of teams. Whether they are a small group of committed individuals in a start-up, a new product development team in a large corporation, or a group of clinical staff on the ward of a hospital, most innovation happens through people working together on shared problem-solving.

But like any group endeavour, simply throwing people together does not make them a team – and in the world of creativity there are many ways in which conflicts, rivalries, peer pressures and a host of other group dynamics can act to restrict the flow of useful ideas. Once again we need to think about the competences and skills underpinning effective working in groups and practice and develop this capability.

So far, so good – and we already have plenty to work with in trying to enhance creativity. But there is another element we will now explore – the *context* in which creativity takes place. What have we learned about building a creative environment, one that supports and strengthens our ability to deploy creativity as individuals and in groups? What factors act to stifle or reduce creativity? How might we design organizations – in terms of structures, physical architectures, policies and procedures – to keep a steady flow of useful ideas flowing? Is there a magic ingredient to having a 'creative climate'?

In this chapter we're going to look a little more closely at the *context* in which this all takes place – and what we might do to provide a supportive environment for creativity.

Why does this matter?

This is particularly important in the many places where we are concerned to develop creative competences and skills inside a larger organization – for example shop floor staff trying to improve their working processes, product and service developers trying to promote new concepts, change agents trying to challenge the way the organization works. These are situations where we certainly need to develop creativity – and while individual and group level skills play a key role, we can also work with the wider environment to help support creativity.

Creativity doesn't happen in a vacuum. Being able to come up with different new ideas is a process which is influenced by a whole series of external pressures which can act as a barrier, pushing our creative ideas back into the bottle.

It's not hard to think of situations where the organization acts as a brake on creative flow – for example being rushed off your feet so there is no time to pause and think of new solutions to problems. Or rigid hierarchies where the dominant rule is 'do as you are told!' Imagine places where procedures and rules – 'the way we do things around here' – are not open to challenge, or organizations in which the risk of things going wrong and the likely consequences mean you'd rather shut up than suggest something new.

There are many ways in which the environment can act as a barrier to creativity – think, for example, about the 'killer phrases' which lurk in the background of many conversations. In different ways they reinforce the reasons why new ideas won't take flight, why the organization would not accept them. They have the same basic structure; 'that's a great idea. . . . .but.' Here are some typical examples and you can almost certainly add your own to the list:

- We've never tried that before.
- We've always done it this way.

- The boss won't like it.
- We don't have the time for that.
- It's too expensive.
- You can't do that here.
- We're not that kind of organization.
- That's a brave suggestion.
- Etc.

Creative activity

Look at the examples in the text and then try and come up with your own list of favourite 'killer phrases'. See how many you can list in two minutes!

All of this suggests that we need to recognize the influence which environment can have on creativity – the good news is that there are plenty of levers which we can work with to develop a more supportive context. To take a gardening metaphor, we can do a lot to prepare the ground to make it a place where ideas find fertile soil in which to grow.

If you'd like to read an example of a 'gardener' at work, you can find the case study of Cerulean on the companion website, which describes Managing Director Patrick McLaughlin's approach to developing a creative culture within his organization.

Building a creative environment

Understanding the many external pressures acting to block creativity is an important step since it gives us an idea of the problems we need to work on. If we want to enable creativity we can do a lot by working with these levers to create a physical and mental environment which is supportive.

It's important to recognize that there are multiple factors combining to limit creativity and many different solutions – it's not a case of one size fits all. Often organizations fall into the trap of thinking they need to copy one element – for example, setting up playful physical environments like those to be found at Pixar or Google. In reality this rarely works; instead we need to understand the particular characteristics of an organization and work with a number of 'levers' to improve the supportive context.

Table 10.1 summarizes some of the key approaches and we'll explore each of these in more detail in this chapter.

Table 10.1 Building a creative environment

Environmental barrier	Ways of dealing with this	Illustrative examples: you can find these on the companion website
Unsupportive physical environment	Make the workplace stimulating	Pixar
	Allow for interaction and bumping into new ideas	Met Office
	Make ideas visible	
	Build a virtual environment	
Lack of time and permission to play	Allow and even require employees time to explore and be curious, to enable incubation	3M
Lack of supporting climate	Create the supporting 'rules of the game'	Redgate
	Core values – everyone can make a contribution	Innocent
	'No blame' culture – encourage experiment	Met Office
	Mistakes = opportunities	Denso
	Chance favours the prepared mind	Veeder Root
Lack of reward and recognition	Reinforce creative behaviours	
Lack of a process for enabling creativity	Make Creative Problem-Solving explicit – establish a process	
Lack of capability – missing competences and skills	Train to develop competences – deploy creativity tools and techniques	See Chapters 2–9 in this book
Lack of / inappropriate leadership	Coaching and supporting the process, moderating and facilitating at different stages, providing an overall direction and focus	

Physical environment

The city of Munich, Germany is home to a complex glass and steel structure which houses the BMW research and development (R&D) centre, where the designs for cars and motorbikes populating the highways of the world are created. The centre is one of the reasons that *Business Week* magazine named BMW as one of the world's most innovative companies in 2006. The R&D centre is not like a conventional office building, but more closely resembles a giant glass cloverleaf with a huge central atrium around which glass-walled offices are spread, each of which looks into the centre and where everyone can see new designs and prototypes, whatever they are doing. As one walks past them to visit the canteen or use the bathroom it is impossible not to notice the prototypes, and the walls are full of sketch boards and spaces for commenting and suggesting ideas. The whole environment seems constructed to bring many people in contact with emerging new ideas and to encourage their contribution.

This is exactly what was in the mind of the architect, Gunter Henn. He was strongly influenced by the work of Thomas Allen in the 1970s (see box) and believed that people interacting was at the heart of creativity and that architecture could force these collisions [1].

Creativity in action: managing the flow of ideas

During the 1970s Tom Allen, a professor at MIT, was interested in how ideas emerged during large complex technical projects. He began studying organizations working for the innovation challenge around the US space programme – finding ways to deliver on Kennedy's original target of putting a man on the moon and bringing him home again safely.

He studied how people shared ideas and how they moved around and across organizations, and laid the foundations for what we now call 'social network analysis' as a way of mapping these interactions. He found, for example, the importance of key individuals (technological gatekeepers) through whom ideas travelled and were disseminated to relevant people. His book *Managing the Flow of Technology* contains a wealth of insights which are of continuing importance in designing today's network-based innovation processes.

One project he undertook explored how the distance between engineers' offices coincided with the level of regular technical communication between them. The results of that research, now known as the Allen Curve, revealed a distinct correlation between distance and frequency of communication (i.e. the more distance there is between people – 50 meters or more to be exact – the less they will communicate). This principle has been incorporated into forward-thinking commercial design ever since, in, for example, The Decker Engineering Building in New York, the Steelcase Corporate Development Centre in Michigan, and BMW's Research Centre in Germany.

It's a long way (10,000 km) from Munich to the West Coast of the United States, but in Emeryville, California, you'd find a similar model of architecture supporting creativity. Pixar Studios is one of the most consistently successful companies in the film business, producing award-winning animated films like *Toy Story*, *Finding Nemo* and *The Incredibles*. Pixar's ability to repeat its success stands in contrast to most studios; its fourteen films have all been both commercial and critical successes and have earned over $8 billion in revenue. This is not a matter of luck; at work is a well-understood and well-managed creative process which keeps the ideas flowing and the output fresh and exciting. One key principle, originating with Steve Jobs (who was a key figure in the early days of Pixar before returning to Apple) was to make the physical geography of the place work to enable the same kind of creative collisions which Gunter Henn uses.

> You can read the full case study of Pixar and its creative process on the companion website.

These days organizations are increasingly recognizing that physical environments which provide space for interaction and which offer stimulation and different perspectives to their employees can act as a powerful catalyst for creativity. The Googleplex is not simply a designer's whim or an attempt to improve employee morale; it is aimed at encouraging creative insights as a part of daily activity. Swiss chemical giant Novartis has designed its offices around principles of communication and idea flow.

In a longitudinal study of workspace design in industry several key elements were being found and described that enhance and foster team and individual creativity [2]:

- Enhancing direct communication by working on the same floor and fostering meeting-points (e.g. copy machines) and face-to-face meetings;
- Modularity: giving flexibility for the workspace according to the task; quiet rooms for concentration or to phone and 'make noise' as well as 'common' rooms for working and interacting;
- Working along the process: office space is allocated along the flow of the process in a company;
- Flexibility of workspace, for example desk-sharing, flexible rooms usable for different tasks (meeting, working space for a project team and so forth).

It's not simply about high-tech California companies; the UK's Meteorological Office is one of the world's leading scientific institutes and is housed in an open glass-framed building with dedicated spaces to try and encourage creative interchange. The Danish public sector has an innovation support agency 'owned' by the Ministries of Taxation, Economics and Employee Affairs. 'Mindlab' is located in a traditional government building but once inside it resembles the same kind of open playful space which Gunter Henn and Steve Jobs were aiming for in their designs.

On the companion website you can watch a video in which Natalie Wilkie and Gary Holpin explain some of the philosophy behind their 'Think Up!' approach to stimulating creativity in the UK Meteorological Office.

One important development in this is the use of virtual space to bring people together and allow for creative interchange. Innovation platforms are now common to many organizations and provide ways in which thousands of employees can engage with each other, suggest and comment, and focus their innovation efforts. While many of these operate within companies there is also a growing trend towards bringing in outsiders to the process – 'crowdsourcing' creative ideas. We discuss this in more detail in Chapter 16.

Time, space and permission to play

We've seen throughout this book that creativity is about long periods of incubation and exploration punctuated by flashes of insight. That's not a process that lends itself to being switched on and off to order, and organizations are increasingly realizing that if they want creativity to happen they must make space for it. 3M is a business with a long tradition of breakthrough innovation – think about Post-it notes, Scotch tape, industrial masking tape and a host of other products we now take for granted. They came out of an organization which has recognized that it needs its employees to be curious, to play and explore, to make odd connections. And in order to do so they need a sense of time being allowed for this and permission to play within that time. 3M operate what is called the 15% policy; employees can use up to 15% of their time on personal projects which don't have to be linked to specific company outputs or productivity targets. This time is not accounted for on timesheets, it's more a signal to employees that creativity is important and that the company trusts them to use the time well.

Much attention has been paid in recent years to Google and their 'innovation machine'. While the business began with a powerful search engine, the company has diversified into many new areas – advertising, web analytics and now in driverless cars, home automation and retailing. Underpinning Google's approach is the same recognition that people need time and space to explore, and so they make it a requirement that their engineers spend at least 20% of their time working on non-core projects. Major successes like Gmail came out of this process of 'permitted play'.

We explore some of the different ways in which organizations are making use of time and space for play together with some of the mechanisms for enabling it in Chapter 16.

Not all organizations can afford the luxury of giving employees the freedom to take their own time; Toyota, for example, is driven by the huge commitment of keeping its production lines running, and interrupting them is costly and disruptive. But they too have their version of allowing time and space for creativity; every team spends fifteen minutes each day before and after its shift in group problem-solving, identifying issues to be worked on and coming up with new ideas to try out during the day. This constant high-frequency, short-burst approach to creativity is called *kaizen* and is central to their success as the world's most productive car maker. Process innovation keeps happening, driven by the creativity of thousands of employees; it's estimated that the company receives on average one useful idea per worker per week and has done so since the 1960s when they began this approach to continuous improvement

On the companion website you can find a number of cases and video/audio media examples of such employee involvement schemes – Kumba Resources, Veeder Root, Redgate Software and Innocent Fruit Juices.

Creative climate

Organizations are much more than a collection of people working together. They have shared beliefs and values and an underlying agreement about 'the way we do things around here'. Whether we are talking about a small start-up or a large corporation, the underlying culture is important because it shapes how people will behave. We can use the metaphor of organizational climate to describe the kind of 'weather system' providing the context in which people work – and this gives us another lever to play with in trying to create a supportive context for innovation.

We have already explored some of the key climate features involved in group-level activity in the previous section. Here we turn our attention to the wider organization and it is important to note the work of several researchers, notably Teresa Amabile and Goran Ekvall.

Teresa Amabile is an American researcher who has extensively explored the role which environment plays in supporting – or stifling – creativity. Her 'componential theory' of creativity suggests that three elements are needed for people to be creative: task motivation, domain-relevant skills and creativity-relevant skills – and they can be looked at an individual level as well as an organizational level.

Work environment or culture is a result of these three elements – a result of different individuals, from top management to individual employees as well as of policies and interactions inside a company. In order to measure the creative climate, Teresa Amabile and colleagues developed KEYS [3]. Besides measuring outcomes, three elements of creative climate are explored:

- Management practices. It is about the orientation of the organization towards creativity; control over one's work; having challenging work; managerial encouragement, and work group support.

- Organizational motivation. Organizational encouragement and lack of organizational impediments – both are focusing on cultural issues, like constructive judgment of ideas.
- Resources. Sufficient resources and realistic workload pressure.

Goran Ekvall described ten dimension of a creative climate [4]. As well as Teresa Amabile's model, it has been repeatedly validated across the world.

- Challenge. Employees participate in the development of long-term goals and are intrinsically motivated.
- Dynamism and liveliness. The atmosphere of a company and how dynamic it is.
- Playfulness and humour. Spontaneity and humour as well as playfulness are an important part of creative culture.
- Freedom. Autonomy, having freedom to act on a day-to-day basis as well as sharing information.
- Risk-taking. It is also about the tolerance of ambiguity as well as taking initiatives; being bold.
- Idea time. Do employees have time to think and elaborate new ideas?
- Idea support. Team members and management listen to ideas and support them.
- Trust and openness. This is about emotional safety, or as we called it, psychological safety.
- Debate. Discussing and fighting for ideas.
- Conflict. This is a negatively correlated dimension. Conflict is described as interpersonal, harming conflicts that build tension between people and in the organization.

As you probably have noticed, this is all about our competence model we described in Sections 2 and 3.

On the companion website you can read about the Cerulean case, which made use of Amabile's KEYS framework to try and develop a culture to support radical innovation.

One area where this organization-wide climate challenge plays out is in the area of 'high-involvement innovation', which we discuss in more detail in Chapter 12. Since everyone is capable of creativity – as we have seen throughout the book –the question is raised as to the kind of organization we might build to engage employees actively in the process. For example a core belief underpinning the Toyota model mentioned earlier is that 'little ideas matter'. This sends out a clear message that every employee can make a contribution and indeed is expected to share his or her creativity. Another example might be an organization which sends out a clear message that mistakes are OK since they provide learning opportunities. We know creativity is about trying things out and experiments often fail; their value lies in helping us move closer towards a useful solution. So building a climate in which people believe that they won't be punished for making mistakes (as long as they don't repeat them!) is an important building block supporting their creativity.

The difficulty with creating this kind of environment is that organizations need to be consistent. Saying 'we're a blame-free organization' and then punishing people who do try things out and make mistakes is not a consistent message, and people quickly see through it.

Successful organizations which have a clear culture for creativity are well aware of the behaviours they want people to practice and the underlying beliefs they want to foster. They make these explicit and they communicate and reinforce them so that they become 'the way we do things around here. 3M's 15% policy, Pixar's approach to creative debate, Toyota's *kaizen* philosophy and Google's 'perpetual beta' approach are all company-specific examples of building a creative climate.

On the companion website you can read cases describing how organizations like Hosiden, NPI and Pixar try to create a climate for creativity.

There is also a tool – the High Involvement Innovation audit – which allows you to explore the climate for supporting creativity.

Creativity in action: employee-led innovation

In a recent study of a wide range of UK organizations in which employees at all levels were regularly contributing creative ideas, Julian Birkinshaw and Lisa Duke identified four key sets of enabling factors [5]:

- Time out – to give employees the space in their working day for creative thought;
- Expansive roles – to help employees move beyond the confines of their assigned job;
- Competitions – to stimulate action and to get the creative juices flowing;
- Open forums – to give employees a sense of direction and to foster collaboration.

You can find links to examples of organizations displaying these 'high involvement innovation' characteristics on the companion website.

Reward and recognition

One important aspect of an organization which supports creativity is the use of reward and recognition. While everyone is potentially creative, they may not choose to deploy their skills in the context of the organization unless they feel it is worthwhile doing so. Motivation at this level is not so much about paying for ideas as in giving people a sense of being recognized and valued for providing them. (Indeed one problem with many suggestion schemes is that they can sometimes be divisive; by focusing on the size of the reward, people often hoard ideas rather than sharing them.) Recognition is often a powerful motivator, and many organizations like 3M make a feature out of celebrating their creative individuals and the maverick behaviour which they often exhibit.

At its most basic the ability to implement an idea is a key factor in building a climate for creativity. If people feel they have autonomy, they can choose what they do; they feel in control, whereas in organizations which limit the exercise of individual thinking, the overall effect can be to switch off people's creativity and turn them into robots. In a small start-up or in a 'creative' context like an R&D laboratory or an advertising agency this isn't a problem; the need for a steady flow of interesting new ideas means that people are encouraged to contribute.

But it is a challenge for many organizations which rely on procedures and rules for co-ordinating work – production lines, call centres and retail order processing, for example. Giving people the opportunity to make suggestions and implement improvements risks compromising the systems which ensure productivity and quality. Yet without those suggestions there is little opportunity to make the system better and the resulting impact on morale and motivation is likely to make things worse.

As we've seen, organizations like Toyota or France Telecom (whose 'Idee cliq' online suggestion scheme has around 30,000 participants every day, building on new ideas) have managed to resolve this paradox by simultaneously putting in place frameworks for creative idea input and specifying where those should be directed. This idea – of 'policy deployment' – means that there is an understanding of where improvements are needed and reward and recognition linked to focused creativity in those areas. (For example it might not be a good idea for a worker in a pharmaceutical factory to experiment with the formulation of the drug he or she is making (!), but the same person could have and implement some great ideas around improving workflow or quality.)

> On the companion website you can find a description of 'policy deployment' and some case examples which show this principle in action.

Establish a process

We've seen that creativity involves a journey, and one useful way of supporting it is to make the process of travelling along it explicit. Having an explicit process is particularly important where people may not have much experience of a structured approach to problem-finding and solving. Many high involvement innovation systems, such as the Toyota model, make use of simple frameworks which everyone is trained to use. The 'quality' revolution which did so much to strengthen the competitiveness of Japanese industry in the 1970s emerged from systematic application of models like the 'Deming Wheel', and more recent impact has come in manufacturing and service organizations through the use of Six Sigma as a formal process. We'll explore some framework methodologies like Design Thinking in the next chapter.

On the companion website there are descriptions of some framework methods – Deming Wheel, Six Sigma, Lean thinking and Continuous improvement – together with some activities so you can try using these.

There are also case examples including Torbay Hospital, Hosiden, Forte, NPI and Veeder Root.

Training and skills development

We've seen that creativity is a natural capability but also that it can be unlocked and developed through the use of tools and techniques. Throughout the book we've tried to introduce you to a wide range of these. So it makes sense within organizations not only to provide structures and frameworks which support people being creative but also to invest in extending and developing those skills. Creativity training is a large field and ranges from simple inputs designed to give people a sense of the core process and experience with applying it (Six Sigma and Deming Wheel, for example) through to more elaborate inputs designed to stretch thinking skills (lateral thinking, TRIZ and Synectics, for example) to leadership programs and worldwide cultural change programs consisting of exercises and coaching around our set of competences.

On the companion website you can find an example of a leadership training program (LTP) and its effects on the innovation capability of a medium-sized enterprise.

Leadership

It is easy to see creativity as a democratic open process in which everyone's ideas are exchanged and built upon. But there is also a need for leadership in organizations – not in the sense of strong authoritative direction but in guiding and shaping the process towards a goal and doing so while balancing resource demands like time and money. And it's not about the leader as being the creative hero so much as the need for leaders as coaches, facilitators and enablers of the creative process.

There are multiple roles a leader can take regarding fostering creativity [6]. It is not only their support and guidance (think back to Chapter 8) that counts but also the co-ordination role leaders can take on in teams (think back to Chapter 6). Leaders can influence the whole process of innovation, from idea generation towards implementation of ideas. But leaders in the role of managers also influence the whole life cycle of employees, from hiring to leaving the organization [7].

Next to the creative competence set, described in Chapters 2–9, leaders need most of all the ability to process complex information and, next to this ability of diagnosis, the ability to reflect and act upon these competences [8]. So, fostering creativity and enhancing innovative capability of an organization needs the same personal initiative than most other tasks of leaders [9]. But the most important part seems to be managerial tolerance of change [10]. But there are also true differences between creative workers and leaders of creative work. One does not have to be a creative worker (or the best one) in order to lead people in creative work. It is much more about leading change, fostering other people to be good at their job and building an environment/culture where creativity can grow and blossom.

On the companion website you can watch interviews with Hugh Chapman (Veeder Root), Emma Taylor (Denso) and Piers Ibbotson who talk about their approach to guiding and supporting creativity.

End of chapter summary

- Managing creativity involves a series of individual and group-level competences, but these are not deployed in a vacuum. We also need to consider the context within which creativity takes place and how far contextual factors can support or block creativity.
- Typical barriers and blocks to creativity include unsupportive physical environment, lack of time or permission to play, negative climate for creativity, lack of skills in creativity, lack of reward or recognition, lack of a framework process to enable repeated creativity and lack of appropriate leadership.
- Physical environments can support creativity by providing stimulus and opportunity for networking and idea flow.
- Allowing time and signalling permission to explore is strongly associated with creative success, and an increasing number of organizations are deploying such approaches.
- Climate for creativity relates to the group and organizational context – rules, norms and so forth – which encourage or inhibit a steady flow of good and implemented ideas.

- Although the skills and competences for creativity are well understood and supported by extensive research, there is still a need to equip people with these and to invest in their development.
- Reward and recognition are powerful motivating factors, and organizations wishing to mobilize creativity need to explore different ways of delivering this.
- Delivering a steady stream of creative ideas requires some kind of framework process, especially with people who are relatively inexperienced, for example in shop-floor teams.
- Leadership for creativity is less about being a creative role model than providing coaching and support, helping to create the context in which people can deliver their best creative performance.

References

[1]   Allen, T. & Henn, G. (2007). *The organization and architecture of innovation.* London: Taylor & Francis.
[2]   Coradi, A., Heinzen, M., & Boutellier, R. (2015). A longitudinal study of workspace design for knowledge exploration and exploitation in the research and development process. *Creativity and Innovation Management, 24*, 55–71.
[3]   Amabile, T.M., Burnside, R., & Gryskiewicz, S.S. (1995). *User's guide for KEYS: Assessing the climate for creativity.* Greensboro, NC: Center for Creative Leadership.

Teresa Amabile, T., Conti, R., Coon, H., Lazenby, J. and Herron, M. (1996). Assessing the work environment for creativity. Academy of Management Journal, 39, 1154–1184.

[4]   Ekvall, G. (1996). Organizational climate for creativity and innovation. *European Journal of Work and Organizational Psychology, 5*, 105–123.
[5]   Birkinshaw, J., & Duke, L. *https://www.london.edu/faculty-and-research/lbsr/ employee-led-innovation*
[6]   Mumford, M.D., & Licuanan, B. (2004). Leading for innovation: Conclusions, issues, and directions. *Leadership Quarterly, 15*, 163–171.
[7]   West, M., Borrill, C., Dawson, J., Bordbeck, F., Shapiro, D., & Haward, B. (2003). Leadership clarity and team innovation in health care. *Leadership Quarterly, 14*, 393–410.
[8]   Chatman, J.A., & Kennedy, J.A. (2010). Psychological perspectives on leadership. In N. Nohria & R. Khurana (Eds.), *Handbook of leadership theory and practice* (159–181). Boston, MA: Harvard Business Press.
[9]   Frese, M., & Zapf, D. (1994). Action as the core of work psychology: A German approach. In H.C. Triandis, M.D. Dunnette, & L.M. Hough (Eds.), *Handbook of industrial and organizational psychology* (Vol. 4, 2nd ed., 271–340). Palo Alto, CA: Consulting Psychologists Press.
[10] Damanpour, F. (1991). Organizational innovation: A meta-analysis of effects of determinants and moderators. *Academy of Management Journal, 34*, 555–590.

Section 5

## Chapter 11

User innovation

What is user innovation?

The pickup truck. It is famous throughout the world and a workhorse found in places as diverse as farms, factories and film sets. But where did the idea originate? It began life not on the drawing boards of Detroit but rather on the farms and homesteads of a wide range of users who wanted more than a family saloon. They adapted their cars by removing seats, welding new pieces on and cutting off the roof – in the process prototyping and developing the early model of the pickup. Only later did Detroit adopt the idea and begin the incremental innovation process to refine and mass produce the vehicle. They were typical examples of *user innovators* – creating something which met their needs.

It is easy to fall into the trap of thinking about innovation as a process in which user needs are identified and then something is created by someone else to meet them. This assumes that users are passive recipients – but this is often not the case. Often it is users who are ahead of the game – their ideas plus their frustrations with existing solutions lead them to experiment and create something new. And sometimes these prototypes eventually become mainstream innovations.

A host of other examples support the view that user-led innovation matters – for example petroleum refining, medical devices, semiconductor equipment, scientific instruments, a wide range of sports goods and the Polaroid camera.

Eric von Hippel of Massachusetts Institute of Technology has made a life-long study of this phenomenon. He has plenty of examples but also has tried to map out the pattern of user-led innovation – it isn't a random event but what he believes to be a powerful complementary alternative to mainstream innovation models.

You can find a link on the companion website to Eric's website, where you can watch some video of him explaining his ideas and download and read his book *Democratizing Innovation*.

Von Hippel makes the point that user innovators:

- Have a high incentive to innovate – they want the result (goals and vision);
- Have a willingness to experiment – prototyping and problem exploring;
- Are tolerant of failure – perseverance;
- Openly share and improve ideas with others.

It's easy to see how closely this fits the profile of the kind of creative individual we looked at earlier in the book. Sometimes the motivation is personal – for example looking for something to provide a better user experience. Sports innovators are a great set of examples here – people seeking thrills (= incentive to innovate) experiment with crazy ideas and mash-up surfboards on wheels (which became skateboards), sails on surfboards (= windsurfing), flying bed sheets (= paragliding) and so forth – all imperfect (and often dangerous) prototypes which eventually stabilize into a more widely used form and become a popular sport.

User innovation can also be born out of frustration. We saw in Chapter 2 how James Dyson's annoyance at the poor performance of his vacuum cleaner led him on a five-year creative journey to come up with a better version. But he isn't alone – much of the course of user innovation history is one of 'frustration-driven innovation'. Most of the smartphones in the world run on a version of the Linux operating system. This is not the product of R&D labs in the depths of the giant Linux Corporation – its origins are in the efforts of Linus Torvalds and other frustrated users who over the years have built and continue to innovate in a community of users. Estimates suggest Linux has a market value of around $25 billion.

Creativity in action: frustration as the mother of invention

Dr Tim Craft is an anaesthetist who got frustrated with anaesthetic equipment and how much it varied from theatre to theatre, hospital to hospital. So he collected ideas from colleagues similarly frustrated and sketched out the basis for products which have since been produced by the company he set up and sold all round the world. There's an audio interview and transcript on the companion website where Tim talks about this process of user innovation.

Megan Grassell was shopping with her mother trying to find a bra for her 13-year-old younger sister. Their frustration at not being able to find anything suitable reminded her of her own experiences at that age and she began to explore founding a company to create suitable underwear for this 'tween' market. Her company Yellowberry was launched via Kickstarter and is now a successful and growing business. You can read more about this case on the companion website.

Sometimes it's necessity which forces a different approach – finding solutions to problems. It could be something simple – think about the experience of looking after a baby and the various challenges that poses! Many innovations – for example the drinking cup which doesn't spill over a clean set of clothes when the baby falls asleep. Owen Maclaren was an aeronautical engineer who saw his daughter's frustration at trying to manhandle a pushchair in and out of small spaces. His experience in designing retractable undercarriages for the Spitfire and other wartime aircraft inspired him to work on her behalf to develop the folding buggy.

Tad Golesworthy is perhaps an extreme example – his incentive for innovation came from the fact that he was dying! Diagnosed with a heart condition he decided to design and then have implanted a new valve; fortunately for him and many others with a similar condition he is alive today.

> You can see a TED Talk about this via a link on the companion website.

Many patients suffer from severely debilitating chronic diseases but an increasing number of them (and their carers) are coming up with ideas based on their own experiences to help make living with their disease easier. Such patient innovators are the subject of a fascinating study and database co-ordinated by Pedro Oliveira and colleagues [1]; another example is the 'rare disease community', which is an online platform bringing together people sharing ideas about living with and treating diseases which are too rare to qualify for mainstream attention in the health innovation system.

> You can find a link to the Patient Innovation website and examples, together with a report on the rare disease project on the companion website.

Creativity in action: patient innovation

One day Louis Plante had to leave a concert because of excessive coughing while sitting in proximity to a large speaker. Using his skills as an electronics technician, Louis developed a device that could generate the low frequency vibrations (Oliveira 2012). His primary goal was to develop a treatment he would benefit from. Much later, he decided that his tinkerer efforts were actually so useful that he created a firm (Dymedso) to commercialize his solution. So in the end, he also became a user entrepreneur.

In line with this example, consider the personal story from Hanna Boguslawska who developed chest percussion with electrical percussion and founded a firm named eper ltd to commercialize it:

> My daughter, 26 with CF, depended for most of her life on us, her parents to do her chest physiotherapy. So her independence was constantly compromised and she hated it. On the other hand, we not always delivered the best physiotherapy; simply because we were tired, or didn't have all this time required, or were sick. Sure, you know all of this. [. . .] Many times I was thinking about a simple solution, which would deliver a good physiotherapy and wouldn't require a caregiver. And I am very happy I could do it. My daughter uses my eper 100 (stands for electrical percussor, and 100 symbolizes all my percussion ideas which were never realized) all the time. According to her it is much better than the human hand and she can do it alone.
>
> (Hanna Boguslawska, mother of CF patient
> and founder of eper ltd)

But it's not just hero/pioneer inventors. Many studies suggest there's a lot more user innovation about than that and that 'ordinary' people do it. One obvious place is in the workplace – while the innovation spotlight is often on the glamorous dramatic new product a lot of important change happens slowly behind the scenes. In Chapter 12 on 'high-involvement innovation' we describe that continuous improvement of processes is what keeps costs low, improves quality, improves design and so forth – and this is often the result of people who work closely with the process every day (users in this context) adding their ideas for a continuous stream of innovation.

And it's not just in the workplace. The UK Think Tank NESTA published research which suggests that in 2010 8% of the population was involved in product innovation and 15% in process innovation as users.

> You can find a link on the companion website to a TED Talk by Charles Leadbeater where he describes the opportunities offered by engaging with user-led innovation.

Studies of 'hidden innovation' suggest that a significant and growing number of people are involved in such innovation and it accounts for a surprising number of new ideas. And the idea doesn't stop with products – it is very relevant to services and the public sector. For example, the Danish government has had considerable success with engaging users in innovations around the tax system!

> You can find a video interview with Helle-Vibeke Carstensen describing the experiences of user innovation in the Danish tax system.

Technology is also empowering users to become creators. Think about the world of smartphone apps – essentially we have a platform in our hands across which all sorts of applications can move from developers to widespread use. Put the coding skills in the hands of users and there is an explosion of possibilities. Examples here might include humanitarian innovation where users create mash-ups quickly to deal with urgent problems – for example Ushahidi (crisis mapping), open street mapping (to create new maps of damaged and safe areas), apps to reunite families separated by the crisis, apps to enable food and medical supply distribution and so forth.

You can find examples of this approach on the companion website.

Other platforms could include 3D printing – these days everyone can have access to their own version of the Star Trek–style 'Replicator' – if you can think of a design it can be made.

You can find a link on the companion website to a TEDTalk by Chris Anderson of *Wired* magazine where he talks about the power of the new 'maker movement' of user innovators.

The process of user innovation

User innovation is beginning to challenge the conventional view of how the innovation process operates. Where the old models tend to involve a funnel, where ideas are winnowed down and refined and eventually shoot out to create value at the far end, the new model is more one in which users not only provide rich ideas at the front end but also act as continuous innovators, modifying and adapting things once they are launched into the market place. The resulting picture is more like a tube with funnel mouths at both ends (see Figure 11.1).

This isn't a new idea – Jamie Fleck suggested a model of 'innofusion' back in the 1980s when researching early users of industrial robots [2]. He noted that the innovation process there was one of user adaptation and fiddling, often leading to new and certainly better designs. Eric von Hippel has written extensively about it – and we are now beginning to see it happening on a large scale [3].

There are two important points where user input becomes important; first in increasing the richness and range of ideas at the 'front end of innovation'. Here the fashion for 'crowdsourcing' isn't just a marketing hype but one which can give smart firms much clearer insight into underlying trends and interests. 'Not

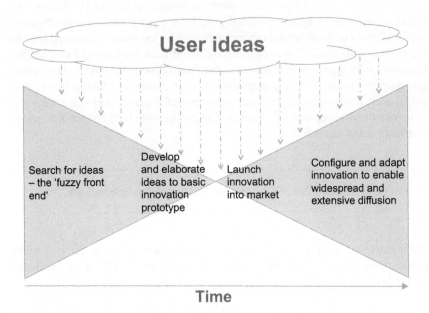

Figure 11.1 Process of user innovation

all the smart guys work for us' is the mantra of open innovation, and in the case of users they are a rich potential source of ideas [4].

The second important point is around the 'back end' of innovation – accelerating and extending diffusion. A key problem in innovation is around enabling the spread of a new product or service to a wide-enough market. Moving to scale is the focus of extensive research around what is called adoption theory – and a key element of that is that innovations diffuse only if they are perceived to be compatible with the context into which they will be placed [5]. So ensuring a good fit between the receiving population and the innovation is critical, and that's where user innovation comes in. By involving users they shape the design so that it is more likely be compatible, attractive to 'people like us'.

So involving users = more ideas and more widely accepted innovation. The big question – which we have learned a lot about in the past ten years – is how?

Enabling user innovation

User innovation is increasingly recognized as important, tapping into creativity and focusing it in different ways. A number of approaches have been developed to try and harness this powerful source of creativity in systematic fashion, including:

- Lead user methods;
- Working with co-creation communities;
- Crowdsourcing ideas;
- Working with extreme users.

Lead user methods

Characteristic of many user innovators is that they appear very early on the adoption curve for new ideas – they are concerned with getting solutions to particular needs and prepared to experiment and tolerate failure in their search for a better solution. So a powerful strategy is to identify and engage with such 'lead users' to co-create innovative solutions.

An example is the 3M company which already has a strong track record in creativity drawing on the ideas of its own employees. In the mid-1990s they extended their approach by bringing in lead users, engaging them in working on early prototypes, suggesting their own ideas and modifications and generally becoming part of the 'front end' innovation team. The results were powerful: a 2002 study suggested that this approach generated an average of \$146 million worth of business after five years, almost eight times higher than the average value for ideas developed only in-house.

You can find more information on lead user methods on the companion website together with a link to video in which Eric von Hippel explains in detail how they are applied in the context of 3M.

LEGO is another company which has worked to engage a community of co-creators, in this case focusing on the children who buy and play with their products. Over a decade they have been developing ways of enabling ideas from children to be articulated and shared across various platforms; this has not only provided benefits in terms of closer customer relationships but has also helped them develop profitable new products. Part of their success is that these products have emerged from the community and have been shown to be popular within that community – the innovations are a good fit with their context.

You can find a case study of LEGO and its approach on the companion website.

Creativity in action: user involvement in innovation

One of the key lessons about successful innovation is the need to get close to the customer. At the limit, the user can become a key part of the innovation process, feeding in ideas and improvements to help define and shape the innovation. The Danish medical devices company, Coloplast, was founded in 1954 on these principles when nurse Elise Sorensen developed the first self-adhering ostomy bag as a way of helping her sister, a stomach cancer patient. She took her idea to a various plastics manufacturers, but none showed interest at first. Eventually one, Aage Louis-Hansen, discussed the concept with his wife, also a nurse, who saw the potential of such a device and persuaded her husband to give the product a chance. Hansen's company, Dansk Plastic Emballage, produced the world's first disposable ostomy bag in 1955. Sales exceeded expectations and in 1957, after having taken out a patent for the bag in several countries, the Coloplast company was established. Today the company has subsidiaries in twenty countries and factories in five countries around the world, with specialist divisions dealing with incontinence care, wound care, skin care, mastectomy care and consumer products (specialist clothing, etc.) as well as the original ostomy care division.

Keeping close to users in a field like this is crucial, and Coloplast have developed novel ways of building in such insights by making use of panels of users, specialist nurses and other healthcare professionals located in different countries. This has the advantage of getting an informed perspective from those involved in post-operative care and treatment and who can articulate needs which might for the individual patient be difficult or embarrassing to express. By setting up panels in different countries the varying cultural attitudes and concerns could also be built into product design and development.

An example is the Coloplast Ostomy Forum (COF) board approach. The core objective within COF boards is to try and create a sense of partnership with key players, either as key customers or key influencers. Selection is based on an assessment of their technical experience and competence but also on the degree to which they will act as opinion leaders and gatekeepers – for example by influencing colleagues, authorities, hospitals and patients. They are also a key link in the clinical trials process. Over the years Coloplast has become quite skilled in identifying relevant people who would be good COF board members – for example, by tracking people who author clinical articles or who have a wide range of experience across different operation types. Their specific role is particularly to help with two elements in innovation:

- Identify, discuss and prioritize user needs;
- Evaluate product development projects from idea generation right through to international marketing.

Importantly COF boards are seen as integrated with the company's product development system and they provide valuable market and technical information into the stage gate decision process. This input is mainly associated with early stages around concept formulation (where the input is helpful in testing and refining perceptions about real user needs and fit with new concepts). There is also significant involvement around project development where involvement is concerned with evaluating and responding to prototypes, suggesting detailed design improvements, design for usability and so forth.

You can find more details of the Coloplast case on the companion website.

Building co-creation communities

Sometimes user led innovation involves a community which creates and uses innovative solutions on a continuing basis. Good examples of this include the Apache server community around web server development applications, Mozilla (browser software), Propellerhead and other music software communities and the emergent group around Apple's i-platform devices like the iPhone.

Within some communities, users will freely share innovations with peers, termed 'free revealing'. Some examples are online communities for open source software, music hobbyists, sports equipment and professional networks. Participation is driven mostly by intrinsic motivations, such as the pleasure of being able to help others or to improve or develop better products, but also by peer recognition and community status. The elements valued are social ties and opportunities to learn new things rather than concrete awards or esteem. Such knowledge-sharing and innovation tends to be more collective and collaborative than idea competitions.

On the companion website you can find video interviews with Michael Bartl of Hyve, a major German company providing software and support for such crowdsourcing and innovation contests, and with Catherina van Delden of Innosabi, a company which mobilizes communities of innovators across a Facebook platform to co-create a range of products including cosmetics, fashion accessories and foodstuffs. There is also an audio interview with David Overton of the UK's Ordnance Survey talking about the challenges in opening up a national geographic information resource to co-creating new development ideas. David Simoes-Brown of 100% Open talks about his company's work in bridging different communities across this 'open innovation' space, while Helle-Vibeke Carstensen discusses how this approach is working in the Danish public sector.

Public sector applications of this idea are growing as citizens act as user-innovators for the services which they consume. 'Citizen-sourcing' is increasingly being used; an example is the UK website fixmystreet.com, in which citizens are able to report problems and suggest solutions linked to the roads infrastructure. The approach also opens up significant options in the area of social innovation – for example, the crisis response tool 'Ushahidi' emerged out of the Kenyan post-election unrest and involves using crowdsourcing to create and update rich maps which can help direct resources and avoid problem areas. It has subsequently been used in the Brisbane floods, the Washington snow emergency and the aftermath of the tsunami in Japan.

Communities of this kind not only offer frameworks for co-creation but represent powerful sources for mainstream innovators. For example, Local Motors is a co-creation community of people interested in automobiles and components. They have not only developed their own cars for sale (including one which can be 3D printed!) but also offer a powerful additional resource for ideas which the mainstream car companies can draw upon.

You can find a case study of Local Motors on the companion website.

Using the crowd

Not everyone is an active user, but the idea of the crowd as a source of different perspectives is an important one. Sometimes people with very different ideas, perspectives or expertise can contribute new directions to our sources of ideas – essentially amplifying. Using the wider population has always been an idea, but until recently it was difficult to organize their contribution simply because of the logistics of information processing and communication. But using the internet new horizons open up to extend the reach of involvement as well as the richness of the contribution people can make.

In 2006, journalist Jeff Howe coined the term crowdsourcing in his book *The Power of Crowds* [6]. In crowdsourcing, an organization makes an open call to a large network to provide some voluntary input or perform some function. The core requirements are that the call is open, and that the network is sufficiently large, the 'crowd'. Crowdsourcing of this kind can be enabled via a number of routes – for example innovation contests, innovation markets, innovation communities.

Open collective innovation (OCI) of this kind is not new but being able to put it into practice has become much simpler. Take for example the case of 'innovation contests' – sourcing good ideas from the crowd. Early examples of such contests included a UK competition to help develop a reliable portable chronometer for naval navigation in the early eighteenth century and a French competition in 1869 to find a substitute for butter (which led to the invention of margarine). But the costs and scale of organization at that time made this a complex and significant undertaking; by contrast it is now possible to set up and run innovation contests rapidly and frequently using well-established and proven software platforms and supporting organizational routines.

Similarly the principle of collaborative research in which perspectives are shared is not new; James Watt developed his steam engine designs with extensive reference to earlier work by Newcomen and others. But once again, today's environment enables widespread 'broadcast search' to diverse players and a corresponding high variety of different perspectives on innovation problems. For example the innovation marketplace at Innocentive.com has a population of around 250,000 regular solvers offering their input to a diverse range of challenges running across the platform.

You can find more details about Open Collective Innovation on the companion website.

Table 11.1 gives some examples of the significant acceleration in innovation potential offered by such models.

Table 11.1 Emergent properties associated with 'open collective innovation'

Emergent property – resulting from OCI convergence	Examples
Lowering of entry barriers – widespread cheap communications allows democratization of innovation, bringing many more players into the innovation game.	Innovation contests – fast and easy to set up, low cost so available to anyone wishing to host one, robust platforms on which specific contests can be configured, high reach in terms of volume and variety of contributors.
Increasing reach – OCI enfranchises many more people, giving them access to the process of innovation and the tools to enable it.	People at the base of the pyramid – the five billion on very low incomes who have traditionally been excluded – are now able to access goods and services and use OCI tools to co-create solutions for their needs. Mobile access to internet allows distributed local solutions and access to global networks.
Increasing involvement – it is quick to build communities around key themes, and if these achieve critical mass there is a degree of long-term sustainability.	Collaborative communities like Linux, Apache, Propellerhead and Wikipedia provide powerful and continuing engines for innovation. Significantly, this community-building is often driven by non-financial motives and enables extensive social enterprises and innovation.

(Continued)

Table 11.1 (Continued)

Emergent property – resulting from OCI convergence	Examples
Increasing range of ideas – OCI spreads the net more widely and the resulting flexibility offers more different starting points for development of ideas and new insights and inspiration across different worlds – recombinant innovation.	Cross-sector learning opportunities such as using manufacturing concepts in healthcare or 'servitization' of product businesses.
Co-creation with users takes the user-led mode further, because it is now cost-effective to bring multiple users into the process. Extent of user-involvement is deepened – moving from cosmetic customization to deep design involvement.	User-input and co-creation – LEGO working with children as designers, patients as a key source of healthcare innovation.
Accelerating diffusion – innovation markets, communities and groupings are simple to establish and quickly reach a scale of connectivity with significant effects in terms of idea generation, idea development – and rapid viral spread across communities.	Online communities can be quickly mobilized. For example Facebook users enabled the website to be translated into multiple languages in a period of weeks. ALNAP provides a networked community for fast sharing and diffusion of best practice in humanitarian emergency aid.
Extending reach to previously uneconomic solutions – OCI facilities managing the long tail problem.	Amazon with books, music, etc. New approaches to dealing with rare diseases by mobilizing communities, etc.

The value of opening up to the crowd is that it can not only amplify the volume of ideas, but also the diversity and evidence is emerging that it is particularly this feature which makes the crowd a useful additional source of innovation.

Extreme users

An important variant which picks up on both the lead user and the fringe needs concepts lies in the idea of extreme environments as a source of innovation. The argument here is that the users in the toughest environments may have needs which by definition are at the edge – so any innovative solution which meets those needs has possible applications back into the mainstream. An example would be antilock braking systems (ABS), which are now a commonplace feature of cars but which began life as a special add-on for premium high-performance cars. The origins of this innovation came from a more extreme case, though – the need to stop aircraft safely under difficult conditions where traditional braking might lead to skidding or other loss of control. ABS was developed for this extreme environment and then migrated across to the (comparatively) easier world of automobiles.

Looking for extreme environments or users can be a powerful source of stretch in terms of innovation – meeting challenges which can then provide new opportunity space. As Roy Rothwell put it in the title of a famous paper, 'Tough Customers, Good Designs' [7]. For example, stealth technology arose out of a very specific and extreme need for creating an invisible aeroplane – essentially something which did not have a radar signature. It provided a powerful pull for some radical innovation which challenged fundamental assumptions about aircraft design, materials, power sources and so forth, and opened up a wide frontier for changes in aerospace and related fields. The 'bottom of the pyramid' concept mentioned earlier also offers some powerful extreme environments in which very different patterns of innovation are emerging. And the crisis innovations emerging from sites of disasters via humanitarian agencies offer another powerful set of examples.

References

[1] Habicht, H., Oliveira, P., & Scherbatuik, V. (2012). User innovators: When patients set out to help themselves and end up helping many. *Die Unternehmung – Swiss Journal of Management Research, 66*, 277–294. See also *www.patient-innovation.com*.

[2] Fleck, J., Webster, J., & Williams, R. (1989). *The dynamics of IT implementation: A reassessment of paradigms and trajectories of development* (No. 14). University of Edinburgh, Research Centre for Social Sciences.

[3] Von Hippel, E. (2005). *The democratization of innovation*. Cambridge, MA: MIT Press.

[4] Rogers, E. (2003). *Diffusion of innovations*. New York, NY: Free Press.

[5] McClure, D., & Gray, I. (2015). Scaling: Innovation's missing middle. *ThoughtWorks*. See *https://thoughtworks.fileburst.com/articles/scaling-innovations-missing-middle-dan-mcclure-ian-gray.pdf*

[6] Howe, J. (2008). *Crowdsourcing: Why the power of the crowd is driving the future of business*. New York, NY: Three Rivers Press.

[7] Rothwell, R. and Gardiner, P. (1983). Tough customers, good design. *Design Studies, 4*, 161–169.

## Chapter 12

High-involvement innovation

In an uncertain world there can't be many organizations which don't recognize the importance of innovation – and the need to mobilize as much effort behind that task as possible. One of the great opportunities open to all of them is to engage the creativity of all employees in the organization – as one manager memorably put it, the big benefit is that 'with every pair of hands you get a free brain!'

There's plenty of evidence to back this up. Some of it comes from individual companies like Toyota, which since it began asking its employees to contribute ideas in the 1960s has received around 50 *million* suggestions for improvement (and implemented the vast majority of them) [1]. And some of it comes through sector and national studies which regularly highlight the contribution employees can make to sustained continuous improvement. It's not just manufacturing – all sectors, including public services, can mobilize the same effect [2].

The idea that people can contribute to innovation through suggesting and implementing their ideas isn't new. Attempts to utilize this approach in a formal way can be traced back to the eighteenth century, when the 8th Shogun Yoshimune Tokugawa introduced the suggestion box in Japan. In 1871 Denny's shipyard in Dumbarton, Scotland, employed a programme of incentives to encourage suggestions about productivity-improving techniques; they sought to draw out 'any change by which work is rendered either superior in quality or more economical in cost'. In 1894 the National Cash Register company (NCR) made considerable efforts to mobilize the 'hundred-headed brain' which their staff represented, while the Lincoln Electric Company started implementing an incentive management system in 1915. NCR's ideas, especially around suggestion schemes, found their way back to Japan where the textile firm of Kanebuchi Boseki introduced them in 1905.

But although it was a simple principle it was neglected in most Western organizations until the last part of the twentieth century. In Japan, on the other hand, it thrived and became a powerful engine for innovation. Firms like Kawasaki Heavy Engineering (reporting an average of nearly 7 million suggestions per year, equivalent to nearly 10 per worker per week), Nissan (6 million/3 per worker per week), Toshiba (4 million) and Matsushita (also with 4 million) testify to the importance placed on the approach. Joseph Juran, one of the pioneers of the quality movement in the United States and Japan pointed out the significance of 'the gold in the mine', suggesting that each worker in a factory could potentially contribute a valuable and continuing stream of improvements – provided they were enabled to do so [3].

This kind of approach is what we call 'high-involvement innovation' (HII; see Figure 12.1). It's about harnessing the creative skills of individuals and groups across an organization and focusing them on the challenges which the organization faces.

You can find some short videos explaining HII on the companion website together with links to a number of case examples.

Building HII capability

It's a simple idea – but making it happen isn't as easy as it sounds. Yes, everyone can be creative and has plenty of ideas for improving things within the organization. But, as we saw, enabling them to do so – and sustaining their involvement – depends on creating an environment in which it can flourish. A major international research programme during the late 1990s looked at this challenge across many countries and the key finding was that HII is not a binary thing, an on-off switch. It needs to become a core part of the culture – 'the way we do things around here' – if it is to have a sustained impact and become a strategic resource. And that depends on building nine core capabilities:

- Establishing HII as a core value – little improvements from everyone (LIFE) matter in this organization.
- Promoting recognition and reward – this core value is reinforced by relevant incentives (and this is less about money than about being listened to, empowered, enabled to contribute).
- Training and development – to support learning about how to be an effective innovator.
- Establishing a core process to enable HII to happen – including allowing time and space for it to operate.
- Implementing idea management systems which give feedback and action to ideas.
- Facilitating and supporting HII – coaching, training, structures and so forth.
- Promoting leadership – entrepreneurial responsibility and walking the talk.
- Providing strategic direction – policy deployment where bottom-up capability meets top-down clear direction about where and why improvements matter.
- Building dynamic capability – continuously reviewing and updating the HII approach.

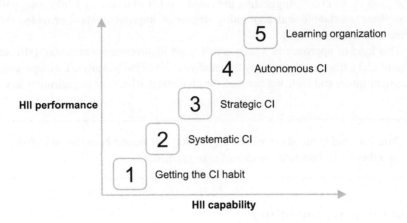

Figure 12.1 High-involvement innovation

We can see close parallels to many of the key competences we have been talking about in the book so far. Creativity is not just going to happen; there has to be a structure and a set of skills which can be learned and developed. People for whom the skills of problem exploration and solving are unfamiliar need a process, a simple cycle they can follow. Their efforts need to be oriented towards a shared goal, and the big stretching target needs to be broken down into achievable targets to guide them. There are many simple tools which can help support the development of thinking skills around Creative Problem-Solving, but these need to be trained and people need to feel confident in using them. Much depends on the context, a supportive environment in which it is OK to experiment and take risks, and to learn from failures – and this poses a big challenge to managers within the organization.

It's worth noting that much of the work of Michael West and colleagues which provided the framework for earlier chapters in this book was carried out looking at workplace teams trying to evolve an HII culture.

Research suggests that moving to HII involves a journey rather than a sudden shift and it's possible to use a 'maturity model' to map the stages in the evolution of capability along this road [4].

Characterizing levels in the HII maturity model

Key elements which characterize each level can be summarized as follows (see Table 12.1):

Table 12.1 Stages in the evolution of HII

HII level	HII level – explanation	Characteristic behaviour patterns
Level 1 – getting the habit	Interest in the concept has been triggered – by a crisis, by attendance at a seminar, by a visit to another organization, etc. – but implementation is on an ad hoc basis	Problems are solved randomly No formal efforts or structure for improving the organization Occasional bursts of improvement punctuated by inactivity and non-participation Solutions tend to realize short-term benefits No strategic impact on human resources, finance or other measurable targets Staff and management are unaware of HII as a process
Level 2 – structured HII	There is formal commitment to building a system which will develop HII across the organization	HII or an equivalent organization improvement initiative has been introduced Staff use structured problem-solving processes A high proportion of staff participates in HII activities Staff has been trained in basic HII tools Structured idea management system is in place Recognition system has been introduced HII activities have not been integrated into day-to-day operations
Level 3 – strategic HII	There is a commitment to linking HII behaviour, established at 'local' level to the wider strategic concerns of the organization	All the above plus: Formal deployment of strategic business goals Monitoring and measuring of HII against these goals HII activities are part of main business activities Focus includes cross-boundary and even cross-enterprise problem-solving

(Continued)

Table 12.1 (Continued)

HII level	HII level – explanation	Characteristic behaviour patterns
Level 4 – autonomous/ proactive HII	There is an attempt to devolve autonomy and to empower individuals and groups to manage and direct their own processes	All the above plus: HII responsibilities devolved to problem-solving unit High levels of experimentation
Level 5 – the learning organization	Approximates to a model 'learning organization'	All the above plus: Extensive and widely distributed learning behaviour Systematic finding and solving problems and capture and sharing of learning Widespread, autonomous but controlled experimentation

In the following sections you'll find some examples of 'archetypes' – descriptive models of organizations at different stages towards maturity. They offer an opportunity for self-reflection and mapping where next to move in terms of building HII capability.

There's a self-assessment tool (High Involvement Innovation audit) on the companion website which will help you explore an organization's HII maturity level, together with some suggestions about actions to build capability.

Level 0: trying out the idea . . .

You believe that people have a much bigger contribution to make to finding and solving problems than they are currently able to make. There must be ways of getting them to chip in their ideas for improving things instead of leaving it up to you and your specialists.

Perhaps you have seen examples in other organizations; perhaps you have read about it; perhaps you have been told by one of your customers that they'd like to see more evidence of this. Everyone seems to be doing it, and there is some logic in trying to get people to contribute their ideas for improvements – rather than hanging up their brains on the coat hook as they come in in the morning!

You're not sure how to put this into practice but you are prepared to give it a try – 'nothing ventured, nothing gained.' It's probably going to take more than just talking to people to get them to chip in their ideas, and you are prepared to invest a bit of time and money in training, perhaps with the help of a consultant.

Your expectations are not too high – this is only an experiment, and if it doesn't work you can always go back to the tried and tested ways of working in the organization. You don't really have a strategic view on this – if it takes off, then there will be time to put some real resources behind it. As long as it doesn't rock the boat too much, and particularly doesn't get in the way of the real tasks of the business, it's worth a try.

Level 1: getting the HII habit

For whatever reasons you have decided to try and do something about involving people in problem-finding and solving within your organization. You're reasonably convinced by the experience of others and by the idea that 'with every pair of hands you get a free brain!' – your problem is how to put that into practice. You are trying a few things to get the idea across but you are also aware that this is a big change to the established 'way we do things around here', so it isn't going to be easy.

You've started with a pilot activity rather than trying to change the whole organization in one go. You've picked a group or groups of people as 'guinea pigs' – some of them are more enthusiastic than others – and they are going through a short programme of training and project work on simple problem-finding and solving. You may be doing this on a do-it-yourself basis, but the chances are that you have hired in some expertise to help with the training and other activities.

People seem to be having fun and they are learning some new tools and techniques; they are also keen to try and make a difference in the project areas they have been tackling. The results are interesting and in some cases you are agreeably surprised by what they have been able to achieve in a relatively short period of time. Many of the solutions they have introduced have a 'why didn't we think of that before?' quality about them – and you are encouraged to think that it might be worth trying to capture this latent knowledge and capability on a more systematic basis.

But therein lies your dilemma. Up till now it has been a (relatively) low-cost exercise – an experiment which has not really disrupted things and which has motivated people and produced some interesting results. It confirms your views that it might be worth going down this path further – but the next step is a much bigger one. Somehow you have to spread the activity and enthusiasm across the rest of the workforce, and make the problem-finding and solving a part of their day-to-day activity rather than just a one-off project. And if you're going to do that then you need to put some structure into the programme – you need regular training, you need some way of helping and supporting the groups, you need to think about how to manage the flood of ideas which might result so you don't turn people off when their ideas don't get implemented – the list goes on and on! And there is the big question which someone is bound to raise – 'what's in it for me?'

People are bound to ask what they are going to get in return for giving their good ideas – so you need to think carefully about some form of recognition for their participation.

On top of that you have to convince your colleagues that this is a worthwhile investment – because it is clear that moving to the next stage will cost time and money, not to mention the need for continuing top management support. All in all, what started as an interesting experiment has now led you to a major strategic decision – the potential benefits have been shown by the experiment, but now you have to decide whether to move on to a much higher level of commitment.

Level 2: systematic HII

You have been working in fairly systematic fashion with the idea of employee involvement in 'continuous improvement' for a while now. You originally set up a project team with the responsibility for designing and implementing a HII system within the organization, and your role is primarily to provide support and backing (not to mention finding the resources to keep it going!). The team is made up of staff from various parts and levels in the organization and they are seconded for a significant part of their time to the HII programme. They originally designed a system which they spent several months planning before launching, first in a pilot project and then rolling it out to the rest of the organization. Their work now is around monitoring and fine-tuning it which they do through a monthly review meeting which you also attend.

The 'HII system' is made up of the following:

  A small group of facilitators (drawn from the project team) whose role is to help train and support the various HII teams. Initially their role was very much 'hands on' but as the teams gain in confidence so the facilitators can work on fine tuning, helping introduce new tools, helping extend participation and so forth.

  A problem-finding and solving approach which defines a systematic process for all the teams to use. This is a simple variation on Deming's famous 'plan, do, check, act' which the project team have modified to suit the organization. Everyone receives training in this at the start of their involvement in the HII programme, and they are encouraged to start using it immediately on workplace problems.

  Training in a suite of simple problem-finding and solving tools which teams can quickly use to help them in their HII activities. Examples of the tools are fishbone charts, brainstorming and process mapping.

  A team-based approach, where groups of five to six people are drawn from a work area and trained together to become a HII team. To help them work as a group they are given some basic training (half day) in tools to help run meetings – agenda setting, action planning and so forth. Initially the facilitators help them run their HII sessions but the teams gradually take over and become self-managing; most try and meet once a week for about forty-five minutes.

An idea management system (IMS) which the project team designed to deal with the high volume of ideas which began to flow once the programme got under way. Essentially the system is geared to try and provide some response to anyone who has made a suggestion as quickly as possible. The response may be simple – an acknowledgement and a go-ahead for implementation by the team itself. (This accounts for a substantial proportion of all ideas.) The next level is those ideas which need additional help or resources – perhaps a skilled craftsman or technician. These are acknowledged and put on a priority list for action when the relevant resource people become available. Finally there are those major changes which form the basis of a special action team – a cross-functional group aimed at tackling a big problem issue. (The IMS also has mechanisms for helping say no quickly and clearly to those ideas which – for whatever reasons – are not feasible or desirable.)

A recognition system which aims to help maintain motivation among the staff to contribute their ideas. Although the group looked at a monetary-based reward system (linked to the value of improvements suggested) they decided that this would not be the most effective, not least because it might be divisive and would tend to encourage people only to offer their 'big' ideas. Instead the system is designed to try and encourage the behaviour of suggesting – which it does by providing simple token rewards for any suggestion made (without attempting to evaluate them). The rewards here vary but include a free cup of coffee, a coffee mug, a T-shirt and so forth; one of the most successful has been a scheme where the company contributes €1 to a nominated charity for every idea suggested in the HII teams. For those ideas which have more significant potential there is a bigger reward, the size and nature of which is decided upon by a panel including the HII project team; this award is made to the group as a whole. (Examples here include money, but also other things like a meal out for all the team members or a place on a training course for each member of the team.)

A communication system, where the results of individual projects can be shared with others. This takes several forms – teams make up 'storyboards' about their particular projects which they display in their areas, there is an in-house newsletter and so forth.

Things are going fairly well with the current system – the majority of people are involved although there is a spread of enthusiasm from a few fanatics right across to a handful of people who are really not interested and in some cases actively hostile. Overall it seems as though people have got the hang of the basic problem-finding and solving approach and the tools which support it; if you look around the organization you can sometimes see the evidence in the form of flip charts or pictures on the walls, or people going into a huddle during a coffee break to try and crack a particular problem issue. There have been one or two big wins – projects where the team has been able to make a significant impact on a particular area, and these big hits in terms of improved quality or reduced costs help you to keep the rest of the management team convinced that the (still significant) investment in HII is worth maintaining.

Although it has gone well and has undoubtedly started to change the way people think and behave around the organization, you have some concerns which the HII team in different ways share. The programme isn't really going anywhere – and in some cases it appears to be falling back. When you started around a year ago there was a lot of enthusiasm, but things now feel a little stale. In the same way, whereas people used to make time and give priority to HII sessions, these are increasingly being pushed aside as urgent work comes along. The team can do some things to help maintain momentum – for example extra training sessions and the introduction on some new tools – but there is a growing sense that the programme is running out of steam.

This isn't helped by the fact that many of the projects which teams have been proposing are put into the queue for specialist action teams – and there simply isn't enough capacity among the specialists to respond quickly. The growing delay between teams suggesting things and something getting down about their ideas is setting up a climate where they start to ask whether it's worth bothering – no-one does anything with our ideas anyway.

You are also concerned that the benefits, although useful in terms of overall morale, are not really producing a big impact on the bottom line. Most of the gains are modest and confined to a local level – and you are finding it increasingly difficult to justify continuing to commit resources to HII when the matter comes up for discussion among your senior colleagues.

You can find some case studies and video material describing organizations at this level on the companion website. The kinds of tools used to support HII can be found in the CI toolbox, also on the companion website.

Level 3: targeted and focused HII

Your organization has been systematically working at involving staff in problem-finding and solving for some time, and there is a well-developed framework to support such activity. This includes:

- A HII project team, whose task is to monitor and support the continuing development of employee involvement in problem-solving;
- A common systematic approach to problem-finding and solving which is used by teams and individuals;

- Regular training and updating in the use of simple tools and techniques for problem-finding and solving;
- An idea management system to manage and progress the various suggestions made from different groups;
- A recognition system which provides feedback and some form of acknowledgement/reward to individuals and teams contributing suggestions;
- A communication system which captures and shares some of the ideas and experiences.

After operating such a systematic approach for a while it became clear that there was a lack of strategic focus to the problem-solving activity, and that as a consequence the benefits achieved were confined to a local level. In trying to move on from this and to break out of a growing sense that the HII activity was running out of steam the organization embarked upon a policy deployment programme. This was a major exercise involving linking the 'top-down' strategic planning of the business to the 'bottom-up' capability for finding and solving problems.

In essence the process involves a top-level set of clear business objectives and targets which provide the focus for the HII activity. These clear targets are then broken down into project areas and further disaggregated into individual improvement tasks; in other words the overall strategy is systematically broken down into 'bite-sized' chunks which different HII teams can work on right across the organization. The process of developing this is interactive, with briefing sessions cascading down through the organization so that everyone knows what the objectives are and why they are chosen, and so that everyone can explore how they and their HII activity can make an impact on these targets.

The result is an extended matrix of potential HII projects, each of which links to a strategic objective. The effect is to connect up the 'engine' of problem-finding and solving with the current strategic needs of the business – for example, for cost reduction, quality improvement or time saving.

A key component in making this approach work has been the introduction of a 'measurement culture'. In the early days of HII some teams had used local measures to help guide their improvement activities but this was not done on a widespread or systematic basis. But in policy deployment it is essential that measurement is introduced throughout the process, otherwise there is no way of knowing whether or not the objectives have been achieved. The types of measurement vary from very simple counting and checking through to more complex and precise approaches, but the underlying principle is the same – to ensure that progress is being made and to identify how much further improvement is needed. This has important implications for the problem of 'proving' the value of HII to the bottom line; once strategic targets are set and progress against them is monitored and measured it becomes possible to 'prove' the value of investing in HII.

In general the system works very well; clear targets are now set and reviewed regularly and the HII teams 'buy in' to the overall strategy and translate it into particular objectives for their problem-solving work. Much of the monitoring and measurement work is done by the groups themselves, and the contribution of individuals to HII activity towards these organizational objectives now forms part of the annual appraisal process. In this way HII has become much more part of the day-to-day 'way we do things around here' than a special initiative.

There are some areas where it could develop further. It still works best within specific areas and the distribution of enthusiasm and involvement varies across the organization. There are some cross-functional projects and even some which involve working with people outside the firm on joint projects – but these are still in their infancy. Increasingly it seems as though the 'big hits' are likely to come from dealing with problems like these which span different areas and organizations.

HII also still needs quite a bit of external support and facilitation – helping define and agree on objectives, providing training and development support to teams, and steering and guiding the process. It is also very much about achieving performance improvements through a lot of small ideas, often resulting from a systematic attack on and elimination of all sorts of waste and inefficiency. While this is of immense positive value, there might be scope for extending the process to a more proactive search for radical new ideas.

Level 4: delegated/autonomous HII

Your organization has been working with HII for some time and has established the basic process of finding and solving problems as a key part of 'the way we do things around here'. HII is not a special initiative but part of the way of life in the organization and groups often find and solve problems in systematic fashion without consciously thinking about how they do it. It is normal to go into groups, do some brainstorming, collect some data and follow a systematic approach – that's just how we do it.

While there is a high degree of involvement in problem-finding and solving activity it is linked to the overall strategy of the business. There is a clear process of policy deployment where the top-level objectives and targets are shared with everyone in the organization (so people know why certain things have to be improved); these high-level targets are broken down systematically into projects with which different HII teams can engage. Monitoring and measuring of progress towards achieving them is handled by the teams themselves and the results are displayed and shared so everyone has a sense of progress towards meeting the strategic objectives.

Teams are experienced and the organization continues to invest in regular training and updating of skills relevant to HII. For this reason they are largely self-facilitating, able to take on loosely defined strategic projects and use a variety of different approaches to carrying them out. They feel empowered to experiment with different solutions (not all of which work) and they share the results of their efforts with other teams so that there is little reinventing of the wheel and so that groups can avoid falling into the same traps as their colleagues. There is a sense of top management support which extends to empowering the groups to choose how their solutions will be implemented and often to spending the money to get something done. There is a high degree of trust – the underlying thinking being that the teams are well trained in HII, they have a clear sense of the strategic objectives and they will try different approaches to find a solution, so they do not need a heavy hand on the tiller from outside.

The 'buy-in' to the strategy is helped through the reward system, which acknowledges that if the organization can achieve its (stretching) strategic objectives it must have done so as a result of the collective efforts of the HII teams. For this reason there is a simple bonus scheme based on a profit-share over and above the agreed target levels. This provides a powerful incentive to the teams themselves.

This approach has worked well and there is a high degree of motivation among the workforce. Labour turnover is low and performance levels are high. There are still areas for further development, however, particularly between different areas within the organization and certainly outside in its relationships with others. Problem-finding and solving in the value stream is an important priority. A second area for extending the approach is in the development of new products and services; at present almost all the HII work has concentrated on making processes efficient and lean – high quality, fast and low cost. But there is also scope for using the ideas and techniques – the HII capability – in other areas and aspects of the business.

Level 5: the learning organization

The organization has been involved in HII for some time and has established systematic finding and solving problems as a key part of 'the way we do things around here'. This approach is strategy-linked – improvements are made regularly and continuously and they make a contribution to the various strategic objectives of the organization. There is a clear link between overall strategy and its deployment down to the various problem-solving teams. HII is also part of individual behaviour – people are often involved in several different activities from a personal level, through a work-group team to cross-functional and even inter-organizational teams. The whole ethos is one of change – constantly searching for ways to improve things and not leaving things as they are unless there is a good reason. The motto could almost be 'if it ain't being fixed, it's broke'! – recognizing that the world outside is constantly moving on and survival and growth of the organization depends on constant learning and change.

People feel a high degree of empowerment – they are skilled and the organization invests regularly in training and equipping them with the skills they need to understand, find and solve problems. They are also not afraid to experiment – the organization takes the view that it is important to make mistakes while trying things out and that this is to be encouraged, not blamed. The only 'crime' is to make the same mistake twice, so people are encouraged to capture and share whatever they learn through experiment.

Knowledge is at the heart of this organization. It is constantly looking for better ways of doing things, for better ideas in its products and services, and it has people skilled and experienced in the tools and techniques of systematic problem-finding and solving to support this. But it also ensures that the lessons of this constant learning process are captured and shared for others to use – accomplishing this through regular meetings and discussion, documentation, displays, newsletters and other communications media, and so forth.

Part of the looking process involves getting access to new sources of information and seeing things from new perspectives. So the organization encourages job rotation and secondment, brings in people with deliberately different backgrounds to get fresh perspectives, sends them out to visit and talk with customers, supplier, competitors and so forth. It is very open to new sources of ideas and knowledge and to ways of seeing the existing patterns in different ways.

Not only is systematic and strategically aligned HII a way of life, it pervades every aspect of the organization. Involvement levels are very high and the approach is used within work areas, between different areas and out into the supply and distribution chain. The concept of value streams and the strategic improvement of these rather than local problem-solving is central.

Making the HII journey towards maturity

As the archetypes suggest, progress towards HII maturity is not simply a matter of time. It requires investment in structures and processes to enable it and time to train and reinforce new ways of behaving in the organization. Table 12.2 highlights some of the key enablers of transition between levels [5].

Working at the HII frontier

HII is not a new idea – examples of attempts to engage employee creativity go back centuries. And at one level the need for it is self-evident – in a complex and uncertain world the one resource any organization needs is creativity! As we've seen in this brief review, making HII happen is not a simple matter of time and good intentions, it requires effort to construct and maintain a culture of continuous improvement.

The challenges in doing so which we've outlined remain pretty much the key starting points for anyone thinking about implementing HII today. But one of the big shifts in the context for HII is the powerful role which new technology is playing in creating enabling platforms. Where the old HII schemes often fell down was in idea management – simply capturing and processing suggestions in a largely manual system led to delays, lack of feedback, patchy implementation and eventual fall-off in interest and enthusiasm.

Now there are many platforms which not only allow employees to make suggestions but also enable others to comment and build on those suggestions. They can go further, volunteering their help in implementation, providing experienced

Table 12.2 Enablers for HII

Behaviour/routines	Blockage	Enablers
'Getting the HII habit' – legitimating and embedding basic problem-solving behaviour	Lack of suitable starting point/project to move from concepts into action No formal process for finding and solving problems Ideas are not responded to Lack of skills in problem-solving Lack of motivation No structure for HII Lack of group process skills	Simple HII activities focused on workplace – for example, 5S techniques PDCA or similar structural model plus training Simple idea management system, based on rapid response Training in simple HII tools – brainstorming, fishbone techniques, etc. Recognition system Simple vehicles, based on groups Facilitator training
'Focusing HII' – getting strategic benefit from HII	No strategic impact of HII Lack of measurable benefit	Policy deployment techniques – to focus problem-solving on strategic targets Hoshin kanri tools Introduce training in monitoring and measurement Statistical process control Process mapping and ownership
'Spreading the word' – extending HII beyond local level	Lack of co-operation across divisions Lack of inter-firm HII Lack of process orientation	Cross-functional HII teams Inter-firm development initiatives Process modelling tools and training
'Walking the talk'	Conflict between espoused and practised values	Articulation and review
The learning organization	No capture of learning	Post-project reviews Storyboard techniques Encapsulation in procedures
Continuous improvement of HII	Lack of direction Running out of steam	Formal HII steering group and strategic framework Regular HII review and relaunch

evaluation and creating teams willing and able to move entrepreneurial ideas forward from the inside. Linking such platforms and the capability they release to key strategic targets for the organization – policy deployment – can provide a powerful new innovation engine.

References

[1]   Meier, D.P., & Liker, J.K. (2006). *The Toyota Way Fieldbook: A practical guide for implementing Toyota's 4P*. New York, NY: McGraw-Hill.

[2]   Schroeder, A., & Robinson, D. (2004). *Ideas are free: How the idea revolution is liberating people and transforming organizations*. San Francisco: Berrett-Koehler Publishers.

[3]   Boer, H., Berger, A., Chapman, R., & Gertsen, F. (1999). *CI changes: From suggestion box to the learning organisation*. Aldershot: Ashgate.

[4]   Bessant, J., Caffyn, S., & Gallagher, M. (2001). An evolutionary model of continuous improvement behaviour. *Technovation, 21*, 67–77.

[5]   Bessant, J. (2003). *High involvement innovation*. Chichester: Wiley.

Chapter 13

Design thinking

Design thinking (DT) is a popular and widely used framework approach to creativity. It uses many of the competences we have been discussing in an explicit way and deploys various tools and techniques to help with this. Importantly it has emerged as a methodology which can be taught and practised – there are many training programmes and several universities now have a 'D-School' on their campuses. Many organizations have begun to embed this as an innovation approach, both in the public and private sector. And it lies at the heart of many consulting offerings, providing client companies with a systematic approach to finding novel solutions to product, service and process innovation.

> You can find a link on the companion website to the 'd.school' at Stanford (its correct name is the Hasso Plattner Institute of Design), which offers a free ninety-minute video-led cruise through their methodology for anyone interested.

DT is an approach to innovation which involves building and testing ideas in a sequential developmental fashion. Its origins lie in the work of the US Nobel Prize–winner Herbert Simon who worked on various aspects of decision-making. He defined it in his 1969 book *The Sciences of the Artificial* as the 'transformation of existing conditions into preferred ones' [1]. He originally suggested a seven-step process for this: Define, Research, Ideate, Prototype, Choose, Implement, Learn.

But the number of stages is less important than the idea of building towards a solution by a formal method. In essence it takes human creativity and focuses it via a process to solve a problem – in other words it is a methodology for innovation. Many writers have contributed to the approach from a number of different disciplines including Nigel Cross (architecture, one of the founders of the journal *Design Studies*), Sydney Gregory (engineering, author of *The Design Method* [1967]), Rachel Cooper (industrial design) and Robert McKim (*Experiences in Visual Thinking* [1973]) [2–3]. The approach drew on many of the tools

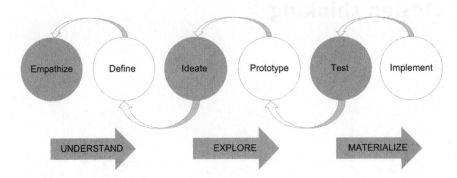

Figure 13.1 IDEO's design thinking process

and techniques for industrial design but applied them to more generic forms of problem-solving, extending the range of application from making products look and feel more interesting and attractive to applying creativity in structured fashion to solve a wide range of business and social problems.

One of the pioneering firms in this field was IDEO (Figure 13.1), founded by an engineering professor at Stanford University, Dave Kelley [4].

The IDEO approach is described in Dave Kelley's book *The Art of Innovation*, and on the companion website you can find a link to an excellent example of the methodology at work. In this video based on an ABC News feature, the IDEO team were challenged to demonstrate their innovation process in front of TV cameras.

But there are others models out there as well. One which we think equally noteworthy is the double diamond model by the British Design Council, developed in 2005 on the basis of case studies of eleven global firms. It describes in four phases the design process from problem to solution (see Figure 13.2). The way the phases are visualized clarifies the way of working in these phases. Starting from a defined problem or challenge, we open up and 'discover' (phase 1) the problem in more detail; just after that a convergent process is going on (define). The problem is clearly described and boiled down to a key challenge. This is again the starting point for another divergent phase: develop. Here it is about collecting ideas, opening up to see all kinds of possible solutions. And then another convergent phase is starting to emerge: deliver. It's about testing and evaluating, about making the concept ready for implementation. At the end stands a solution to the initial problem.

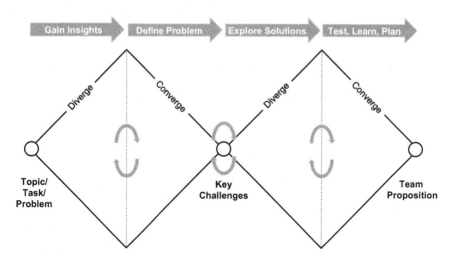

Figure 13.2 Double diamond model

Design thinking follows certain 'ground rules' regardless the modelling of the phases. For example, all innovation is based on the need of the user, innovation is developed best in teams, and iterations are necessary in order for a successful innovation. Group processes like sharing insights and knowledge, supporting ideas of others, pushing the frontiers of an idea to make it 'wow', getting and receiving feedback from the group and from potential users, and felt psychological safety within the 'design team' are all vital elements to the idea of design thinking. So, competencies are the backbone of design thinking.

Overview of the phases

Typically DT involves working through a series of stages, but it is also about recognizing the *cyclic* nature of creativity – learning from testing and implementation helps refine and elaborate. We describe the key phases of the IDEO model in the following section. The phases are:

- Empathize
- Define
- Ideate
- Prototype
- Test
- Implement
- (and repeat).

Empathy – drawing on fields like anthropology emphasis is placed on understanding how people actually behave in a situation, what their experiences of a problem are, creating solutions which work for them in their context. One of the problems in innovation is that we often make assumptions about what users want rather than developing a clear understanding of their context. This is complicated by the fact that what people say – for example in response to a market survey or in a focus group – is not necessarily what they actually do!

Tom Kelley of IDEO explains the DT approach they take in this area:

> We're not big fans of focus groups. We don't much care for traditional market research either. We go to the source. Not the 'experts' inside a (client) company, but the actual people who use the product or something similar to what we're hoping to create . . . we believe you have to go beyond putting yourself in your customers' shoes. Indeed we believe it's not even enough to ask people what they think about a product or idea . . . customers may lack the vocabulary or the palate to explain what's wrong, and especially what's missing.

Creativity in action: users know best

One of the dangers in humanitarian innovation is that well-intentioned providers make assumptions about what end users actually need, and what will actually work in their context. Inappropriate solutions provided with the best intentions litter the sites of disasters – complex equipment which cannot be maintained, supplies used for different purposes. (For example researchers from the Oxford University's Humanitarian Innovation Project found that in Ugandan refugee camps people were using emergency mosquito nets not as an anti-malarial aid but as a source of rope with which to build the shelters which they felt were a more urgent need.)

Underpinning this is an assumption that solutions can be designed far from the context in which they are to be implemented. What is needed is a recognition of the importance of user perspectives – for example how people actually behave under crisis conditions, how they prioritize their emergency needs, how best they can support themselves and so forth.

And empowered users are a rich source of ideas – many important humanitarian innovations arose in this bottom-up fashion. For example the crisis-mapping app Ushahidi emerged from users mashing up Twitter and other social media feeds to help provide a reliable information platform in the post-election violence in Kenya. The app has subsequently been used all around the world including in the Brisbane floods and the Fukushima disaster.

You can find a video interview with Michael Bartl on the companion website where he describes using ethnographic techniques in new product development, together with a detailed description of some of the tools for doing so.

Developing a deep understanding can generate new insights – for example Tim Brown of IDEO writes about the company's work with the Japanese cycle manufacturer Shimano. Working to try and understand why so few (less than 10%) of US adults rode bicycles they uncovered a variety of concerns including intimidating retail experiences, the complexity and cost of sophisticated bikes, and the danger of cycling on heavily trafficked roads. This led to a new concept – 'coasting' – which drew on people's happy memories of childhood biking and which influenced various aspects of the subsequent offering including new in-store retailing strategies, a public relations campaign to identify safe places to cycle and a reference design for cycle companies to use in producing 'coasting' bikes [5].

Creativity in action: understanding user needs in Hyundai Motor

One of the problems facing global manufacturers is how to tailor their products to suit the needs of local markets. For Hyundai this has meant paying considerable attention to getting deep insights into customer needs and aspirations – an approach which they used to good effect in developing the Santa Fe, reintroduced to the US market in 2007. The headline for their development programme was 'touch the market', and they deployed a number of tools and techniques to enable it. For example, they visited an ice rink and watched an Olympic medallist skate around to help them gain an insight into the ideas of grace and speed which they wanted to embed in the car. This provided a metaphor – 'assertive grace' – which the development teams in Korea and the United States were able to use.

Analysis of existing vehicles suggested some aspects of design were not being covered – for example, many sport/utility vehicles (SUVs) were rather 'boxy' so there was scope to enhance the image of the car. Market research suggested a target segment of 'glamour mums' who would find this attractive and the teams then began an intensive study of how this group lived their lives. Ethnographic methods looked at their homes, their activities and their lifestyles – for example, team members spent a day shopping with some target women to gain an understanding of their purchases and what motivated them. The list of key motivators which emerged from this shopping study included durability, versatility, uniqueness, child-friendliness and good customer service from knowledgeable staff.

Another approach was to make all members of the team experience driving routes around Southern California, making journeys similar to those popular with the target segment and in the process getting first-hand experience of comfort, features and fixtures inside the car, and so forth.

A good example of the DT approach comes from work in the UK's Luton and Dunstable hospital (L&D) which involves using design methods to create a user-led solution to the challenge of improving patient care among neck and head cancer sufferers. Part of this project involves patients and carers telling stories about their experience of the service; these stories provide insights which enable the team of co-designers to think about designing *experiences* rather than designing services. Importantly the role of designer includes all of those involved in the collaborative process: patients, staff, researchers and improvement leaders as well as design professionals [6].

Experience-based design (EBD) of this kind involves identifying the main areas or 'touch points' where people come into contact with the service, and tries to identify areas of exceptional practice, and areas where systems and processes need to be redesigned to create a better patient experience of health services [7]. These touch points effectively help to prioritize actions. Working together patients, carers, doctors, nurses and hospital administrative staff can begin to design experiences rather than just systems or processes. The process is enriched by taking into consideration the different skills, views and life experiences of the patients, carers and others involved.

In the L&D such co-design has led to changes – for example patients and carers have changed project documentation so that it better reflects their needs, and clinic staff and patients have worked together to redesign the flow of outpatients in the consulting room. Various methodologies were used to encourage patient involvement in the process, including patient interviews, log books and film-making. This enabled patients to show their experience of the service through their own lens, and bring their story to life for others. In total thirty-eight improvement projects were identified.

You can find audio and a transcript of an interview with Dr Lynn Maher describing this approach on the companion website. There are also other cases – RED and Open Door – which describe applications of DT in healthcare innovation.

Definition – recognizing that what appears to be the problem may in fact be a symptom of a wider problem and that exploring and playing with different definitions can help set up the conditions for successful solution. As we saw in Chapter 2 problem exploration and discovery is a key part of the creativity journey and DT provides a systematic way of managing this. There is a particular link with the competence around building shared vision, gaining agreement about and commitment to the problem we are trying to solve.

You can find an example of using reframing in the context of medical innovation in the DOME – designing out medical error – case on the companion website.

Taking time out to redefine the presented problem in different ways and from different perspectives is an essential part of design thinking. Tools like 'how-to' statements, problem redefinition, root cause analysis (fishbone technique), process mapping and levels of abstraction are used. But again, trying to express different viewpoints reflecting the concerns of the defined stakeholders is core to the process.

In the double diamond model a key challenge from the standpoint of the user is defined at the end of the second phase. So, at the end we have not only defined the user we are looking to 'help' to satisfy his/her needs but also defined the challenge we have to overcome to have a successful 'product' at the end. This will be the starting point for our ideation process in the next phase.

You can find details of a key challenge and a template on the companion website.

Ideation – in this stage various approaches are used to come up with suggested solutions and pathways to be explored. These include the use of 'wild ideas' as a stimulus for others, 'brainstorming' as a careful process of suspending/postponing judgment, and the use of visual aids to capture and make people's ideas available to others. Again this stage draws extensively on creativity research including the powerful role played by unconscious processes in forming novel associations. But it also builds on group competences like striving for excellent ideas and the constructive controversy within that.

DT is not about a single technique but about skilled teams able to open the ideation toolbox and find different resources to help – they recognize the difficulties around setting effects, functional fixedness and other barriers to creativity and can deploy techniques to help counter them. Similarly although brainstorming is a central approach it is carried out in a way which allows for extensive challenge and debate but in a supportive context. And diversity is seen as an important element in team composition to try and maximize the range of experiences and domain expertise on which the team can draw.

An important element in DT is the explicit recognition of users as central to the process – both in terms of understanding their needs (empathy) but also as sources of relevant ideas which will also be compatible. The previous chapter on user innovation highlights this key role.

Prototyping – rather than seeking to plan and develop a perfect solution, design thinking involves a series of interactive experiments which allow for learning around prototypes.

We saw the importance of this approach in earlier chapters; it provides a way of moving from vague notions, hunches, half-formed ideas towards something more workable. Prototypes offer a series of stepping stones, bridges, scaffolding – essentially playing with ideas about the problem. As James Dyson, reflecting on his company's approach, points out, 'prototypes allow you to quickly get a feel for things and uncover subtle design flaws.'

The clue is in the name – proto-type. It's not about the finished object but a stepping stone, a test bed for learning, some way of exploring in laboratory/ experimental mode. Kids do this naturally – from the moment they can start to hold and examine an object they begin to explore it, trying out all its possibilities. And when they play together they multiply the possible options in inspiring fashion – a humble cardboard box can become a spaceship, a shop, a stage, an article of clothing, and it can change its identity with impressive speed!

Prototyping offers some important features to help in the creative process:

- It creates a 'boundary object', something around which other people and perspectives can gather, a device for sharing insights into problem dimensions as well as solutions.
- It offers us a stepping stone in our thought processes, making ideas real enough to see and play with them but without the lock-in effect of being tied into trying to make the solutions work – we can still change our minds.
- It allows plurality – we don't have to play with a single idea, we can bet on multiple horses early on in the race rather than trying to pick winners.
- It allows for learning – even when a prototype fails we accumulate knowledge which might come in helpful elsewhere.
- It suggests further possibilities – as we play with a prototype it gives us a key to open up the problem, break open the shell and explore more deeply.
- It allows us to work with half-formed ideas and hunches – enables a 'conversation with a shadowy idea'.
- It allows for emergence – sometimes we can't predict what will happen when different elements interact. Trying something out helps explore surprising combinations.

Prototypes can take many forms, from simple sketches and models through to complex simulations. German researcher Bernhard Doll offers a helpful map on which different kinds of prototype can be mapped – the important point in DT is not the form but the way in which the prototype is used to help build shared ideas. This approach also helps draw in user experience since the prototype becomes a 'boundary object' around which various people can provide their ideas and input (see Figure 13.3) [8].

Test – the next stage from prototyping is trying those ideas out on end users. 'Fail often to succeed sooner' is a motto only used at IDEO which characterizes this approach of learning through testing; it builds on the idea of rapid cycles of experimentation rather than planned launch of an exhaustively developed idea. The core idea is around hypothesis testing and gradually learning through a series of build-test-refine loops which allow for fast learning.

Examples can be found in beta testing in software and the 'lean start-up' approach where a core tool is the 'minimum viable product' – an early test of

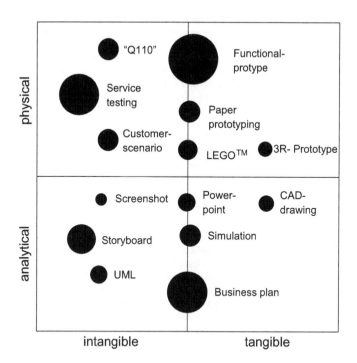

Figure 13.3 Boundary objects

the idea designed to get feedback and information. We'll discuss these 'agile' approaches in more detail in Chapter 15.

Implement – put the idea into practice. Although this might appear to be the end of the journey the reality is that moving an idea into implementation restarts the process, allowing refinements and improvements, identifying other dimensions of the problem which could be addressed. One of the key lessons around diffusion of innovations is that as ideas spread out and scale so they are changed by the interactions with the adopting population [9].

It's easy to see DT as a simple and logical progression through a series of stages. But innovation in real life is not like that – it is a meandering journey involving backtracking, blind alleys and sudden sprints. So DT as a framework methodology should be seen as something involving multiple cycles and extensive feedback between these stages.

Tools for design thinking

DT is a framework methodology with some core underlying principles like empathy, constructive controversy and prototyping. The underlying competences are very much those which we have explored in the book and the good news is that

Table 13.1 Useful tools and techniques for design thinking

Stage in DT Cycle	Useful tools and techniques
Empathize	Ethnography User-led innovation Lead-user methods Customer journeys Storytelling Outcome-driven innovation Empathic design Netnography Kano methods Repertory grid Personas
Define	Five whys Fishbones How-to statements Process mapping Value curves Competitiveness profiling Abstract-driven search Value curves Value stream analysis
Ideate	5Rs Brainstorming Lateral thinking Analogy and metaphor Recombinant innovation Attribute listing Morphological analysis TRIZ
Prototype	Prototyping methods Serious play, simulation, storytelling Lean start-up Living labs
Test	Lean start-up and hypothesis design 5×5×5 Lead-user methods Getting feedback
Implement	Beta to scale Building communities Learning logs

there is plenty of equipment in the gym to help train and develop skills. Table 13.1 gives some examples and you can find details of all the tools and techniques on the companion website.

References

[1] Simon, H.A. (1969). *The sciences of the artificial.* Cambridge, MA: MIT.

[2] Gregory, S. (1965). *The design method.* Oxford: Butterworth.

[3] McKim, R.H. (1972). *Experiences in visual thinking.* Monterey, CA: Brooks/Cole.

[4] Kelley, T., Littman, J., & Peters, T. (2001). *The art of innovation: Lessons in creativity from IDEO, America's leading design firm.* New York, NY: Currency.

[5] Brown, T. (2009). *Change by design: How design thinking transforms organizations and inspires innovation.* New York, NY: Harper.

[6] Bessant, J., & Maher, L. (2009). Developing radical service innovations in healthcare: The role of design methods. *International Journal of Innovation Management, 13,* 555.

[7] Pickles, J., Hide, E., & Maher, L. (2008). Experience based design: A practical method of working with patients to redesign services. *Clinical Governance: An International Journal, 13,* 51–58.

[8] Doll, B. (2009). *Prototyping zur Unterstützung sozialer Interaktionsprozesse.* Munich: Gabler.

[9] Fleck, J. (1994). Learning by trying. *Research Policy, 23,* 637–652.

## Chapter 14

Creativity under extreme constraints

As we've seen, creativity isn't always about throwing resources at a problem. Some of the most inspiring ideas emerge from contexts which seem to close off mainstream ways of solving problems – they force our thinking in new directions. Google has a slogan – 'creativity loves constraints' – and this does seem to be borne out in practice. Sometimes the lack of availability of resources provides a powerful context for innovation.

In this section we'll look at two versions of the extreme constraint context and show how these conditions effectively provide a very different framework within which creativity can flourish. Understanding how it takes place in these worlds can also give us clues about how we could learn and adapt our approaches. For example, the huge Hyundai conglomerate built a core capability around the idea of 'constructed crisis' – effectively thinking about future worlds with very challenging conditions and using this to drive new ways of thinking about products and services it would need to create [1].

Frugal innovation

'Frugal' is a word which means 'careful with resources', and in the business world it is increasingly used to describe an approach to innovation which is simple and sustainable. It grew out of experiences in locations where shortages of key resources required ingenious solutions to problems and where the simplicity of such innovations permits their widespread diffusion.

For example the problem in many shanty towns and temporary settlements is how to provide light when there is rarely any electric power available, and even if there were people could not afford it. By the simple use of an old plastic bottle with some liquid inside (containing bleach to keep the bottle clean), a window can be made in the roof through which light can pass. Alfredo Moser, a Brazilian mechanic, is credited with this idea which has diffused widely; over a million homes in Brazil now make use of this idea.

The underlying ideas of frugal innovation are to simplify products and services to the point where they are good enough to meet widespread needs but not wasteful in terms of excess or unnecessary functions. The approach has become important in meeting the needs of the emerging world where large populations represent significant markets but where individual purchasing power is limited. The management researcher Coimbatore Krishnarao Prahalad wrote persuasively about this in his 2005 book *The Fortune at the Bottom of the Pyramid*, arguing that while several billion people lived on incomes of less than $2/day, this did not mean that they did not share needs and desires for goods and services, only that the ways those were designed and delivered would need to change [2].

This challenge to innovation has become increasingly visible and important in many sectors, from consumer goods to cars, telecommunications and healthcare. Different labels have been used – for example '*jugaad* innovation', which refers to a Hindi word which means improvisation and flexibility to solve an urgent problem [3].

But it would be too easy to dismiss frugal innovation as only being about simple products and services for low wage economies; in fact there are some powerful lessons and messages of much wider relevance [4].

Here are some examples:

- The Miticool ceramic refrigerator, designed to be made using local materials and skills and providing an effective alternative for places without reliable electricity.
- The Chotukool refrigerator, addressing the same problem, offering a simple, low-cost portable device aimed at large local market.
- The Aravind eye care system, a dream of a retired eye surgeon to bring low cost safe and reliable cataract care to the poor of India. The system now delivers better quality care than most Western hospitals at a fraction of the cost ($25/operation); as a result over 12 million people who would otherwise be blind can now see. The model developed systematically, borrowing and adapting ideas from the world of McDonalds and fast food, and gradually expanding into a highly integrated system in which lenses, instruments and other elements are produced for use in the growing number of Aravind hospitals. Products and services are exported to 87 countries.
- The Narayana Health (NHL) approach followed similar lines and was pioneered by Dr Devi Shetty, who took the principles and used them in complex operations like open-heart bypass surgery. The same results apply: massive lowering of costs without compromising on safety. And again the idea is to develop a system, a platform with high levels of integration and across which frugal ideas are constantly being explored. The model has extended to health insurance, where twelve million farmers can pay a monthly micro-insurance premium of twelve cents and receive widespread healthcare benefits, and to advanced telemedicine where the problems of skill shortages and expert coverage across a vast subcontinent are dealt with using sophisticated IT infrastructure. The successful model is now beginning to have an impact in mainstream markets; in 2016 Narayan opened a facility in the Cayman Islands to offer reliable, low-cost health care to neighbouring US citizens.

- While frugal innovation is associated with emerging market conditions where purchasing power is low the potential for such ideas to transfer back to industrialized markets is high. GE developed a simple electrocardiogram machine (the MAC 400) for use in rural India. The machine became widely successful in that context but has since become a best seller in other markets because of its simplicity and low cost. It was developed in eighteen months for a 60 per cent lower product cost and retails for around $800 versus $2,000 for its nearest competitor. Significantly it is becoming very popular as a low-cost, 'good enough' machine for use in international markets around the world.
- Siemens took a similar approach in developing its Somatom Spirit, designed in China as a low-cost computer body scanner (CAT) machine. The target was to be affordable, easy to maintain and usable by low-skilled staff; the resulting product costs 10 per cent of a full-scale machine, increases throughput of patients by 30 per cent and delivers 60 per cent less radiation. Over half of the hundreds sold each year go to international markets. In particular Siemens took a 'SMART' approach based on key principles – simple (they used a Pareto view of the main functions required rather than going for stateof-the-art functions), maintainable, affordable, reliable and a (fast) time to market.
- Neusoft in China are pioneering the use of advanced telemedicine to help deal with the growing crisis in which half a billion people will need health care. Instead of building more hospitals the plan is to develop an advanced IT-supported infrastructure to offer a network of primary care – a 'virtual hospital' model at much lower cost and with much wider outreach.
- Back in India the Mangalaayan Mars orbit spacecraft was successfully launched 2013 at the first attempt. Despite the complexity this was developed three times faster than international rivals and for a tenth of their costs. Its success is attributed to frugal principles – simplifying the payload, reusing proven components and technology, and so forth.
- In the automobile industry there have been significant moves in the frugal space, pioneered by Renault-Nissan among others. Their chairman, Carlos Ghosn, coined the term 'frugal engineering', built on the success of a frugal model (the Dacia/Logan platform in Europe) and established a design centre in Chennai aiming to build a car for the Indian mass market. The Kwid was launched in 2016 selling at €4,000 and has broken sales records with a healthy order book and despite strong competition.

Frugal innovation – framework principles for creativity

Underpinning this model is the application of some core principles which we have already seen in this book.

- Vision driven – frugal conditions force a clear and challenging goal around which teams can focus their problem-solving efforts. Examples include cutting medical costs by a factor of ten (Aravind, NHL), providing another car for the twenty-first-century Everyman (Tata/Renault), bringing needed goods and services within reach of the lowest paid (CEMEX, Lifeline Energy), putting a spacecraft in orbit around Mars in half the time and at half the cost of competitors (Mangalaayan), and so forth;

- Recombination – adapting and reusing elements of solutions from elsewhere – for example GE's ultrasound scanner, Siemens' CAT device;
- Task orientation and striving for excellent ideas – innovations emerging from high performing teams debating and arguing about solutions;
- Prototyping and learning from and with users;
- Perseverance – crisis conditions clearly a strong negative motivator.

The essence of the frugal approach can be expressed in some core principles:

- Simplify – exploring the problem and developing solutions which deal with the key required functionality – this isn't 'dumbing down' so much as distilling the essence of a solution into core elements.
- Focus on value – avoid overshoot, avoid waste.
- Don't reinvent the wheel – adopt, adapt, reuse, recombine.
- Think horizontally – open up the innovation process, more minds on the job.
- Platform thinking – build a simple frugal core and then add modules (a good example is the low-cost airline industry which is now constructing various options on the core basic low-cost platform).
- Continuous improvement.

You can find more information about this approach in a 'deeper dive' on the companion website together with case studies of Aravind, NHL and Lifespring.

Crisis-driven innovation

Innovation is all about survival – how often do we hear versions of that line? But in the field of humanitarian aid this really is the case. Innovation can sometimes be a matter of life and death. It's a world characterized by crisis – but it's also somewhere from which we might learn some new lessons to help manage innovation.

When disaster strikes – whether natural or man-made – we need innovation and we need it fast. And often the mainstream solution pathways are blocked so we have to invent radical alternatives; we have to improvise.

Think about an earthquake, after which the problem of moving food and medicine around becomes massively more complex when the roads are unrecognisable lumps of rock and gaping fissures. How do you handle water and sanitation when pipes are broken and smashed? How do you communicate when your phone lines are down? How can you provide healthcare when the hospital is in ruins? How do you house thousands of people whose homes are part of the wreckage? Under these conditions we need as much creativity as we can get – and we need it fast.

The good news is that there are some impressive examples of innovation in this context. For example:

- Emergency shelters erected using lightweight durable materials which can be assembled fast and by unskilled people;
- 3-D printing technologies being used to provide critical parts to keep broken infrastructure operating;
- Simple low-cost hygiene products to avoid sanitation-linked infection and provide clean drinking water;
- Novel healthcare solutions to prevent the spread of disease and treat victims fast and effectively;
- Cash-based options (via vouchers or mobile phones) to give people resources to procure what they need to feed, clothe and care for their families.

The process is one we would recognize as core to innovation – taking knowledge and configuring it to create value to end users. Sometimes it's the result of novel research and development, for example using drones to carry relief supplies over damaged terrain, or big data to help in the management and logistics of large temporary settlements like refugee camps. But much of the time it is adapting and configuring existing knowledge to new purposes. A good illustration of this kind of innovation is in the use of mobile phones:

- Creating an 'instant' banking system through which people can access cash and use this to buy food, medicines and other essentials;
- Open street mapping to provide up-to-date information about affected populations, damaged infrastructure, key emergency locations and so forth;
- Reuniting displaced persons;
- Crisis mapping and emergency communications;
- Creating online access to key information but also to provide employment opportunities;
- Of course, providing resilient and fast-to-implement voice communication.

You can find a short video outlining the concept and a wide range of examples and case studies of humanitarian innovation on the companion website. In particular the M-PESA example shows how crisis-driven innovation forces new trajectories and possibilities, something which Suzana Moreira also discusses in a video interview about her social enterprise Mowoza.

At its heart all of this depends on creativity – bringing together diverse people; exploring, ideating and elaborating around a compelling vision; and doing so in a context short on time and other key resources. Managing HI is not a different art form so much as a variation on the core theme – essentially how to manage innovation under crisis conditions. Crisis-driven innovation is characterized by

- Extreme conditions forcing a radical rethink of solution approaches, potentially opening up new innovation trajectories;
- Users and context are critical – HI requires user participation in configuring solutions;
- Rapid prototyping and learning are a key feature; HI is linked to entrepreneurial experimentation;
- Rapid diffusion – a combination of urgency of need, configuration of appropriate solutions by engaged users, and resource backing from major aid agencies to drive adoption to scale;
- Recombination – the failure of existing solutions under crisis conditions forces a rethink and wider search space, opening up potential for cross-sector learning.

Once again we can see similarities to themes explained earlier in the book – around problem exploration, openness and search for radical new directions, recombination and bridging between different worlds, and so forth. While crisis-driven innovation of this kind is of value in its own context there is also considerable scope for learning from it as an approach to be more widely deployed.

> You can find some examples of crisis-driven innovation on the companion website.

References

[1] Kim, L. (1998). Crisis construction and organizational learning: Capability building in catching-up at Hyundai Motor. *Organization Science*, *9*, 506–521.
[2] Prahalad, C. K. (2009). *The fortune at the bottom of the pyramid.* Upper Saddle River, NJ: Wharton School Publishing.
[3] Radjou, N., Prabhu, J., & Ahuja, S. (2012). *Jugaad innovation: Think frugal, be flexible, generate breakthrough innovation.* San Francisco: Jossey-Bass.
[4] NESTA (2012). *Frugal innovation.* London: NESTA (National Endowment for Science, Technology and the Arts).

## Chapter 15

Agile innovation and lean start-up

Agile innovation is a term used to describe a series of methods which originated in the field of software development [1]. It has been increasingly applied to other development projects for new products, services and even process re-engineering. At its heart is an approach which emphasizes focused high-intensity team work (often called 'scrum'), stretching goals and rapid cycles of prototyping, testing and learning. Where conventional project management techniques set a goal and then break down the various tasks needed to complete it into key activities and allocate resources to them, agile methods are more open-ended, allowing considerable creativity and flexibility in the execution of activities which will move nearer to the stretch target.

The basic framework in an agile approach involves setting up a core self-managed team, drawing on different functions and with a clear and stretching target. The team use various creativity tools (such as brainstorming and design thinking) to generate a list of key features which they think will be of value to the end user. Two key roles operate – a team leader who represents the end user's point of view and ranks these features from that perspective, and a process facilitator whose role is to help manage the support and psychological safety aspects of the team.

Once the stretch goal (vision) is broken down into a ranked list of contributing projects, the team work on short problem-solving cycles ('sprints') around these issues. Typically there is a short review meeting at the start of each day to explore progress, challenge and strengthen ideas, and develop experiments which they then test out during the day. The results of those experiments provide feedback and data to fuel the next day's review meeting and drive the sprint forward. Experiments may be of a technical nature – for example writing code or developing a working prototype – or they may be market tests, trying out the ideas with potential end users. In both cases the idea is to move through a fast cycle of experiment and learn, with the prospect of failure seen simply as a learning opportunity rather than a block to further progress.

Agile methods work – various reports suggest time savings of between 10 per cent and 40 per cent, and the quality of solutions is often much better [2]. Much of this success comes from focused teamwork, and once again we can see many of our core competences being deployed. The stretch target, the psychological safety which comes from having an autonomous and empowered group with the licence to experiment, the constructive controversy which emerges during the scrum process, the supporting and reflecting of ideas during the review meetings after a sprint are all critical success factors in the agile approach. In agile approaches creative teamwork is strongly promoted because without our described competences this approach will not work. Team reviews on the level of what did work and what not as well as on the level of collaboration and co-operation within the team are standard procedures in agile innovation.

Lean start-up

Lean start-up (LSU) is a similar approach for entrepreneurs developed by Eric Ries and popularized by him and Steve Blank in various books and articles [3]. It draws on his own experience as an entrepreneur and his reflections on what went wrong with the process. At its at heart is the view that starting a new venture is about a series of short fast experiments rather than a carefully planned and executed big project. Each cycle is carefully designed to generate information and test ideas out on the market – and after each prototype the venture idea is adjusted. Key principles are the 'minimum viable product' (MVP), which is a simple basic version of the overall product idea which can be tested on users to gain feedback, and the 'pivot', which involves changes in direction as a result of that feedback.

For a link to a talk of Eric Ries speaking at LSE go to the companion website.

The origin of the 'lean' idea comes from the low-waste approach pioneered in manufacturing and widely used across all sectors. It has been applied to product development to reduce time and resources spent and in software in particular has been allied to a second principle, that of 'agile' development. Here the main project is broken down into a series of fast short cycles of prototypes and learning, with the development team effort concentrated in fast bursts of intense activity – the 'scrum'.

LSU developed in the field of software and web applications but the underlying philosophy can be applied in any project. There are some core elements to the approach, as discussed in the following sections.

Build-measure-learn

The principle here is to design a hypothesis to test an idea and then adjust the project on the basis of that feedback. So, for example, it can be used to test a particular feature where the hypothesis is that people will like and value it: if they do, then retain the feature; if they don't, drop it.

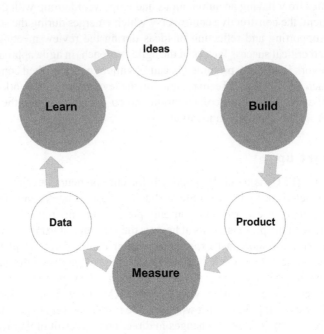

Figure 15.1 Lean start-up

Minimum viable product (MVP)

This is the minimum configuration of the new venture idea which can be used to run a build/measure/learn cycle – a simple prototype whose purpose is to generate data which helps adjust the core idea for the venture.

Validated learning

An important element of LSU is to work with data which provides useful information and helps learning about the venture. Ries talks about the problem of 'vanity metrics' which might appear to be measures of success but don't actually reveal anything useful. The number of people visiting a web page for example is not helpful in itself, but the amount of time they spend or the features they click on may be, because it gives information about the underlying things that people are valuing – at least enough to spend some time on. Equally the number of return visitors is a useful metric.

Innovation accounting

Linked to validated learning is the idea of using data to ensure resources are being well spent. To do this requires establishing a baseline and then improving on the performance linked to that by varying elements in the MVP – a process Ries calls 'tuning the engine'. For example a simple baseline could be set by a market survey which asks people if they would buy a product or service. Then launching an MVP cycle would generate data which suggested that more (or less) of them would be interested – and the core concept could be pivoted before a retest cycle. In this way the scarce resources associated with innovation can be carefully tracked.

Pivoting

The core assumption in LSU is that the only way to get closer to what customers actually need is to test your idea out on them and adapt it according to feedback from several learning cycles. So there is a need to use data from experiments to adjust the offer – the idea of a pivot is not that you change the idea completely but pivot it around the core so that it more exactly meets market needs. YouTube was originally a dating site on which one of the many features offered was the ability to share short video clips. During MVP tests it became clear that this feature was particularly valued so the original idea was adapted to put this more up front; further tests showed it was sufficiently valued to make it the core feature of the new business venture.

The essence of pivoting and MVP could be summed up as 'launch and see what happens' – inevitably something will and if the experimental launch is well designed it will help sharpen and refine the final offering without too much resource waste. Even if the MVP is a 'failure' there is valuable learning about new directions in which to pivot.

Ries talks about several versions of the pivot:

- *Zoom-in pivot*, where a single feature in the product now becomes the entire product (as in the YouTube case);
- *Zoom-out pivot*, where the whole product becomes a single feature in something much larger;
- *Customer segment pivot*, where the product was right, but the original customer segment wasn't. By rethinking the customer target segment the product can be better positioned;
- *Customer need pivot*, where validated learning highlights a more important customer need or problem;
- *Platform pivot*, where single separate applications converge to become a platform;
- *Business architecture pivot*, essentially changing the underlying business model – for example from high margin, low volume to low margin, high volume;
- *Value capture pivot*, where changes involve rethinking marketing strategy, cost structure, product and so forth;
- *Engine of growth pivot*, where the start-up model is rethought. Ries suggests three core models for this – viral, sticky or paid growth – and there is scope to change between them;

- *Channel pivot*, where different routes to reach the market are explored;
- *Technology pivot*, where alternative new technologies are used but the rest of the business model – market, cost structure and so forth – remains the same.

Lean principles used in the concept lean start-up

- Single unit flow

  An idea which originated in the Toyota Production System and is one of the cornerstones of 'lean' thinking [4–5]. In essence it is about working in small batches and completing the tasks on those rather than working in high volume. Think about doing a mailshot which would involve stuffing envelopes, addressing them, stamping them, posting them and so forth. Doing this in high volume one task at a time runs the risk of being slow and also of errors being made and not detected – for example, spelling someone's name wrong. Working one unit at a time would be faster and more accurate.
  Applied to LSU the idea is to work at small scale to develop the system and identify errors and problems quickly; the whole system can then be redesigned to take out these problems.

- Line stop/Andon cord

  Another idea drawn from Toyota is the ability to stop production when an error occurs – in the giant car factories this is done by means of a cord and a light which flashes above the place where the employee has found a problem. In LSU it is the principle of making sure there are error checks and that the process is stopped until these are fixed.

- Continuous improvement

  Another Toyota-based principle which is to keep reviewing and improving the core product and the process delivering it. By working in small batches it is possible to experiment and optimize around the core idea.

- *Kanban*

  Yet another 'lean' feature, this refers to the system of stock management associated with just-in-time production. Applied to LSU it puts improvement projects around the core product/venture idea into 'buckets' which are processed and progressed in systematic fashion. It is a powerful aid to managing capacity since new projects cannot be started until there is room for them in the system.

- Five whys

  A powerful diagnostic tool (see Chapter 2 for more), this helps find root causes of problems and directs action towards solving those problems rather than treating symptoms.

References

[1] Morris, L., Ma, M., & Wu, P. C. (2014). *Agile innovation: The revolutionary approach to accelerate success, inspire engagement, and ignite creativity.* New York, NY: Wiley.

[2] Altringer, B. (2013). A new model for innovation in big companies: Why injecting veteran entrepreneurs into an established organization can work wonders. *Harvard Business Review*, November 19.

[3] Ries, E. (2011). *The lean startup: How today's entrepreneurs use continuous innovation to create radically successful businesses.* New York, NY: Crown.

[4] Blank, S. (2013). Why the lean start-up changes everything. *Harvard Business Review, 91*, 63–72.

[5] Monden, Y. (1983). *The Toyota production system.* Cambridge, MA: Productivity Press.

Section 6

## Chapter 16

The future of creativity

Throughout the book we've been stressing some core messages about creativity:

- It's not a flash of magic but a journey.
- It's a journey which involves skills – to make it repeatedly we need to learn and develop these skills.
- It's not doing one thing well but involves building a repertoire of linked competences.
- It's not just a solo act; it's very often about a team and there are additional skills/competences at that level which result from interaction effects. The creative team is more than the sum of its parts.
- The wider environment in which creative individuals and teams operate is also part of the puzzle – and there is much that can be done to create supporting conditions and to allow the further development and practice of core skills.

None of this changes – it represents hard-won lessons from research and experience. But what does change is the *context* in which creativity is deployed. In particular new opportunities emerge for new tools and even new complementary approaches, and this is the focus of this last chapter. It involves looking along the current frontier and trying to do a little future-gazing about what might affect creativity in years to come.

Key points of interest along this frontier

The rise and rise of digital creativity

With the widespread availability of connectivity new possibilities have come for supporting creativity, both in terms of incrementally upgrading existing skills, tools and techniques but also in more radical forms. For example, as we saw in Chapter 8 brainstorming represents a powerful approach to Creative Problem-Solving. But while it ought to offer scope for novel ideas arising from diversity and different perspectives, its advantages can often be blunted by negative group effects. For example people feel unable to express ideas as a consequence of hier-archical or peer group pressures to conform, and if they do speak up it is often with 'safe' uncontroversial ideas. The idea of postponing judgment to allow ideas to incubate can quickly become distorted into a 'no criticism' policy which mili-tates against the kind of 'constructive controversy' which we have seen is such an important feature of high-performing creative teams.

One promising line to emerge in the late twentieth century was the use of online nominal groups, online voting and related tools to help get the best out of groups. A modern version of this are virtual teams and the ways they interact. Online collaboration platforms for teams are enabling teams to work in problems without being in the same room. Brainstorming sessions can be held via these devices and nominal group work with all its advantages in idea generation is combined with exchange possibilities that foster team collaboration.

Another variant on this is the idea of digital suggestion boxes – dealing with some of the limitations of employee involvement which emerged when a physical idea had to be posted and extracted, explored and decided upon. Now it is possible to collect thousands of ideas across a workforce – and to provide feedback and further progress very quickly.

These days online tools allow for various forms of debate, elaboration, criticism and refinement – automating some of the constructive controversy which we have seen is a valuable resource. And adding competition elements and time constraints means that idea challenges can now be organized through which teams quickly form, create and refine solutions to targeted stretch goals. Variants on the approach allow for others to act as judges and idea evalua-tors, offering constructive commentary and focusing the best ideas towards the final goal.

It's worth contrasting the early days of idea competitions with today's examples. Back in the eighteenth century the British Navy had a problem with its ships – it kept losing them! Navigation was not a precise art which meant that errors were made, sometimes with tragic consequences. In 1707 a fleet of ships heading towards Plymouth harbour ended up dashed on the rocks off the Scilly Islands and this prompted the Admiralty to offer a prize of £20,000 (equivalent to around £2.5 million today) to anyone who could come up with a solution. The challenge lay in measuring longitude accu-rately and this required the development of a reliable portable chronometer. The winner was a carpenter and joiner from Norfolk, John Harrison, and his beautifully engineered design is still visible in the Navy Museum at Green-wich in London.

Across the Channel the Emperor Louis Napoleon lent his support to a simi-lar contest, this time to improve the provisioning of his army. Nicolas Appert developed the principles of food canning in 1810 and was awarded the FF12,000 prize; later, in 1869 the chemist Hippolyte Mège-Mouriès developed margarine as a substitute for butter; both innovations made significant difference to military logistics. These and other examples remind us that the fashion now for 'innovation contests' is not something new; the difference is that it now takes very little time to organize such activities across organizations or even to source external ideas. Several organizations have specialized in providing the platforms on which such activities can take place, combining elements of suggestion schemes, online voting and team building with processes which allow for rapid elaboration and refinement.

> You can find on the companion website a case study of the Liberty Global Spark programme as an example of such an online contest.

Co-creating with the crowd

To some extent these applications of information and communications technology augment approaches which already existed. But digital technology also enables very new approaches to creative working which were simply not possible at an earlier stage. In particular, the idea of working with the crowd not only as a source of ideas but also as co-creation partners across a platform.

Consider the case of LEGO – a company which has reinvented itself to work far more closely with its customers. LEGO's business has always been based on storytelling and imagination, encouraging children to play with their bricks and toys and create their own imaginary worlds and creatures with these elements. The name LEGO itself comes from the Danish meaning 'play well'. What they have been learning to do is use online platforms to encourage children to design their own toys using LEGO components and increasingly to share these ideas with others to help refine and improve the designs. LEGO provides an environment and tools (like online computer design tools and interactive platform websites); their 'market' then brings their ideas and co-develops them with LEGO. One such iteration along a journey which has already lasted ten years is LEGO Ideas; here the invitation is to submit ideas which will be displayed so that others can 'like' and comment on them. If an idea attracts over 10,000 'likes' then LEGO will explore actually producing that idea. So the lines between professional designers in the company and children as designers co-creating with LEGO have become increasingly blurred.

The same thing is happening in many areas, facilitated by digital technologies which enable design and manufacture and above all sharing and co-creation across communities. If you have an idea for a piece of jewellery or an item of furniture, if you have a solution to a nagging problem at home, if you think you can improve the public services you consume – if you have creative input of any kind, there is probably a website where tools like computer-aided design and 3D printing can help you realize this.

You can read more about the LEGO case on the companion website together with other examples like Threadless and Adidas that are trying to engage co-creation with their customers.

Back in the early days of the internet Philip Evans and Thomas Wurstner suggested a model in which many traditional markets would be disrupted because the new technology would enable the traditional trade-off between richness and reach to be resolved. By 'richness' they meant the depth of engagement between an organization and an individual – for example, working with their individual ideas, and by 'reach' they meant the ability to work with many people simultaneously. Their ideas have now moved to centre stage as platforms of the kind described earlier become increasingly visible and where crowd creativity is beginning to emerge [1].

Co-creation with the crowd is not confined to the front end of innovation, souring new ideas at an early stage. Platforms typically allow for communities to form around an idea, challenging and refining it, shaping and configuring it as it develops. This has the advantage of adapting it to suit the particular circumstances of those involved in the process – making the idea 'compatible' with their world. Research has shown that this is a key factor influencing the rate and extent of diffusion of innovations – so co-creation with the crowd means faster and more widespread acceptance.

You can read about a number of examples of such co-creation in the report Open Collective Innovation on the companion website.

The other advantage of such digital platforms is that they facilitate building communities of innovators. These communities may remain online – for example the powerful Linux operating system (which runs most smartphones and a host of other applications) is the product of a community of co-creators continuing to work together to develop and refine their software. It has been running as an extended online group since 1991 when Linus Torvalds began writing an alternative to the mainstream systems of that time [2].

Others operate as a hybrid using the platform to communicate and share across large distances but also enabling face-to-face meetings and activities. For example Local Motors is a community of car enthusiasts who collectively design, build (and now sell) a range of high performance co-created vehicles.

You can read a case study of Local Motors on the companion website.

Democratizing innovation

These trends are accelerating. Eric von Hippel began commenting thirty years ago on the phenomenon of user-led innovation and identified a number of groups where this was an important pattern – for example farmers and medical instrument production. But recent studies have begun to highlight the extent to which user input is shaping the innovation agenda – a NESTA study in the UK, for example, suggested that a significant proportion of product and even more process innovations began life as user ideas [3]. The trend has been enabled in part by technology – as we said earlier it becomes much easier to mobilize the ideas of the crowd and to work with them, elaborating and refining them in a process of co-creation. But it is also a consequence of social shifts towards a more networked 'sharing economy' in which ideas are trafficked freely. An important element of the work that Von Hippel and colleagues have been doing is in trying to understand the motivation for participating in user-led co-creation, and it appears that there is a high degree of altruism, of sharing ideas without expecting a direct financial return. Instead the incentive to innovate and the belief that sharing ideas will help amplify them across a community (with the results benefitting everyone) provide the momentum behind continued and active participation. He calls this process the 'democratization of innovation' and suggests that it is a growing and powerful movement, operating not only in the world of commercial innovation but having a significant impact on social innovation as well.

Gamification – playing with innovation

In parallel with digitalization has come renewed interest in bringing play to the forefront of innovation. Motivating people to want to participate in idea contests and other co-creation activities comes in part from their desire to contribute – but it can also be released through engaging them in some kind of game playing. Gamification of problem-solving, making the quest fun and rewarding progress along the way with tokens and other incentives is becoming an increasingly important element of open/crowd-based creativity [4]. Introducing an element of competition between groups can have a positive effect on creativity as we saw earlier; increasingly online innovation contests build in this feature as a way of stretching the teams towards better ideas. (Unfortunately sometimes the element of playing games moves beyond the original objectives of the contest organizers; research suggests sometimes players become creative at developing strategies which help them win by various forms of cheating and manipulation of the rules! [5].)

There's another area where the concept of play is becoming increasingly relevant – at the fuzzy front end of innovation where safe exploration of very early ideas and problem formulation takes place. We've seen throughout the book the importance of this front end of the creative journey – problem exploration. In different ways we need to find ways to discover the underlying problem and possible solution pathways, and then as we generate solutions we need to be able to play further to help the process of refinement and configuration. This puts the idea of play centre stage.

Patrick Bateson and Paul Martin describe and explore connections between play/playfulness and creativity in their book [6]. It is easy to follow that playing and creativity have features in common, like breaking rules, goofing around, or flow while playing respectively being creative. They also look at 'creative' people like Feynman, Mozart, and Crick and Watson who all embraced playfulness as a way to create something. Francis Crick and James Watson, in their autobiographical book *The Double Helix*, describe how dubious people were watching them going for long walks, playing around before they received the Nobel prize for their creative achievement of modelling the double helix structure of DNA [7]. A similar approach to academic achievement is reported about Richard Feynman, Nobel Prize winner in physics. After a successful start in academia, he got bored with physics and started to think about other career options, when remembering why he liked physics – playing around. He started 'new' and became one of the most influential physicists of modern times.

One of the key elements in play is prototyping. We move from vague notions, hunches, half-formed ideas towards something more workable not by a single leap but by a series of stepping stones, bridges, scaffolding – essentially playing with ideas about the problem. And it helps to have an object or device to enable us to do this. The artists in the study by Mihaly Csikszentmihalyi and Jacob Getzels picked up objects, weighed them, turned them around in their hands and looked at them from different angles [8]. Dyson's method was the same – create a *prototype* to help focus the exploration: 'prototypes allow you to quickly get a feel for things and uncover subtle design flaws' [9].

As we saw earlier, prototyping offers some important features:

- It creates a 'boundary object', something around which other people and perspectives can gather, a device for sharing insights into problem dimensions as well as solutions.
- It offers us a stepping stone in our thought processes, making ideas real enough to see and play with them but without the lock-in effect of being tied into trying to make the solutions work – we can still change our minds.
- It allows plurality – we don't have to play with a single idea; we can bet on multiple horses early on in the race rather than trying to pick winners.
- It allows for learning – even when a prototype fails we accumulate knowledge which might come in helpful elsewhere.
- It suggests further possibilities – as we play with a prototype it gives us a key to open up the problem, break open the shell and explore more deeply.
- It allows us to work with half-formed ideas and hunches – it enables a 'conversation with a shadowy idea'.
- It allows for emergence – sometimes we can't predict what will happen when different elements interact. Trying something out helps explore surprising combinations.

Prototyping has always been an important part of innovation – even when the solution trajectory is clear there is plenty of room for using test pieces to refine the product and get the bugs out. But rather than seeing this as a late stage tool to help polish a solution we should look more closely at its role at the very fuzzy front end of the innovation process. Effective innovators need a variety of skills to help them create value from ideas – and, as writers like Michael Schrage (*Serious Play*) and Stefan Thomke (*Experimentation Matters*) suggest, learning to play could be an important addition to their repertoire [10–11].

Prototypes can take many forms – physical models, sketches, simulations, even stories which can be adapted and retold. Their key feature is that they provide some interface around which different stakeholders can explore and contribute – they enable *co-creation*. Their importance is increasingly recognized – and this has also placed attention on the spaces where it can take place.

Creating space for innovation

Building spaces for innovation is a hot topic these days. Whether you call them innovation hubs, living labs, maker-spaces, fab-labs, accelerators or hotspots you can hardly turn a street corner or a magazine page before you bump into another example. The names may vary but the underlying idea is the same – a place where people can meet to get inspired and supported by each other, to articulate and co-create; an environment in which ideas can be explored and played with.

This is becoming a very fashionable new direction for innovation. Companies looking to reinvent themselves no longer set up corporate venture units – they establish their own Silicon Valley–style start-up garages and lofts. City and regional governments rebrand their incubators as innovation hubs and build lab-style environments with support facilities to allow a new generation of entrepreneurs to realize their dreams (and hopefully deliver local economic growth as a by-product). Fab-labs and maker-spaces abound; run-down old warehouses and industrial buildings are being reinvented as shells within which new forms of entrepreneurial life can flourish.

And with this has come a renewed interest in diversity – attracting a mixture of different people to these innovation spaces. Networking and making new connections, harnessing energy and ideas to fuel a start-up culture and revitalize organizations, opening windows to let in some fresh air to the boxes they have become stuck in.

But this isn't a new idea. Back in the seventeenth century places like Oxford were full of coffee houses, sometimes called 'penny universities' because that was the price of admission including coffee. It wasn't the hot beverage which drew people but rather the opportunity to mix and exchange ideas – a place where the 'normal' rules of society governed by status and economic position were left aside and people could meet and explore new possibilities on an equal footing.

And they weren't just about talking; in 1680 Edward Lloyd's premises hosted a mixture of ship owners, captains, merchants and others with links to the maritime world. New ventures were explored and support for them secured – an early version of today's venture capital pitching. Today's towering Lloyd's building has its roots in that start-up meeting place. A few blocks away, Jonathan's Coffee House became the favoured meeting place for another group of potential investors and entrepreneurs – the foundation of the London Stock Exchange. Isaac Newton was a fan of the Grecian coffee house where experimental scientists liked to gather – and where he once dissected a dolphin on the table! And today's branch of Starbucks on Russell St, London, is on the site of Button's coffee house, where in 1712 poets, playwrights and journalists gathered around long wooden tables drinking, thinking, writing and discussing literature into the night. We might think 'open innovation' is a new idea but it was alive and very much kicking three hundred years ago!

It wasn't only coffeehouses; similar hotspots for innovation could be found in the swishy drawing rooms of Paris, St Petersburg and Milan. Under the careful management of women like the redoubtable eighteenth-century hostess Madame Geoffrin, such salons became home to progressive ideas and creative conversations, incubators of new thinking in music, visual arts, theatre and science.

And a slightly less plush context – Gordon French's garage in Menlo Park, California, in the mid-1970s – was home to the Homebrew Computer Club, an informal group of electronic enthusiasts and technically minded hobbyists who gathered to trade parts, circuits, and information about DIY construction of computing devices. One of the regular members was Steve Wozniak, who credits this as the place where the Apple I was born.

What these all have in common is that they were much more than simply meeting points – somehow they came alive and became powerhouses for innovation. It's the search for that magic spark that can turn a 'dead' property into a 'live' crucible for creativity which lies behind the upsurge in current interest.

Boundary objects, agents and spaces

Prototypes alone aren't enough – to work effectively with them we also need boundary *agents* – someone to bring relevant people together and enable them to have useful conversations (Figure 16.1). Their role has long been recognized as important in innovation – for example the sociologist Ronald Burt developed an elegant theory around the role of brokers in bridging between networks. They are 'boundary spanners' – able to operate in different networks but also to see relevance and make connections between them. He gave them the rather odd label 'structural holes' – but despite this strange name tag their importance in innovation continues to emerge [12]. From Thomas Allen's pioneering work on 'technological gatekeepers' during the NASA moon landing program to Procter and Gamble's extensive use of 'technology entrepreneurs' as part of their 'Connect and Develop' framework, they are central to effective open innovation [13]. And there's a whole growth industry of consultancies and platforms aimed at providing bridging and brokering services.

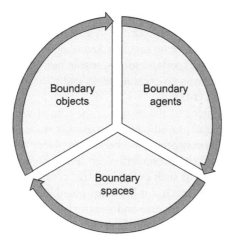

Figure 16.1 Boundary elements

Successful entrepreneurs do this – a key skill lies in being able to infect others with their vision and then getting them to engage in shared exploration and articulation. And – back to our eighteenth-century salons – the secret was not simply in inviting guests and setting out refreshments. It lay in finding ways to bring people together, to act like a marriage broker for creative minds, catalyzing innovative conversations.

Which brings us back to boundary *spaces* – where does all of this happen? And can we create spaces which actively stimulate and enable innovation? Research by NESTA in the UK suggests that it's much more than a simple physical space – just like a theatre we can provide the basic stage but it is the particular arrangements of scenery, lighting, properties and above all actors and directors which bring it to life. There is a growing body of experience around configuring boundary spaces – for example in terms of physical environments aimed at enhancing creative collisions (think of the BMW Research and Innovation Centre in Munich or Pixar's Emeryville studios). Innovation accelerators flourish not just because of the equipment and facilities available to users but also because of the networking and mentoring which goes on within what is a creative community of practice.

Part of the story is in seeing boundary spaces as prototypes in themselves – places where we can learn more about the approach. A recent study by Cambridge University has looked at the lessons offered by Joseph's – a 'drop-in' innovation lab in the heart of downtown Nuremburg (complete with coffee bar where new ideas for refreshments are prototyped!). Operated as a joint venture with the local university and the nearby Fraunhofer Institute, Joseph's has been running for nearly two years, during which a variety of 'theme-worlds' have been explored – for example, 'smart living', mobility, personal health and fashion. Each theme-world involves a mixture of physical and virtual prototypes, workshops, seminars and spaces to support informal conversations; it's a bit like a museum or art gallery with different exhibitions throughout the year. A key element is the attempt to bridge different worlds – to bring together Saturday morning shoppers, weekday schoolchildren, company experts, students, researchers and entrepreneurs, and to try and engage with them in co-creating ideas and prototypes for future product and service innovations [14].

Another important piece of the puzzle is the role of *virtual spaces* in which ideas can be explored and played with. Increasingly we are seeing platforms not just as software to support suggestion schemes but places where communities can be built and interact and where innovation can and does emerge. Think Linux and many others as examples of such online creative communities. A key advantage in such platforms is their reach – it becomes possible to open up conversations and co-creation with a truly diverse and geographically far-flung community. In many ways they offer a 21st version of the Oxford coffee shops of three hundred years ago.

You can find a case study of Joseph's and a description of Living Labs on the companion website.

Big Data and pattern recognition

A key theme and theory in creativity is around pattern recognition. We saw earlier how many theories suggest that when confronted with a problem we first search back in our 'library' for something which looks like this – pattern matching – and then try and deploy the solution we developed for that situation. Where we don't have an exact match we modify and extend or, occasionally, come up with a novel solution. But pattern recognition is central to the model – and, as we've seen with many examples, it's a rich source of solution possibilities.

Think about reframing – the ability by abstracting a problem to its core features to see the potential for applying solution approaches based on the underlying pattern. The Aravind Eye Care system using the same approach to surgery as McDonalds do to fast food preparation and Henry Ford did to building cars. Hospital operating theatres applying the same solution principles to improve utilization of scarce resources as low-cost airlines do in fast turnarounds, manufacturers use in reducing set-up times of big machines and Formula 1 motor racing teams deploy in fast pit stops.

Recent developments in Big Data have provided new tools to help us do this and to automate/mimic the process. For example, data analytics across very large volumes of data helps to uncover hidden patterns and direct solution search more effectively. Putting simple sensors at road junctions can identify the underlying root cause of traffic management problems. Analyzing thousands of patient records can detect otherwise missed clues in medical diagnoses. Google's Deep Mind division is now using advanced analytics and machine learning in partnership with the UK National Health Service to identify patterns in health records and develop preventive measures to help avoid the costs and pain of problems which emerge if diseases are not treated early enough.

Johannes Eichstaedt and colleagues looked at Twitter accounts to predict heart-disease rates on the county level in the United States [15]. They looked at language patterns and found strong correlations between negative social relationships in tweets and heart-disease mortality, for example. In fact, a resulting model could predict AHD mortality better than a model that combines ten currently used predictors, for example demographics, health risk factors and socioeconomic variables.

Big Data will change our view of the world and will probably also help us to be more creative and to know more about how creativity comes into this world and can be fostered.

As we've seen there's significant scope for recombination of solutions based on underlying patterns; this lies at the heart of methodologies like TRIZ and Morphological analysis.

You can read more about these on the companion website.

Harnessing the power of Big Data analysis has opened up new possibilities for such approaches, ranging from simple online patent searches to sophisticated platforms which try to match problem patterns with known solution pathways.

Artificial intelligence (AI) – and 'artificial imagination'

Back in the 1970s researchers like Marvin Minsky and Ray Kurtzweil began to talk about the possibilities of intelligent machines, drawing in part on the theories of Norbert Wiener and other cyberneticians. At the time computers were primitive, and although artificial intelligence (AI) was an interesting concept its practical realization was fraught with difficulty. Even simple tasks were beyond the ability of machines to 'think' their way around [16].

AI as science fiction has gradually become AI as everyday fact, driven by increases in computing power and decreases in costs together with a much more sophisticated understanding of how human beings solve problems, especially via the use of 'neural networks'. The result is an inexorable move towards the era of widely applied AI, with milestones being ticked off along the way. IBM's Deep Blue machine managed to beat the world chess champion in 1996, deploying something of a brute force approach. But by 2016 Google's Alpha Go model managed to beat the world champion Lee Se-Dol at the much more complex game of 'Go'. The significance of this was the embedding of massive machine learning capability – the problem was solved by applying and experimenting with strategies and learning from them so that the computer improved each time.

Several influential reports now suggest that AI is likely to have an increasingly significant impact on employment – no longer is it a case of robots taking over manual work but now 'thinking machines' can replace many white collar jobs which require elements of judgment and decision-making [17]. This impact is likely to be felt right across the economy – accountants, nurses, drivers, retailers, craftsmen, air traffic controllers – the list is extensive and there are likely to be more as AI develops.

While one optimistic argument is that removing human beings from the drudgery of work may allow them to spend their time in more creative pursuits there are challenges at this frontier too. Major research projects are trying to develop machine learning algorithms and programs which emulate creative activity – for example in trying to write stories or compose music. At an auction in February 2015 a picture sold for $8,000 – the surprising fact was that this had been created by Google's DeepDream software!

As Jang Dae-Ik, a science philosopher at Seoul National University, told the *Korea Herald* after AlphaGo's victory:

> This is a tremendous incident in the history of human evolution – that a machine can surpass the intuition, creativity and communication, which has previously been considered to be the territory of human beings. . . . Before, we didn't think that artificial intelligence had creativity. . . . Now, we know it has creativity – and more brains, and it's smarter.
>
> [18]

In conclusion . . .

This 'whistle-stop tour' along the creativity frontier opens up some interesting questions about the future of creativity. We could pursue it further into the realms of science fiction – brain implants, trans-cranial stimulation, and mind-enhancing drugs as alternatives to the rise of the intelligent machine, for example. But we'll close here with three simple reflections on creativity which we hope have been illuminated in our book.

- *Creativity is a journey, not a magic event.* We hope we've helped put the myth of divine inspiration to rest and provided at least a sketch map of the landscape through which we need to travel.
- *Everyone can undertake the journey.* Again, another myth which we hope to have dispelled – everyone is fitted with the standard equipment necessary to be creative.
- *Getting fit for the creativity journey matters.* Creativity involves a set of

competences and underlying skills. And the important thing here is that we can work on our 'creative fitness' developing skills and stretching creative competences.

We hope the book helps. . . .

References

[1]   Evans, P., & Wurster, T. (2000). *Blown to bits: How the new economics of information transforms strategy.* Cambridge, MA: Harvard Business School Press.
[2]   Torvalds, L., & Read By-Diamond, D. (2001). *Just for fun: The story of an accidental revolutionary.* New York, NY: Harper Audio.
[3]   NESTA (2010). *Measuring user innovation in the UK.* London: NESTA.
[4]   Zichermann, G., & Linder, J. (2013). *The gamification revolution: How leaders leverage game mechanics to crush the competition.* New York, NY: McGraw Hill.
[5]   Scheiner, C., & Baccarella, C. (2016). *Don't underestimate the power of the dark side – Moral disengagement in idea competitions.* Working paper, Friedrich Alexander University, Erlangen Nürnberg.
[6]   Bateson, P., Bateson, P.P.G., & Martin, P. (2013). *Play, playfulness, creativity and innovation.* New York, NY: Cambridge University Press.
[7]   Watson, J. (2012). *The double helix.* New York, NY: Hachette.
[8]   Csikszentmihalyi, M., & Getzels, J.W. (1971). Discovery-oriented behavior and the originality of creative products: A study with artists. *Journal of Personality and Social Psychology, 19,* 47.
[9]   See the Dyson company website, *www.dyson.com*
[10] Schrage, M. (2013). *Serious play: How the world's best companies simulate to innovate.* Boston, MA: Harvard Business Press.
[11] Thomke, S.H. (2003). *Experimentation matters: Unlocking the potential of new technologies for innovation.* Boston, MA: Harvard Business Press.
[12] Burt, R. (2005). *Brokerage and closure.* Oxford: Oxford University Press.
[13] Allen, T. (1977). *Managing the flow of technology.* Cambridge, MA: MIT Press.
[14] Groves, K., & Marlow, O. (2016). *Spaces for innovation.* London: Frame3.
[15] Greve, K., Martinez, V., Jonas, J., Neely, A., & Moeslein, K. (2016). *Facilitating co-creation in living labs: The JOSEPHS study.* Cambridge: Cambridge University Institute for Manufacturing.
[16] Eichstaedt, J.C., Schwartz, H.A., Kern, M.L., Park, G., Labarthe, D.R., Merchant, R.M., . . . Seligman, M.E.P. (2015). Psychological language on Twitter predicts county-level heart disease mortality. *Psychological Science, 26,* 159–169.
[17] West, D.M. (2015). *What happens if robots take the jobs? The impact of emerging technologies on employment and public policy.* Centre for Technology Innovation at Brookings, October, 1–22.
[18] Simonite, T. (2016). Ok computer, write me a song. *MIT Technology Review,* June 8. See *https://www.technologyreview.com/s/601642/ok-computer-write-me-a-song/*

Index